CHASING 193

Vol. II

The Quest to Visit Every Country in the World

By
Ryan Trapp
&
Henrik Jeppesen

Copyright © 2016 Ryan Trapp & Henrik Jeppesen
All rights reserved.

Table of Contents

Foreword i
Michael Runkel, Germany 1
Karin Sinniger, Switzerland 15
Lawrence Williams, The Gambia 32
Jorge Sanchez, Spain 57
Paulo Mansur Raymundo, Brazil 73
Bart Hackley, U.S.A. 99
Jack Goldstein, Colombia 117
Kolja Spöri, Monaco 150
Bob Parda, U.S.A. 165
Thomas Buechler, Switzerland 193
Claus Qvist Jessen, Denmark 208
Jack Wheeler, U.S.A. 238
Henrik Jeppesen, Denmark 260
Harald Buben, Austria 284
Watson E. Mills, U.S.A. 299
William Baekeland, Ireland 322
Paul Hurwood, England 345
Luis Filipe Gaspar, Portugal 358
Artemy Lebedev, Russia 373
Jagannathan Srinivasaraghavan, India & USA 385

Foreword

My love of traveling began when I was in my early teens. Growing up in Juneau, Alaska I think lent to the feelings of wanderlust that I had and the desire to leave my small island town behind and see the world. Early trips for me meant road trips through the Yukon Territories and British Columbia areas of Canada and to Washington state. That was enough to always have my eye towards the road and want to see more. Later, in my late teens, I lived in a variety of states and began using every opportunity possible to head out to neighboring states, and then overseas. There soon came a point when traveling and having adventures was the most important thing to me, and over the proceeding 15+ years, I have turned that interest into some incredibly memorable moments in dozens of countries around the world and remote island groups. My love of adventure has lead me into meeting some like-minded people and to the realization that these people were some of the most interesting individuals in the world. This got me to thinking that these people's stories need to be shared and told. And that's where this book comes in.

Over the two-year-plus journey of compiling and editing together this *Chasing 193* series, I have had the pleasure of speaking with and getting to know some 54 world-class travelers (34 from the previous edition and 20 from this one). I have become friends with a lot of these people, traveled to far-off places with some of them, and come to respect and admire them all. Like a lot of readers, I am left in awe of those that have truly given traveling their all and seen more in their lifetimes than most could ever imagine.

It is no easy feat to pull together some of the world's busiest and most active people – especially those that routinely are oceans and many time zones away – and get their cooperation in an interview which is lengthy and covers their past, present and future. I give my heartfelt thanks to those who gave me so much of their time and energy.

My primary objective with these books has been to ignite the fire within those people that want to see this world in-depth and motivate them to keep striving for more and to recognize that it is possible to go 'everywhere.' Equally important to me is to give these eclectic and extraordinary people the recognition they deserve and let their unique stories come out to the world in their own words. It has been my goal from the beginning not to have a 'watered down' fairy tale of life on the road where everything goes perfect, but instead to acknowledge the good and also reveal the painful side of this challenging and time-consuming pursuit. I hope that is has been achieved.

As you are now about to head into another set of interesting life stories and tales from 20 fascinating individuals, I also give thanks to the readers for coming along on the journey through the lives of some of the best-traveled people in the world. May this give you the spark to head in the direction of your dreams, whatever they may be.

Sincerely,

Ryan Trapp

Michael Runkel, Germany

(In Papua New Guinea)

Where did you grow up, and what was your early life like?

I grew up in a small town near Nuremberg, Germany, in a middle-class family of teachers. When I was nine, I discovered the 19th-century German author, Karl May, who wrote adventure novels exploring Eastern Europe, the Middle East, Africa and the American Old West. He had never traveled to any of these regions but portrayed them so well in his writing that most people thought he had been there himself. He created figures like Kara Ben Nemsi, a kind of Indiana Jones character of that time and sparked my passion for adventure and world cultures. By age 10 I had read all of them, about 80 books.

We traveled with my parents very regularly but never outside of Europe, so I was sure that as soon as I finished high school, I would go on my own adventures. My first trip was traveling around Europe and Morocco by Interrail, the modus operandi of young European travelers at that time.

What was the first international trip you took, and what do you remember most about it?

My first trip was an Interrail trip down to Morocco in 1988, right after high school. We were traveling with two blonde Austrian girls in the precarious town of Asilah, not far from Tangier. What I remember about this trip was our initial experience. We needed to change money and were approached by a group of young men. They told us they'd take us to a bazaar at a souvenir shop where we could exchange, but when we got there, they pressured us into buying something. We were on a very tight budget and tried to leave the shop, but one of the young guys took out a knife and threatened me into buying something. That was my first experience with the 'wild west' of travel.

When did you go from traveling casually to making this a full-time goal, and what motivated you to travel to every country?

I never doubted that venturing out would become a part of my life. In university, I had my own business, so I was able to fund my travels half the year and study the other half. I collaborated with Adidas early on, where I was photographed in the company's gear at Mt. Everest Base Camp, Salto Cara (Angel Falls) waterfalls in Venezuela, and the Hussaini Hanging Bridges in Pakistan. By reselling them back, I was able to offset a lot of my travel costs from the beginning.

Traveling to every country was never really important to me. I was much more curious about a place – it's political, economic and cultural climate and exploring versus checking a place off the list. But in 2008, a friend introduced me to the Most Traveled People (MTP) site, and we had a meeting with some of the most-traveled Germans in Munich, plus Charles Veley and Jorge Sanchez, organized by Kolja Spöri. That was the day I thought to myself: 'I've been to so many places, why not try to visit every country?'

What have you done in your life to gain the freedom and finances to pursue as much travel as you have?

I work as a freelance travel photographer selling my photos via stock agencies, tour operators and on assignments. I'm also a high school teacher, which allows me to travel four months per year and take a sabbatical leave once in a while.

Has there ever been a time where you considered abandoning your travel goals?

Never for one second.

What do you consider to be your two favorite travel experiences, and why?

One was meeting my wife on an icebreaker in the Antarctic Peninsula. She is a pop singer and was giving an impromptu concert on board, and the rest, they say, is history. We decided to travel together for the next nine months through South America, New Zealand, Micronesia and the Pacific Rim.

Another was in Cambodia right after the war. I arrived a week after the 1993 elections with a journalist couple from New Zealand. Everything was cleared out – no tourists, no souvenir stalls. We were the only foreigners among monks and soldiers. It was as if we'd time traveled to a century earlier.

What are the main things you seek to experience when you travel (culture, cities, nature, animals, adventure activities, etc.)?

My primary intention is to try and see everything our planet has to offer. Photographing UNESCO World Heritage Sites is a big passion of mine, and taking portraits of people across all cultures and backdrops. Another favorite is visiting cultural festivals, like the Sing-sing in Papua New Guinea or Mindelo Carnival in Cape Verde. Capturing people in their authentic spirit is something, as a photographer, I particularly gravitate to. You can see some of my work on my website, Michael Runkel Photography (www.michaelrunkel.com).

Looking back from when you started traveling to where you are now, in what ways, if any, has travel changed you?

Over the years, I've definitely gotten more experienced when handling certain situations – unpredictable circumstances due to the nature of the country or encounters with precarious people. Developing a sixth sense about a place takes some trial and error. I've also fostered a better understanding of the world. After seeing a place with your own eyes you will form a much different opinion, as opposed to reading about it in the paper.

Today the world is more globalized, and it's easier to travel anywhere. I'm glad I was able to see a few places when they were untouched.

Do you speak any foreign languages, and if so, which have been the most useful for you besides English?

I am fluent in English, French, Spanish, and my mother tongue, German. I can also get around well with Portuguese, Italian, Russian, and Indonesian. In my opinion, if you speak

English, French, Spanish and Russian you can, aside from China, cover most of the planet.

What was the longest extended trip you have ever taken, when was it and where all did you go?

I've done five RTW ('Round the World) trips, the longest being 13½ months in 2011 and 2012. It was through Singapore, Papua New Guinea, Solomon Islands, Vanuatu, New Caledonia, all the provinces of Australia including Lord Howe Island, New Zealand, Argentina, Chile, Antarctica, Brazil, Paraguay, the Philippines, Micronesia (Yap, Guam, Chuuk, and Pohnpei), the Northern Marianas, South Korea including Jeju Island, Malaysia, Indonesia (Sumatra, Java, Bali), Tonga, Samoa, American Samoa, Fiji, Kiribati, five islands of Hawaii, California, Baja California, all central plain states of the U.S., Winnipeg, all the U.S. states from Newfoundland down to New York, and the ABC islands (Aruba, Bonaire, Curaçao) in the Caribbean.

What two countries have exceeded your expectations and which ones left you feeling underwhelmed, and why?

I feel that the Stan' countries, despite the harsh police climate there, are completely underrated. They have so much to offer, and very few people visit them. On the contrary, Australia is slightly overhyped. It has some stunning natural spots like Bungle Bungle Range and Ayers Rock, but in between there is not too much.

When you travel, do you prefer to go with others or solo, and why?

I usually travel with my wife or with a friend. Sometimes, but seldom, I go by myself. In places like Bhutan or Kamchatka, I usually get a group of friends together. I love to share the experiences, and with all of my camera gear, it's a bonus to have extra models on the trip...

What has been your most uncomfortable mode of transportation?

My most unpleasant method of travel was riding a camel for five days in Rajasthan. I had amoebic dysentery, and the slowest camel of the group, so you can imagine how I would've needed the guide to bring the camel down. Every time my stomach would give me a sign, I'd just have to wait and press my butt cheeks together.

What is the strangest thing you've seen/experienced while traveling?

The strangest thing I've experienced was the 'Jumping of the Bull' ceremony of the Hamer tribe in southern Ethiopia's Omo Valley. The tradition goes, when a woman fancies a man, he is supposed to beat her with four wooden sticks until they break. Apart from a basket skirt, she is naked. The man of her liking beats her and breaks the skin all over her body. She usually withstands the pain, smiling at him instead of crying. Once the sticks are broken, the man accepts her. In this tribe's tradition, the women have a lot of sexual experience before they get married, so you see most women and girls with huge scars on their backs and breasts.

Once that rite of passage is over, the men separate from the women and lead a group of bulls into a field. The line them up in a row – one man holding its tongue and another, its tail. A young boy, completely naked, is brought into the field – he knows that if he wins the challenge he will be a man, but if he loses, he will be a failure. This challenge is to walk across the back of the bulls four times without falling off. If he succeeds, he will be able to choose a girl for the night.

What are the best and worst meals you have ever eaten while traveling, and where was it?

I've eaten a lot of outlandish things in my life, but the worst was in Lamalera, on the Alor Archipelago in Indonesia. Because of its remote location, the people are allowed to hunt whales when they migrate past their village each year. The Lamalerans hunt in the way of Moby Dick, holding long spears in their hand with a rope attached. They jump on the whale and impale the spears into its body. The whale dives down and pulls the boat with it. Once the whale comes up again, the hunter will try to spear it again. That can go on for many hours. When the whale dies, they bring it to shore and cut in into pieces. There is no electricity there, so no way to preserve the meat. For that tribe, the only preservation is by laying it out in the sun to dry. I was invited by the village elder there to have some of the whale while half the village watched – it smelled as if it had been lying out in the sun for three months. I only ate a small portion before I had to run and vomit, as the smell of that meat kept me away from any other meat for weeks afterward.

The second most peculiar meal I had was raw marmot in Mongolia. We were traveling through central Mongolia and met a group of hunters emerging from the middle of nowhere on horseback. They had been hunting marmots, but we invited them to join us for some fish we had caught an hour earlier. After dinner, they felt compelled to counter-invite us to their yurt the next morning for "breakfast." We drove to their yurts the next morning and were greeted by all the families. We were used to eating strange meat there but were definitely not prepared for marmot in the raw. They peeled the skin off and removed the intestines and served it to us for breakfast. Again, this was an invitation, so we couldn't refuse. To cope with that taste, we cut some raw onion up and took a big bite before we filled up our mouth with the meat.

A day later we heard that a plague had broken out, and it was, of course, transferred by marmots. Luckily nothing happened, but for a minute, we were worried because we were a few days from the capital, Ulaanbaatar.

Out of the thousands of places you've stayed around the world, what have been your best and worst accommodations?

My favorite place I ever stayed was in a tree house in Tanna, Vanuatu. The dwelling was right below the active Mount Yasur, so you could look out over the erupting volcano. It was an outstanding experience.

My stay with a tribal elder in Irian Jaya, a village some three days away from the Baliem Valley, was particularly memorable. In this tribe, the men and boys stay on the upper-level of their huts, while the women and pigs, which are considered holy, sleep below on the ground. Since the upper level was already filled, I had to sleep down below next to a giant mother pig. She had cozied up next to me, fallen asleep and started snoring. I tried jolting her awake, but no reaction. In the end, I gave up and chalked it up as a night to remember.

What is your favorite "off the beaten path" destination, and why?

I love traveling to Yemen – it's one of the only places that hasn't changed much in the last 20 years. The people are, contrary to how it's portrayed in the media, extremely friendly, and the landscape and cultural sites are incomparable. Nowadays, while many extraordinary places are flocked with tourist groups and hotel complexes, Yemen remains unaffected.

What were your most challenging countries to visit, and why?

In 1991, while traveling in Pakistan, I met some Mujahideen in Balochistan. One spoke English quite well, and we came along. They invited me to visit their home village in Afghanistan, where at that time a civil war was raging. Since I was always curious about Afghanistan (and a bit of a fool), I decided to go with them, hiding in the back of a pick-up truck across the border. I was wearing Pashto clothes and had a beard, so I was able to pass as an Afghani, but the entire time I was afraid of being caught. If anyone had talked to me, it would have been over.

Of which travel accomplishments are you most proud?

On December 26, 2003, I survived a major earthquake in Bam, Iran, where tens of thousand of people were killed, and the entire city was completely destroyed. The earthquake came in the night; I'd been in another earthquake before, so was able to sense it and get myself out of the guesthouse I was staying in before it collapsed. For the next 12 hours, and with the help of my friend and the guesthouse's owner, I dug out the surviving tourists from the rubble and rescued ten lives. Hours later we managed to bring them to Tehran, where they got medical attention and survived. I got a lot of attention through this and was able to raise enough funds to return to Bam to build a school and fund a women's project for the restoration.

Do you remember encountering particular people who left a lasting impression with you?

In 1994, I traveled to Lhasa, Tibet. Word had spread that a few hours away was a "Living Buddha." I thought this would be nothing less than an interesting experience and loaded into an old Chinese bus packed with Tibetan pilgrims to that remote monastery. After the prayers, we slowly made our way to the top of the monastery to a room where, to my surprise, a fairly young boy was sitting. The vibe was really spiritual and the pilgrims I'd traveled with seemed totally devoted to him. He gave me a piece of red string, which I tied around my wrist, and even wore for a while after. Six months later I found out that he was well-known reincarnation and the movie *The Living Buddha* was made about him.

In 2004, I had a private audience with Shirin Ebadi, the Nobel Prize winner and human rights activist from Iran. She was small in size but had an incredible presence, especially knowing that every move she made was monitored by the Iranian secret service (SAVAK).

If you could travel back in time, to which era and place would you go, and why?

I would go back to the 70s when it was easy to travel through Afghanistan on the old 'Overland Trail' to India. Another would be to travel through the Sahara, all the countries like Niger, northern Chad, and southern Algeria that are pretty much off limits now.

Can you describe any particular situation where you felt completely out of your comfort zone?

I got arrested once in Karachi, Pakistan. At customs, as I went through the x-ray, someone tapped my shoulder to see what I was carrying in my bag. I'd had some crazy travel moments the previous two months, traveling in war-torn Afghanistan and post-Khomeini Iran. In Afghanistan, a Mujahideen had given me a gift – an antique, non-functioning muzzle-loader from the 1800s. The airport security guard was part of the ISI secret service and asked me to come with him. I explained that it was a gift and didn't work, but he accused me of trying to smuggle it out of the country since it was a historic artifact. The sentence for that was two years. Karachi is not the place you want to be in jail. I spent the next few days in a detention prison being interrogated. Finally, the morning after my second night in jail, he must have sympathized with me because he came in, gave me the gun back and said I could leave, but to take the gun with me. Keeping the gun would have otherwise been grounds to keep me detained. I've never been more relieved than in that moment. Who knows what would have happened being imprisoned in a Pakistani jail for two years?

What are your three favorite cities in the world, and why?

My favorite city in the world, by far, is Sana'a, the capital city of Yemen. This is where time stands completely still, with its centuries-old mud architecture, olive presses run by camels and men sporting Jambiya swords. It's as if the place has been in a vacuum for the last century.

My second favorite city is Vancouver – there is something about this town that I really connect with. Its location is ideal: you can go skiing and swim in the ocean on the same day, and offers a mélange of natural and cosmopolitan which is hard to rival.

The third is Bangkok. Despite the traffic, Bangkok has the most Oriental feeling, lots of attractions, good shopping, and fantastic food. It is also a hub for Asia and a convenient stopover point to satellite out of.

What is the ideal amount of time you prefer to travel on each trip before you are ready to go home and take a break?

I don't think there is an ideal amount of time. It really depends where I travel and what is on my list. I am happy to go for a day or as much as a year. Some locations have so much to offer I can't get enough, and some I am just happy to have seen once. At one point, I'd traveled for twelve months, and if I'd had more time, I would have extended my trip immediately. Another time I was in West Africa, and I couldn't wait to get my flight back.

In your opinion, where are the most beautiful places on Earth?

Capturing a place in the right light sometimes is more important than the place itself. As a photographer, I am always trying to utilize the best light – it doesn't matter if it's a bustling city or a secluded beach. I try and travel to locations during specific times of the year when I know it will be good weather, and will even adjust my trip if things are looking questionable. It makes such a difference if you arrive at a place in the warm late-afternoon light, as opposed to rain or clouded over.

If you had an unlimited budget and space and time were no object, what would your perfect travel day look like (for example: start your morning in Bora Bora; afternoon on a safari in Kenya; night in Australia, etc.)?

Sunrise on Easter Island; breakfast at the blue lagoon in Rangiroa, French Polynesia. Midday at Jellyfish Lake in Palau; an afternoon seeing the migration in Masai Mara, Kenya; sunset in southern Libya and after sunset; and ending the night with the lava eruptions at Mount Yasur in Vanuatu.

Which three countries would you recommend for adventurous travelers to visit, and why?

(1) Yemen, as mentioned before, is one of the most rewarding countries to travel in every aspect. Socotra Island, the so-called "Galapagos of the Indian Ocean", is a part of Yemen and is one of the most unique places I've seen.

(2) Tajikistan is wild, rough and untouched, so its people still have an openness about them, innocence.

(3) Algeria has Roman ruins, old Kasbahs, the ancient forgotten Islamic sect of M'Zab, and surreal desert scenery in the south.

If you had just one travel story to share with someone, what would it be?

Never kiss an orangutan! In the 90s, I visited Tanjung Puting National Park in Kalimantan, Borneo. The park is known for its extensive orangutan conservation. On the visit I came into contact with a smaller orangutan who took a liking to me – he grabbed my hand and dragged me over to his little domicile, clear that he wanted to become friends. It was quite a show, using my arms as swings and climbing up and down my body. But after some time I had to leave, and he didn't want to have any of it. He climbed up and tried to do some form of kiss, or in other words, sprayed my entire face. A couple of weeks later I was back in Germany and felt a bit off, and I went to the hospital and found out I had heart muscle inflammation. I was hospital-bound and became a test object for a group of scientists before recovering. So, to say the least, don't kiss an orangutan.

Do you ever feel you have missed out on certain aspects of life while away from home as you travel so much?

I've always tried to keep a life back home, even when I'm gone for a long time, so I always felt happy in both worlds. I am happily married now, and we just had our first child.

What advice would you give to others who would like to travel to every country?

Have a short, middle and long-term plan. Start experimenting with your style of travel and what works for you, and don't be afraid to venture into new territories, personally and geographically. Do your research and you'll see that many places considered dangerous by Western standards are much easier to travel through than, say, Detroit.

For someone who has been almost everywhere, what still gets you excited about packing your bags again?

Knowing that I'm going to have a completely new experience, take great photos and embark on an adventure always gets me excited about traveling. I love meeting new people and awaiting what is yet to come, discovering what is over that next horizon. To expect the unexpected.

Looking ahead, what travel plans and goals are you still pursuing, and what is on your "Bucket List"?

My goal is to have visited all countries before I am 50 (currently at 176/193). I photograph UNESCO World Heritage Sites – it would be great to try and visit as many of those as possible in my lifetime. My wife and I just welcomed a baby, and we are excited to show our kids the world. I'd also love to revisit some of the places I've traveled to 20/25 years ago and see how much they've changed.

Karin Sinniger, Switzerland

(Karin Sinniger in a London pool at sunset)

Where did you grow up, and what was your early life like?

I was born to Swiss parents in Hong Kong in the early 1960s during a typhoon. The only doctor available was attending a black tie event at the Governor's Mansion. He delivered me and walked back to the event with some drops of my blood on his crisp white shirt. But he was very gracious and said he preferred delivering babies a hundred times more than attending such events.

A few months after my birth we moved to Malaysia. It was exciting but also scary at times. There were race riots in 1969, and our house in Kuala Lumpur was under a hill where a lot of people were killed. For months, my mother wouldn't let us out of the house in the morning without first checking that there were no body parts in our garden. We also lived close to the zoo, and occasionally animals would escape and walk through our garden. I was only five, but recall my father and mother holding our barking dog on a leash pouring over an encyclopedia to try and figure out what the animal was. On the phone with the zoo, my parents explained that an animal with a long snout was in our garden, and the zoo keepers asked if it was an elephant! It proved to be a giant, albeit harmless, armadillo.

From Malaysia, we moved to the Philippines during the Marcos years. Martial law was declared and during periods of unrest women and children would be sent out of Manila to the calmer beaches or mountains. We were given homework assignments for a month at a time and had to study by ourselves. We also lived through many typhoons – once the roof blew off our house. Another time, we had no water in our neighborhood for weeks. We had a swimming pool and would get water and boil it from the pool and shower in big plastic drums. Our neighbors would bring us chickens in exchange for water. At night, we got about with candles. As kids, we really enjoyed all of this!

But there were also a lot of burglaries, and they weren't as much fun. Most families had security guards, but they would be bribed to take sleeping tablets. I once slept over at a friend's house. Their bedrooms were upstairs and the living room, dining room, and kitchen downstairs. When we awoke everything downstairs had been carted off in the night, bar a glass mixed with some alcohol concoction from the drink cabinet. This signaled what gang had robbed the house – they were that brazen. My mother would also often get calls threatening to kidnap us from school if my parents didn't pay a ransom. But she flummoxed the kidnappers by telling them they would be doing her a favor by keeping us!

From the Philippines, we moved to Japan. The culture was fascinating, and there were few foreigners, so we had to adapt. I then went to boarding school and university in England before moving to the U.S. for my master's degree in law. I worked on Wall Street for six years. From there I eventually joined the oil industry and continued being a gypsy, working in the U.S., Switzerland, Azerbaijan, Angola, and now South Africa.

I believe my childhood gave me a love of adventure and travel. The more exotic the country, the better. My friends and colleagues are amazed that I go to Iraq and Afghanistan on holidays. My mother is sure that I am a spy!

What was the first international trip you took, and what do you remember most about it?

I've been traveling since I was born so remembering my first trip is not easy. A few memories of early trips come to mind:

I was bored at university and cut my classes and lectures every February when the train company would run a half price special and go on day or weekend trips throughout Britain. One weekend I wanted to see Mount Snowdonia. It is Britain's highest mountain, but for a Swiss person, it didn't seem like a mountain. I recall getting off the train and asking where the mountain was! I was so disappointed that I took the train back to university the next day. But I also saw lots of regional museums and learned to appreciate art and history as a result of those trips. I would spend hours looking at portraits in manor houses and imagine the lives of these people.

My first solo trip was to Australia. I worked as an intern lawyer in Sydney and then spent a month traveling around Australia by bus, before flying to Bali for a week. I remember arriving in Bali with $80 USD in my pocket and living in simple digs close to Kuta Beach. A lovely family who owned a warung on the beach rented surfboards and cooked fresh food. They adopted me, and I left the country with $20 still in my pocket. I still have a photo of me with that family. My mother says I look so happy and at home with that family, and I was.

The other early trip I remember was after I graduated from law school. I traveled from London to Kathmandu on a double-decker London bus converted with bunk beds up top and a kitchen and seating area at the bottom. Only three of us and the bus driver could get visas into Khomeini's Iran. A big sign at the border with Turkey saying "Death to the Supper (sic) Powers" and the "Americans are dogs but the British are worse" greeted us. Our vinegar was taken off us as it was considered alcohol. Our cassette tapes (this was in 1987) with female singers were confiscated as they weren't wearing veils. We stayed at a hotel in Isfahan. I whistled while showering and the hotel keeper told me to stop as women weren't allowed to whistle and would get five lashes in the public square for this. We went to the cinema to see Treasure Island in Persian. They cleared out the entire row I was seated on of all the men. The trailer before the film showed Iraqi jets being shot down. You could buy postcards of these downed jets. I sent one to my mother saying, "Wish You Were Here." She didn't appreciate it.

When did you go from traveling casually to making this a full-time goal, and what motivated you to travel to every country?

I was on an expedition to the Chagos Islands in the British Indian Ocean Territories (BIOT) in 2005. There I met a member of the Travelers' Century Club (TCC). It quickly became apparent that as a result of my upbringing and wanderlust, combined with the scuba diving I had done around the world, I had been to more than a 100 territories and could become a member. My friend was an avid stamp collector and combined this interest with traveling. I figured I could do the same with scuba diving and marry my love for traveling and diving in a more systematic way. Once I had a goal to go to every country, I rapidly added to my country count. I would tack on a few days at the end of business trips to dive and travel and visited lots of landlocked countries I would ordinarily not have chosen to go to had I not had a goal.

What have you done in your life to gain the freedom and finances to pursue as much travel as you have?

From my very first paycheck, I've saved. I never wanted to be stuck in a job working for people I didn't like or doing something I didn't enjoy. I wanted the freedom to retire early. I also quickly realized that investing long term in the stock market and buying quality companies and holding them was the only path for a regular wage earner like me to secure the money I needed to live my dreams, short of robbing a bank or winning the lottery. So while my colleague's amassed cars, second homes, and possessions, I saved and amassed stocks and invested in travel and the experiences that come with it. Saving even small sums of money and letting the gains compound over long periods has paid dividends for me. Indeed, Albert Einstein called compounding the best-kept secret. Twenty years from now you will probably not remember the TV or couch you bought, but you will remember your trips, experiences and the kindness of the people you met. So I think investing in travel is well worth it in terms of the education you get and richness it adds to your life and persona.

Has there ever been a time where you considered abandoning your travel goals?

I have been trying to dive in Somalia, but I'm told it is still too dangerous. I'm not giving up, though...

What do you consider to be your two favorite travel experiences, and why?

I recall being in a yurt with an Uyghur family near Urumqi in western China in 1987 and riding horses with them during the day. I had an incredible moment of being one with the world and in the moment. I found that same zen moment in the back of a taxi in Kurdistan in the searing desert heat: there was very little scenery, a tar road and it was over 40C, yet I had an incredible feeling of contentment and the daily chatter in my head subsided, and I felt cleansed.

I also loved diving at dusk with the flashlight fish coming out of the hold of the SS *President Coolidge* in Vanuatu. You have a nitrogen buzz due to the 40-meter depth and see thousands of points of light for a few minutes surrounding you until they disappear into the sea. It's like floating in space. I came back to my hotel room after that dive and didn't even shower as I wanted to keep the salt on my body to hang onto that moment forever.

What are the main things you seek to experience when you travel (culture, cities, nature, animals, adventure activities, etc.)?

I look to experience the best each country has to offer, be it cultural, natural, etc. Of course, I always try to dive in each country too, so there is almost always an element of adventure and nature in my travels.

Looking back from when you started traveling to where you are now, in what ways, if any, has travel changed you?

Travel has made me more flexible and ensured that I am at home anywhere and with anyone.

Do you speak any foreign languages, and if so, which have been the most useful for you besides English?

I speak French, German, Spanish and Portuguese in addition to English. French is useful in North and West Africa, but I have found Spanish to be the most useful after English as it is the lingua franca in Central and South America (other than Brazil), and knowing Spanish enables you to get by in Italy and Portuguese-speaking countries.

What was the longest extended trip you have ever taken, when was it and where all did you go?

I went on a six month trip after graduating from university in 1987. I took a bus from London to Kathmandu and from there went to Tibet, Bangladesh, Singapore, Malaysia and Indonesia. At the end of it, I got a bit bored from traveling and was itching to get back to my studies.

I will soon retire and doubt I will travel full-time. I have learned to slow down and am planning on making several trips every year, but also to spend a lot of time sitting still!

What two countries have exceeded your expectations and which ones left you feeling underwhelmed, and why?

I cut short a trip to Israel in 1985 – the only time I have ever done so. I found the people too rude and chauvinistic to anyone who wasn't Jewish. But I went back three years ago with my nephew and niece and we had a great time.

I wasn't expecting much from Malawi but loved experiencing the age-old rhythms of life along the river as the fishermen got up at dawn and their wives and children cooked and cleaned with no electricity. Luang Prabang in Laos also spoke to me: it is such a peaceful and spiritual place. Ditto with Bhutan. You've got to love a country that measures its success by how happy its people are!

When you travel, do you prefer to go with others or solo, and why?

I have mostly traveled solo, although that has recently changed as I got married. I'm a loner by nature and like being able to meet people when I want to, but also to be alone when it suits me. I also think that people relate differently to you when you are on your own. You are less threatening to others, and if you are a woman, people are often protective over you. You also are often more open to striking up conversations with strangers than if you travel with a companion. I don't like mass tourism and enjoy planning my own trips and going where I want to go rather than where the tour operator wants me to go.

What has been your most uncomfortable mode of transportation?

Traveling in China in 1986 by train. I took a three-day journey from Xi'an to Urumqi in the height of summer across the Taklamakan Desert. The train was delayed, and we ran out of water. Three elderly people were carried off the train dead. Every morning the "East is Red" would blare us awake. I persuaded one of the train attendants to play The Beatles instead one morning. The head attendant came running to switch it off! But the worse was an overnight train ride from Dunhuang to Beijing. Most of it were traveled "hard feet"– meaning standing. Not one nook or cranny on that train was free – whole families were camped in the toilets with their farm animals. The other problem was that passengers from passing trains would throw bottles. So to prevent killer litter, they kept the windows in our train sealed. Every male on the train, including nine-year-old boys, chain-smoked. It was like a sauna and terribly smelly. My white t-shirt was gray upon arrival in Beijing. Something you can only do when young!

An overnight ride in a minibus from Guayaquil to Quito was also uncomfortable and gave me bronchitis. And I hitchhiked a lift in a hay wagon to the Lhasa airport in Tibet. I was in good company shedding farm odor and hay on that plane ride to Beijing.

What is the strangest thing you've seen/experienced while traveling?

I was working as an intern at an advertising agency in Hong Kong one summer. We had a client launch in Macau. The morning after the launch we had a day to sightsee. First stop was the bombed shell of the Portuguese Cathedral in the center of town. I was taking a photograph and all of a sudden I feel a searing hot pain in my foot. Before I had time to call out the pain was gone, but when I tried to walk I couldn't. I looked down at my feet and saw a small hole right through my right shoe and knew I had been shot. I hobbled to my colleagues and asked them to take me to a hospital. They thought the heat was getting to me and didn't take me seriously at first, as no one had heard a shot go off. They finally took me to the hospital, and a Portuguese doctor also couldn't believe I had been shot as guns are illegal in Macau. By that time, I was shaking in shock and fear that I wouldn't walk again despite the immense heat and humidity. They put about ten blankets on me while the doctor took an x-ray and confirmed that I had a bullet in my heel. She smoked the whole time she operated to remove it and halfway through waived the bloody bullet under my nose and asked if I wanted it as a souvenir! However, she quickly recanted and said she had to give the bullet to the police. The police came with sirens blaring to take me from the operating table to the police station. My colleagues, who initially didn't believe I had been shot, suddenly remembered hearing this that and the other. The police developed the film from my camera and from the angle could see where I had been shot from, but nothing could account for why I had been shot. To this day, this remains a mystery.

What are the best and worst meals you have ever eaten while traveling, and where was it?

I'm a vegetarian and survived traveling in China for six weeks, when there was limited food in 1986, by eating old army rations that provided the minerals and salt you needed for a day. The "1958" rations were my favorites – but that isn't saying much.

I love Indian food and The Red Fort in London serves some of the best I have had. I love the avocado shakes in Angola, and the flourless chocolate cake at Oon.dah in Luanda is to die for – even better than my mother's and that IS saying a lot.

Out of the thousands of places you've stayed around the world, what have been your best and worst accommodations?

Amanwana on Moyo Island, Bali; Jao Camp, Okavango Delta, Botswana; Arakur Ushuaia Resort & Spa in Argentina. The indoor pool with piped soft music in the underwater tunnel leading to the outdoor infinity pool looking over the Beagle Channel in the moonlight is a dream. Since it opened nearly 20 years ago, I have been staying at the Sofitel St James in London for business, and we have been growing older together. The hotel is small enough to be intimate and large enough to give you privacy. The decor is wonderful, but what sets the hotel apart is the management and staff. It is exceptional.

My worst accommodation was a Burmese jail. I was transiting a town with no accommodation for foreigners and missed the last bus out. I was therefore put up in a prison. The kindly police assured me the prisoners were "nice", and indeed, there were no cells. It was all open air. They fed me peanuts. I felt as if I was in a zoo. At four in the morning, they bundled me out and set up a road block to put me on the first bus leaving that town.

What is your favorite "off the beaten path" destination, and why?

A flying safari taking in the desert, sand dunes and Skeleton Coast of Namibia due to the diversity of the terrain, breathtaking scenery and witnessing how well-adapted life is even in the harshest environments.

What were your most challenging countries to visit, and why?

Visiting the Chagos Islands, British Indian Ocean Territories was a five-day rough sail from the Seychelles. I didn't realize until later how difficult it was to get permission to go there until I joined the TCC, so I was very lucky that a biologist friend told me to drop everything to dive in that unique location.

I spent a month on a vessel trying to get to Bouvet Island in March 2015, but despite the expedition allowing for two days there, the weather was so bad we couldn't land. We did circumnavigate the island twice, though.

Libya is currently off limits to tourists both from a visa issuance and safety perspective, and Somalia is currently too dangerous to travel to.

Of which travel accomplishments are you most proud?

Setting the world record for scuba diving in the most countries (as of March 2016, I have dove in 144 countries). I dove with an elephant in the Andaman Islands in 2013, and that was the 125th country I dived in. A year later I took my nephew, niece and wife to dive there and we were the last divers to dive with Rajan before he was retired. He had noticeably aged from the previous year but seemed to know it was his last dive. He didn't want to come out of the water, and his mahout had to lead him out.

Do you remember encountering particular people that left a lasting impression with you?

I have few bad memories of people I have met in my travels; they are almost all good.

The family in Bali I mentioned before who befriended me when I was a poor student who needed to make $80 last a week. The old lady in Rome who not only showed me where to catch a bus but paid for my fare. The elderly couple I sat next to on the train to Glasgow, who took me home with them and gave me food and shelter for the weekend.

I also have wonderful memories of the old crab fortune teller I consulted in 2012 in the north of Cameroon on the Nigerian border. I asked him if I would find love and in which country I would make my home. He kissed and sang to his crabs and then told me that within five years I would marry an African and remain in Africa. In May 2015, I married a South African and since September 2015, I have lived in Cape Town. That old man sure knew what he was doing!

If you could travel back in time, to which era and place would you go, and why?

England in the golden age of exploration in the late 19th and early 20th century. So much of the world was still to be discovered, and the public was fascinated by expeditions to find the source of the Nile, the poles, the stories of Stanley and Livingston, etc. and helped fund some of them. The Royal Geographical Society was a focal point for these expeditions and the photographs and dissemination of knowledge stemming from them. You can still access this material today.

Can you describe any particular situation where you felt completely out of your comfort zone?

I was befriended by two youths on a bus in Chittagong, Bangladesh. They offered to take me to the airport to catch my flight to the capital, Dhaka. They hailed a motorbike rickshaw and off we went. About ten minutes into the ride, I noticed that we veered off the main road going to the airport. I shouted to the driver that he made a mistake and that I needed to go the airport. The youths spoke to him, and we continued on the wrong road. Again, I yelled to the driver to go to the airport. He spoke little English but did understand this and an argument started between him and the youths. One of them jumped out of the rickshaw and ran off. It was then I suspected that all was not right, and I proceeded to push the other man out of the rickshaw. Finally, I was by myself and the driver told me that I was lucky he understood some English because the young men had plans to rob me.

Another time was when I was doing my cave diver certification. It was in the blue hole caves in the Bahamas. Our dive master had just died after he went down 300 feet in a cave without taking helium gas to keep his mind clear and couldn't find his way back up. It is important that cave divers can find their reels and the safety lines they lay going into a cave if the cave they are in gets silted, so we train extensively by putting tape across our masks so that we can't see. We were at 80 feet, and before they taped my mask, I saw a white tip circling the cave with little room to maneuver. I was terrified that I would inadvertently corner the shark while looking for the reel. But I live to tell the tale!

What are your three favorite cities in the world, and why?

1) London: so much history and culture and great ethnic restaurants. A very livable city if you can afford it!

2) Cape Town: a city that lifts your soul and spirit with its beauty.

3) New York: my old stomping ground. It's truly a city that never sleeps: it's like stepping into a cup of hot black coffee. I love the wealth of movies you can see in a few block radius. I can scratch my movie itch by seeing movies from 10 AM to 11 PM and just hailing a cab to get from one theater to another.

What is the ideal amount of time you prefer to travel on each trip before you are ready to go home and take a break?

When I was in my early 20s, I spent six months traveling overland from London to Malacca. I was bored with travel at the end of it and ready to go home.

Since then, my travel schedule has been dictated by my work, so it has been tough to get away for more than two weeks. I find that it takes me about that long to get into relaxation mode, so two weeks is too brief.

I was recently on an Antarctic cruise to Bouvet for a month and found that to be a completely relaxing amount of time to be away, particularly as I have started slowing down as I get older and now look for quality experiences rather than rushing around to tick off every sight to see from my list.

In your opinion, where are the most beautiful places on Earth?

My native Switzerland; the Namibian desert; the colors in the caves of Stoltenhoff Island in the Tristan da Cunha archipelago.

If you had an unlimited budget and space and time were no object, what would your perfect travel day look like (for example: start your morning in Bora Bora; afternoon on a safari in Kenya; night in Australia, etc.)?

Sunrise at the crater rim of Mount Yasur, Tanna Island, Vanuatu. It's an easy climb, and they even have a volcano post office to buy your postcard in advance. The sunlight on the magma of the crater rim is fantastic.

Diving in the Solomon Islands.

Visiting the Pitt Rivers Museum, in Oxford, UK.

Enjoying mezze for lunch overlooking the port of Tyre, Lebanon.

The Antarctic Peninsula in the afternoon.

An elephant walk massage at the Glenn Hotel in Cape Town.

Sunset over Angkor Wat, Cambodia.

Indian dinner at the Red Fort in London.

A swim and star gazing over the Beagle Channel in the pool of the Arakur in Ushuaia.

Sleeping at Flamingo Bay Water Lodge, Ponta da Barra, Inhambane, in the midst of the mangroves in Mozambique.

Which three countries would you recommend for adventurous travelers to visit, and why?

Taking a safari in Botswana's Okavango Delta. It's one of the best quintessentially African experiences.

Visiting the Chagos Islands, British Indian Ocean Territories. The history is interesting although tragic; there is some excellent scuba diving, and it is one of the most difficult destinations to get to – so the sense of accomplishment will be high.

Antarctica: even experienced travelers often leave the polar regions for last, which is a pity as it is such a unique destination. The never ending sea, whiteness and life among the harsh environment will touch you to the end of your days.

If you had just one travel story to share with someone, what would it be?

That would be my story of getting shot in Macau, mentioned above.

Do you ever feel you have missed out on certain aspects of life while away from home as you travel so much?

I have only been married recently, so I don't think I have missed much by being away from home. However, I did try and cram the maximum into every day, so often needed to go back to work to recover from my vacation!

Since being married, however, my focus has shifted away from traveling for the sake of traveling to traveling to places where my spouse and I can enjoy an experience together.

What advice would you give to others who would like to travel to every country?

Take the time to smell the roses and value the experiences along the way rather than focusing on getting to your next destination.

For someone who has been almost everywhere, what still gets you excited about packing your bags again?

I love researching each trip and finding out what there is to do in each place I want to visit and the anticipation of what I will see.

Looking ahead, what travel plans and goals are you still pursuing, and what is on your "Bucket List"?

Exploring the northern polar regions and diving in Greenland and Irian Jaya, Indonesia.

Lawrence Williams, The Gambia

(At the DMZ in North Korea, 2015)

Where did you grow up, and what was your early life like?

I grew up in England in a small town on the Surrey/London border in a run-of-the-mill, middle-class family who did not travel outside of the UK for holidays. My maternal grandparents had a holiday caravan on the south coast of England, and I would go there a lot as a child. From a young age I was always getting on local buses and trains, going to nearby towns, and by the time I was 12 I was venturing up to London alone or with friends. I was very much involved in BMXing and skateboarding, and during the early to mid-1980's I would take the train from Hampton Court station to Waterloo every Wednesday night to skateboard on the South Bank. I always had a desire to travel from a young age and had a lot of independence. I was fascinated by Africa from as early as I can remember, and at seven years old my class at school went to the Commonwealth Institute in London, and I was given The Gambia to do a project on, and from there my love of Africa was cemented. I knew one day I would live in Africa, and as soon as I finished university, I moved to The Gambia.

My father introduced me to music from as early as I can remember. He had been a musician in the 1960s and had a passion for music that he passed down to me. I went to my first concert at the age of 14, and by the time I was 16 I was traveling all over the UK and Europe watching live music, and eventually going all over the world to see my favorite bands play. It got to the stage where I started to choose countries that I had not been to before to see the bands, and eventually the music took second place to the country that I was visiting. To this day I still try to see bands play in new countries, often tailoring my journeys to fit in with concert tours. I no longer feel the need to see every concert that my chosen bands play, but I still love to experience live music.

What was the first international trip you took, and what do you remember most about it?

My mom's sister had emigrated to Australia before I was born, and in 1979, she was diagnosed with terminal lung cancer. In early 1980 when I was ten years old, my grandfather took me to Australia to visit her before she died so I could get to know her and my cousins that I had never met. I had just had pneumonia and been bedridden for eight weeks, and then suddenly I was on an 18-hour flight to Australia for a six-week adventure. The first thing about the trip that sticks in my head was landing at the Bombay airport and seeing all the corrugated iron shacks that were people's homes right up to the fence of the airport. There had been an outbreak of cholera just before we arrived so we could not leave the plane. I remember the doors of the plane opening on the tarmac and feeling a blast of heat and the smell of India enter the plane.

The whole trip was marred by the fact my auntie was dying, and ever since then I have had no desire to visit Australia again. I will return one day to visit Tasmania and to leave James there in Australia, but the whole experience of being confronted with a family member dying affected me deeply, and has really warped my view of the country. I have some happy memories of the place and having adventures with my cousin, but mainly I feel a weird sense of loss when I think of Australia.

Two years later my grandparents took me to visit relatives on the East Coast of America for the first time, and that was a totally different experience and started my love of the USA.

When did you go from traveling casually to making this a full-time goal, and what motivated you to travel to every country?

In 1992, when I was in my final year of university, I took a trip to The Gambia with James English. James was my best friend's uncle, who I had known for years and had grown up calling uncle as well; an extended family situation. He was living in Alaska and would pass through the UK on his many journeys around the world, and once I had started traveling properly we would meet up when he was in England and show each other our slides and talk about the trip we had just done, and dreams for future adventures. In 1992, James returned to the UK and was about to do a 9-month expedition through Africa. His first stop was The Gambia, where he was looking for land to build a lodge with his friend. I asked if I could join their journey and we traveled the whole country searching for land. On Christmas Eve, James' friend decided that The Gambia was not the country for him to invest in, so James and I went out to look at one last area on the river, and ended up stumbling across an area of forest that astounded us. Four days later we were business partners and owned four acres of forest in Africa. Eventually, we created a nature reserve out of the area, protecting over 1500 acres of forest and replanting tens of thousands of trees back into the area. In 2004, the Mandina Lodge won an international tourism award, as well as being named "Best New Eco Hotel in the World" by the *Sunday Times* newspaper.

James was the most traveled person I had ever met, and being around him was like taking a crash course in hardcore travel. We started traveling a lot together, mainly to destinations that he had not been to, and soon my country count was rising steadily. Unfortunately, James was diagnosed with skin cancer in 2010, which he was told he had beaten, but a year later it returned and spread throughout his body, and he died eight weeks later in September 2011. At the time of his death, he had been to 232 countries and territories.

We had always said that we would visit every country in the world, and after he had died, I decided to take some of James' ashes to every county that he had not visited. I went through his list of countries and counted that he had 32 left. During the first trip with his ashes, I decided that I would try to leave some of him in every country in the world. On the second journey, I did with his ashes, and I made up my mind to take some of him to every country and territory on the Travelers' Century Club (TCC) list. I had been to over 100 countries when I started my travels with James' ashes, so I will have to return to a lot of places again to leave him there. The good thing about returning to countries that I visited with James when he was alive, is that I know the places that he really enjoyed, so I can jump in and out of a country in a short period of time and have a plan in advance where I want to leave him.

The project, which I call "Travels With My Dead Uncle" has changed the way that I travel, and has given me a purpose behind going to all countries and territories. Sometimes I used to think that I was selfish wanting to travel so much, but now feel like I have a greater purpose to being on the road, and the fact that I am honoring James in the process makes it feel extra special.

What have you done in your life to gain the freedom and finances to pursue as much travel as you have?

From the time I was 15-years-old I always had part-time jobs to fund my music and travel obsessions, sometimes working three different jobs at the same time, as well as going to school and university. My parents would match the money that I would save to help me travel more; they sacrificed a lot so that I could have the freedom to travel and experience the world. Even now I am still in debt to them for my travels. I don't take a wage from my lodge; instead, I constantly reinvest any money made into making the place better and paying off debts. I have taken some quite substantial loans out; my parents have re-mortgaged their house on a couple of occasions, and I use loans to help finance the travel as well. By any means necessary!

Has there ever been a time where you considered abandoning your travel goals?

After James had died I only traveled for business for two years. I lost the need for adventure in my life, and without him to travel with it all seemed like a waste of time and energy. As soon as he died I had his ashes tattooed into the palms of my hands, which was when I decided that I would take some of his ashes to all of the countries, but every time I would plan a trip I would find an excuse to cancel it. Eventually, I booked a flight to Cyprus, and I started off by finishing Europe for him, and the month-long trip that I took ignited my passion for travel again. Since then I have been on a mission to travel as much as possible.

What do you consider to be your two favorite travel experiences, and why?

This is a hard question to answer. There are so many aspects from every trip that I take that stand out in my mind. But if I had to pin it down it would probably be the first trip that I did to Asia, as I had never experienced anything like it before, and everywhere I looked I was in total awe of my surroundings, and I had culture shock on a daily basis for months on end. It was that trip through Southeast Asia that really gave me my love of ancient cultures and gave me the confidence to travel to remote places. The standout point of that journey was taking an old steamboat from the Riau Islands, which are the closest Indonesian islands to Singapore, to Pekanbaru in Sumatra, and sleeping on deck for two nights under the full moon. It was a magical experience.

The second would be driving from London to The Gambia with James in our 1977 Land Rover in 1993. We had nothing but problems with the vehicle. We blew the engine in Spain, and I had to fly back to the UK to get parts. We were stuck for six weeks in total in a small town south of Barcelona, as one thing after another went wrong with the car. Finally, it was ready, and we set off again and crossed from Spain into Ceuta and then into Morocco. At the time, Mauritania was only just opening up to let travelers cross through from Western Sahara. We had to get a letter from the British Embassy in Rabat saying we had notified them of our plans to cross Western Sahara, and if anything happened to us we would not receive any assistance from them. Then we had to buy a non-refundable airline ticket, to prove to the Mauritanian government that we were flying into Mauritania. It was all a plan to make more money for the Mauritanian government, I am sure, but that is what we had to do get the visa.

We joined one of the first ever convoys that left from Dakhla in Western Sahara and ended up in Nouadhibou in

Mauritania. The first night we camped in sand dunes close to the border, and we could hear Polisario fighters talking on the other side of the dunes. There was a heavily landmined area between the rebels and us, but it was a still a very tense night. A couple of days later we were deep in the Sahara Desert in a convoy with two other English Land Rovers. The lead car hit a patch of soft sand and revealed a land mine that was hiding just below the surface. We slowly drove past, staying in the tire tracks of the first vehicle. When we started to look more closely at the terrain around us, we could see the odd land mine sticking out of the ground. We stayed well back from the lead car who were oblivious to the danger around them. That journey felt like a proper expedition to some really untamed territory.

What are the main things you seek to experience when you travel (culture, cities, nature, animals, adventure activities, etc.)?

I am not a great city person; I much prefer to be in nature or off the beaten track. I do think it is important to see a country's capital city, but I like to spend as little time there as possible. Also with globalization, so many cities are losing their individuality. I was in Beijing in 1990; there were very few cars and a billion people on bicycles. I went back again in 2015, and I could not recognize the place. It could have been a city in Europe or America once you are away from the famous tourist spots. I find that quite sad to experience.

I am always looking to meet the local people and experience how they live, especially those who live in remote areas of the world. I love to see wildlife as well and will go out of my way to see animals that really interest me. I love primates and went to Sumatra to see the orangutans, the Democratic Republic of the Congo to see the gorillas, and Guinea to see the chimpanzees. It was a little goal I set for myself, to see all the great apes in their natural habitats. I have a troupe of baboons that live in my forest in The Gambia, and I can watch them for hours. They fascinate me. On my last trip, I went to Sabah to see the proboscis monkeys and to meet the orangutans again.

Looking back from when you started traveling to where you are now, in what ways, if any, has travel changed you?

Travel made me independent and gave me a strength of character that you can only get on the road. Also, by traveling simply on a small budget, I believe you gain so much more knowledge and see the world you are in more clearly and have a greater understanding of what life is like there for local people. It made me unafraid to face my fears head on, and it has also prepared me for any situation that life might throw at me. I can sleep anywhere now, and have slept in abandoned buildings, under buses, in baseball fields and more bus and train stations than I could ever count. Also, once I have been on the road for a couple of days, home comforts are soon forgotten, and in extreme situations, I can go days without worrying about where I can shower or change my clothes. I remember being on a three-day slow train from Mexico City to Tijuana, in the cheapest seats, sitting with local gang members who were going off robbing people on the train. They looked at James and I and decided we had nothing worth taking and we were left alone. Another time in Mexico, again with James, we were on an overnight bus from Acapulco heading up the coast when bandits hijacked the bus at 2 am and driven into a palm forest. One of the bandits discharged his shotgun into the roof of the bus, and ricocheting bullets hit two passengers. The robbers sent the bus driver around the bus to take people's possessions; he took one look at us and turned around without taking anything. We were the only ones on the bus not to lose our money and belongings. I always try not to show any signs of wealth when traveling in developing countries.

Do you speak any foreign languages, and if so, which have been the most useful for you besides English?

I am terrible at foreign languages. My brain will not store the information. I can speak a small amount of French and Spanish, enough to scrape by with, and I can speak some Mandinka, which is the main language in the region where I live in The Gambia. I have always been able to hear more of a language than I can speak, and often I will understand a conversation that is happening around me, but will only be able to answer in English. I am fortunate that English is the most widely recognized language in the world. The only place I have really had a problem with language was in Urumqi in China. I could not find anyone to help me, and for a couple of hours, I wandered aimlessly looking for the bus station to take me to the border of Kazakhstan. Eventually, a Mongolian lady approached me and asked if I needed help, and then went out of her way to guide me to the correct bus station. There is always a guardian angel if you wait long enough.

What was the longest extended trip you have ever taken, when was it and where all did you go?

The longest continuous trip I have taken was just under five months when I was a student and had zero responsibilities. I hitchhiked from Tanzania to South Africa by myself, and then met a friend in Durban for the last part, and we surfed all the beaches down the east coast of South Africa. On that trip, I also spent time in Zanzibar, Malawi, Zambia, and Zimbabwe. I look back on that journey now and can't believe how long I spent in each country, just hanging out and traveling at a leisurely pace. If I had that amount of time now, I would see a whole lot more. I think the more I travel, the more easily I get a feeling for a new country and its people and cram a lot more into a much shorter space of time.

What two countries have exceeded your expectations and which ones left you feeling underwhelmed, and why?

Iraq exceeded all expectations that I had. I was not prepared for the friendliness of the people of Iraq, and also the beauty of the mountains of the north. Everyone that I encountered was so friendly and ready to help. There were a lot of military checkpoints, and at one point we were stopped and asked to leave the car and taken to the commanders office. I had no idea what was happening, and at first, I thought there was a problem with me being there. The commander kept making phone calls and after 30 minutes I was back in the car with the driver. I asked what the problem had been, and it turned out the military were concerned for my well-being and had been phoning through to other checkpoints to make sure the road ahead was safe for me to travel.

Bangladesh was the second place that bowled me over. Despite the poverty, I find it one of the most beautiful, chaotic and open countries in the world. People are in genuine wonder when they see a foreigner, and everywhere that I went I was the center of attention. There are very few social boundaries between people, and if you stop somewhere for a few minutes, a crowd will slowly form around you with people asking questions. I found I could take photographs and film of people, and they would not be at all offended having a camera stuck in their face. I made a journey on the Rocket Paddle Steamer, and when the captain of the boat saw a foreigner was on board, I was invited up to the wheelhouse to see how the boat was controlled. There was a long gangplank that went from the wheelhouse to the front of the boat, and I got to walk the length of this and film from the top of the boat looking down. I had nothing but amazing adventures in Bangladesh.

With regards to being underwhelmed with a country, the only place I have not really enjoyed was China. The first time I went to eastern China in 1990, I loved it. My second time there was in 2007, and I traveled the Silk Road from Pakistan up to Kashgar. I was totally disappointed with what I saw – I was expecting this magic city of the Silk Road and instead I found a big dirty city that had lost all of its culture and charms, with the least friendliest people I have ever met. I vowed never to return to China again, but returned in 2015 to visit Tibet and Hainan Island, both of which I really enjoyed. The beaches on Hainan were a tropical paradise that I was not expecting from China. So I guess the moral is there is always something of beauty and interest, even in the countries you dislike.

When you travel, do you prefer to go with others or solo, and why?

James and I were great traveling companions; we had the same goals and used to like to travel fast, not spend time in museums, but embrace the country and people of the present tense, not wallow in artifacts from the past. Before we started our business in The Gambia, I traveled a lot by myself, and now that James is no longer here I am happy going alone again. It is nice to meet up with friends on the road from time to time. Recently my parents have joined me for parts of my journeys. I am very excited to be able to show them areas of the world they never thought they would visit, especially after all the sacrifices they made for me as a child.

What has been your most uncomfortable mode of transportation?

I think it would have to be the journey from the Dogon Valley in Mali traveling to Burkina Faso. The guidebook at the time said it could take up to a week to travel along the most direct route between the two locations, and it suggested going back to Bamako, the capital, to cross into Bobo-Dioulasso. I was traveling with James on this trip and we had just come from the capital, which we did not enjoy and did not want to return to. We decided to take the adventurous route instead. We arranged a donkey cart to carry our bags out of Dogon Country and made our way to a tiny village where it said sporadic transport would pass through. We met a traveler from Japan who could speak zero French and only a few words of English. When he saw us he started crying out of relief, as he had been stranded for two days and was having a terrible time in Mali.

We waited for a couple of hours and eventually a bus turned up going in the direction of the Burkina Faso border. The bus had no glass in the windows, and the terrain is very sandy. As soon as we set off, it was like being in a sandstorm inside the bus, which went on for hours. There were twice as many people as there should have been crammed inside, and I kept on feeling the guy sitting next to me trying to pick my pocket. The whole journey was a real endurance test, and when we finally got off the bus, we looked like we had been stranded in the Sahara Desert for a month, covered head to toe in sand. We crossed the border into Burkina Faso, and I sat on a wall, exhausted. Next thing I know rocks are flying by my head. I jumped up to see a military guy throwing stones at me. It turned out the wall I sat on was surrounding the flag of the country, and he had taken great offense at me sitting on it.

What is the strangest thing you've seen/experienced while traveling?

It would probably be the burning craters in the middle of the desert in Turkmenistan. In the morning, I was bathing in an underground sulfur lake, and in the afternoon, I was on the back of a motorbike heading into the desert to experience the craters. It was a fascinating thing to see, and the closer you got the sheer size of these holes becomes apparent. When I stood on the edge and peered over it made me think this must be what hell feels like; the heat was unbelievable. The craters are the result of gas exploration by Russia, that then was set on fire by accident. I loved everything about Turkmenistan, and the craters were the highlight of that trip.

What are the best and worst meals you have ever eaten while traveling, and where was it?

I am not a food person. I eat to stay alive, but food does not excite me like it does for so many people. Living in Africa I eat healthy organic food most of the time, so when I leave and go back to Europe, I tend to eat junk food and love it.

The worst meal I ever had was in a shack in the middle of the Sahara Desert in Mauritania, which consisted of raw goats head where you were expected to pick the meat off the skull with the eyes still in place, followed by camel meat in a fat-based stew. Terrible. I had camel again a few days later while still in Mauritania and it was fantastic.

The best meal was in The Gambia, in a rundown shack on the banks of the Hallahin River, that divides Gambia from the Casamance region of Senegal. An old girlfriend had taken me there, promising me the best pizza I would ever taste. I found it extremely hard to believe when I saw the broken down building, as there was no door to the shack, one broken plastic table and a couple of very unstable looking chairs. After 10 minutes an Italian man arrived, set a fire in a tiny brick oven and set about rolling dough on a counter in the corner or the room. One at a time out of the tiny oven he produced the best pizza I have ever tasted. A few months later he opened a slightly bigger place in Sanyang village, still no more than a shack, but here he also started making his own pasta as well as pizza. People would travel from all over The Gambia to sample his food. One day I took some friends there and the place was closed, and it has never opened since. I have no idea what happened to the Italian, but it was a sad day when the place closed.

Out of the thousands of places you've stayed around the world, what have been your best and worst accommodations?

The worst accommodation was in northern Malawi on my first trip to Africa. I stayed in a backpackers hostel in Nakarta Bay, and it was terrible. The outside toilet that was shared by the whole lodge was by far the worst toilet I have ever experienced, and I have stayed in some really cheap and terrible places. There were bed bugs that ate me alive, and the room was the most squalid thing I have ever experienced, with bloodstained sheets from the previous occupants fight with the bed bugs. At the time, there was a roving bank in Malawi, and I had crossed the border from Tanzania and was left stranded with no local money. The guesthouse in question used to allow travelers to stay there and rack up a bill until the traveling bank came to town. They had a captive audience.

The best accommodation I have ever stayed in was my tent on my first journey through Africa. I felt so safe and comfortable while in there, and to know I was self-sufficient and could stop in any village or beach and pitch my tent and have the same feeling of being home every night was priceless. And it saved on money, even if I was paying to pitch it in the grounds of a hostel. I loved that tent. Later on, when I drove with James from London to The Gambia, our Land Rover had a roof tent fitted, and very soon that took on the same magic powers as my first Africa tent. Independence is everything.

What is your favorite "off the beaten path" destination, and why?

I think that would have to be the Bamiyan Valley and Band-e-Amir National Park in central Afghanistan. The sheer ruggedness and beauty of the area was unbelievable. Photos that I took at the lakes look like someone has gone over the top on Photoshop, but they are just snapped on a cheap camera with no filters. Other than the tragedy of the Taliban blowing up the Buddha's, the whole Bamiyan Valley is like going back in time. I have journalist friends who have been to Afghanistan many times and have never really seen the country, other than the areas that are ravaged by war, and that is very sad, as it is one of my favorite countries I have visited. This trip was another one that I did with James, and we had shalwar kameez outfits made for us in Pakistan before we crossed into Afghanistan, so we could blend in more while we were there. James had a big beard at the time, and he was constantly getting mistaken for being Afghan.

What were your most challenging countries to visit, and why?

Turkmenistan and Iran for the visas. It took a long time to organize both, and when we finally got our visas for Iran in Uzbekistan, it then looked like we would not get our Turkmenistan visa issued, which would have meant we could not visit Iran, and weeks of work and stress would have been wasted. We went every day for a week to the Turkmenistan Embassy in Tashkent, each day taking bottles of vodka for the guards so they would put in a good word for us with the embassy staff. We finally got our visas on James' birthday and headed straight for the Turkmenistan border.

Of which travel accomplishments are you most proud?

Every time that I leave some of James' ashes in a new country or territory, I get a huge sense of accomplishment. I have to really plan and execute leaving the ashes, and I have to film the process so I can prove in the future that I have actually left him in all the countries that I say I have. The other thing that gives me great pleasure is feeding stray dogs and cats in developing countries. It is probably the most important thing for me to do when I am traveling, after leaving James' ashes. When I first started traveling with James, he told me that every country you visit you should try to give back to the place, rather than just take. Now I spend roughly half my daily budget buying food for street animals. I also try to give as much as I can to people in desperate situations, but it is mainly the animals that I concentrate on. It makes me mad to see backpackers in developing countries that seem so unaware of their surroundings, normally in a big group of friends, insulated from the realities of what is going on around them for the local people.

Do you remember encountering particular people that left a lasting impression with you?

I was in northern Iraq (Kurdistan) and visited a refugee camp populated with Syrian Kurds who had been displaced by Islamic State and forced to flee their village. I sat in a freezing cold tent, huddled around a tiny gas stove trying to stay warm, and drank tea with a family and listened in disbelief as they told me the story of their predicament. Family and friends were raped and murdered when ISIS took over their village. They fled into the mountains on the Syrian/Iraq border where it was reaching 50 degrees during the day. They spoke of trying to help orphaned children they met on the journey, only to have the children die in their arms from dehydration. It was one of the most moving and sad experiences I have ever had, but I am glad to have experienced what you would normally only see on television for myself. It is something I will never forget as long as I live. Such humble and dignified people who have seen horrors that no one should have to experience.

If you could travel back in time, to which era and place would you go, and why?

I think I would choose the year 1968, and I would go to California for the music, specifically to see The Doors play. Also, the surf scene at that time was truly underground and bohemian, and I think the whole vibe of the peace and love era would have been an amazing thing to have lived through. Things started to change very quickly after this, and by the end of the 60s, the hippy dream was dead. But for a few short years, it seemed like the most exciting place in the world to be.

Can you describe any particular situation where you felt completely out of your comfort zone?

I hitchhiked into Mana Pools National Park in Zimbabwe on my first trip to Africa when I was a student. As I entered the park, I paid my camping fees at the ranger station, and while I was there a group of very loud South African guys arrived. I was listening to their conversation, and they said they were in the park for four nights.

I was shown my camping spot, a few meters from the Zambezi River, and pitched my tent. I knew there was no fence around the camping area, as my friend Jim had visited the year before and had his tent attacked by a hyena. Mana is one of the only parks in Africa where you can walk without a guide, and they have all the big scary animals that will eat you for breakfast. The first evening as the was sun was setting, hippos started coming out from the river and running through the camp, then a pack of hyenas invaded. It was exhilarating but extremely scary at the same time. I went into my tent to listen to music on my headphones, and just as I was about to fall asleep, I felt the ground shaking. An elephant was walking past my tent. I panicked and ran from my tent to the toilet and shower area and locked myself in a cubicle. After 30 minutes or so, I came out of the toilets and felt the presence of something in front of me in the darkness. I shone my torch into the abyss and saw a lioness standing five meters away from me. I ran back into the toilets petrified and spent most of the night locked into my favorite cubicle.

The next morning I wandered past the South Africans campsite and saw they were packing up their tent and leaving. I asked what the problem was, and it turned out that two of their group was sleeping inside the tent while two slept outside. The two outside woke up with hyenas standing on top of them ripping their tent apart trying to get at the food they had stored under the flysheet of the tent. That was too much of a wildlife experience for them, and they left the park instantly.

What are your three favorite cities in the world, and why?

Vancouver, Canada is high on my list. I love the feeling of the city. It is also quite small so you can walk around easily and find your bearings quickly. I also love the fact that you can see mountains, and you have the water there as well. There are also some really nice parks, so you can get the feeling of rural mixed in with the urban.

Tbilisi, Georgia exceeded my expectations by a long way. To stand in the center of town and do a 360-degree spin in the evening and see all the forts, churches and cathedrals all lit up at night on the hill is something to behold. Also, the old town has such character, and the restaurants were amazing. I hope weekend wedding groups from the UK do not find this cultured and beautiful city and spoil it, as they have done in so many European cities. It was also extremely friendly and felt totally safe.

Thimpu, Bhutan is also a favorite. The only capital city in the world not to have a set of traffic lights. It is a small city, not much more than a big town really, with a real sense of its self; it could not be mistaken for any other city in the world. I love the traditional architecture with its painted wood, and the international airport in Paro has the most stunning cultural architecture of any airport I have ever seen.

What is the ideal amount of time you prefer to travel on each trip before you are ready to go home and take a break?

Four to six weeks is the ideal travel time for me. Any longer than that and I start to take travel for granted and can get complacent to my surroundings. I try to move through as many different landscapes and cultures as possible, so I am always being excited by new and different experiences. After a 3-month trip through Central Asia, I did not want to ever see a blue mosque again. It is a shame to get bored with travel, and my experience of Iran is spoiled because I had been on the road too long when I arrived there and was bored with seeing the same sort of sights over and over.

In your opinion, where are the most beautiful places on Earth?

The mountains of the Himalayas are the most stunning I have ever seen. The jungles of Borneo and Sumatra are the wildest and densest I have experienced, and the beaches of Palau are probably the closest I have been to true paradise – the kind of beaches that you see on adverts that you don't actually believe exist, but they do, and you can find them in the Pacific. The Sahara Desert for the sheer size and all of the geographical terrain changes that you experience driving through. On my first journey there in 1993, we saw no sign of any human existence for six days but found a dolphin skull hundreds of miles from the coast.

If you had an unlimited budget and space and time were no object, what would your perfect travel day look like (for example: start your morning in Bora Bora; afternoon on a safari in Kenya; night in Australia, etc.)?

I would start the day at my home, Makasutu in The Gambia, go snowboarding in Hatcher Pass, Alaska for lunch, go surfing in Indonesia late afternoon. I would watch the sunset over the Ngorongoro Crater in Tanzania, and finish the day off with a trip into space on Virgin Galactic.

Which three countries would you recommend for adventurous travelers to visit, and why?

Afghanistan for the beauty and sheer exhilaration of traveling through a country with so much history. Your journey should start with a trip through the Khyber Pass from Peshawar, on to Kabul, and then the Bamiyan Valley in central Afghanistan. This is necessary to really get a feeling for the beauty and scope of the country.

North Korea as it needs to be experienced by anyone who is serious about travel. It is like nowhere else you will ever see, and who knows how long it will be before it changes.

Bhutan for the unspoiled nature and culture. It is another one of those (few) places on earth where you really feel like you have escaped the tourist trail. Even though you are on a government-sanctioned tour, it still feels like a very special experience to be there.

If you had just one travel story to share with someone, what would it be?

In 2015, I took a trip with the amazing Henrik Jeppesen to North Korea. I had just been in South Korea and had left James' ashes in the Demilitarized Zone (DMZ) closest to Seoul, and decided it would be great to leave James in the DMZ in North Korea as well. There is a military presence on the south side, but there are a lot of tourists there, and it feels more like Disneyland than an area technically still at war with its neighbor.

I met Henrik in Beijing where we had a meeting with the tour operator that had organized our trip to DPRK. I explained that I was trying to leave James' ashes in all countries and territories, and asked if they thought it would be a problem. The guy giving us our orientation thought the project was interesting and said he could not see there being a problem, but to run it past our guides before I did anything. The first day in DPRK I casually mentioned my plan to one of the guides, who then went off to find our second guide. After they had spoken together for a couple of minutes, they told me it was illegal to spread someone's ashes in their country, so I was forbidden to do so. I thought that would be the case, and was really mad at myself for even asking them.

Two days later we were heading to Kaesong and the Demilitarized Zone. I have James' ashes sewn into a goat skin juju by a holy man in The Gambia, and each country or territory I visit I tear off a single pouch, open the leather and spread a small amount of ashes. It takes time to do and can bring attention to me as I am doing it. This time, I decided to open the juju in the hotel room before we left, and I had the ashes wrapped in a piece of plastic in my pocket. When we arrived at the DMZ, it was immediately clear that the North Korean side was a lot more serious than the South, and I felt like I was being watched constantly. I saw Henrik engaged in conversation with the guides and a couple of military while we were on a viewing deck. So I took the opportunity and walked off by myself and spread the ashes over the edge of the building. I always film myself while I am doing it, and later on, that night when I watched the footage back, in the background you can see a military officer point at me and walk over to the head guy, who then looks my way and talks into a device hidden in his sleeve. As soon as I had left the ashes, I moved away from where I had been standing, and as I did a group of the military all walked over and started looking over the edge, trying to figure out what I had done.

On the drive back to Pyongyang, one of the guides asked if she could see my camera. I gave it to her, and a couple of minutes later I turned around to ask for it back, and she was going through all the settings trying to figure out how to watch the footage. I took the camera back from her before she had a chance to watch anything, but I knew I had been seen and was expecting trouble.

Back at the hotel I had a bad feeling about being observed and was worried about the footage. Normally I download my film every night onto my computer and then transfer it onto my hard drive, and then delete the footage from the memory card. This time, I downloaded the footage on my computer, gave it a false name, and buried it deep in the trash. I did the same on my hard drive, which I then hid in files not related to travel, and left the footage on the memory card, which I put back in the camera.

The next morning we were flying back to Beijing, and I was really worried about going through the airport in Pyongyang. We arrived, and the guy checking passports recognized me from when I came in initially, gave me a big smile and let me through to check in. I was amazed at how easy I had made it through. Ten minutes later we were queuing for our boarding passes, and I get a tap on my shoulder. I turn around to see one of the guides standing there with a huge military officer. The guide tells me they forgot to check my computer, and I had to follow them to do a routine check. I knew there was nothing routine about it when they took me to a corner of the airport where seven military officers interrogated me. They asked directly to see the footage I had taken on the platform of the DMZ and started going through all the files on my computer. I was playing dumb and pretending I did not know how to use my camera properly. I finally told them the footage was on the memory card, which they removed from the camera and placed in their computer. It did not take them long to find the file of me spreading the ashes, and as they pressed play my adrenaline was racing, and I thought to myself, 'This is it. I am going to be arrested in North Korea'. As I had been filming myself I had been talking to the camera – straight after I drop the ashes I say, 'I expect I will get arrested now.' These words came into my mind as they started to watch the footage, and I really started to panic. They paused the film as I show the ashes in my hand to the camera, and they ask what I am holding. When I told them what I had in my hand, all hell broke loose, and I had the seven military and the guide all shouting at me at once. It was chaos. The head military officer told me I had not only broken all the laws of North Korea but had also broken all the military laws as I had done the terrible act in the Demilitarized Zone. They were all shouting that I had polluted their beautiful and clean country, and at that moment, Henrik turned up looking for me. The expression on his face dropped when he saw what was going on, and he said he would wait with me no matter what happened. I told him to get on the plane; it would not be good to have both of us stuck in North Korea.

Eventually, they started to calm down, and I was apologizing to them for my behavior in their beautiful country. Someone produced a pen and paper, and I was told to write a letter to the Dear Leader, explaining what I had done and apologizing for disrespecting his country. My hand was shaking so much I could hardly write, but I managed to scribble some words out, and they seemed happy. My footage was deleted, and I was given the memory card back and told I could pack my computer and go. I ran to the check in, and I was the last person there. Most people had already boarded the plane, but I could see Henrik still waiting for me to arrive.

I got my boarding pass and made it out of DPRK without being thrown in prison, and I still managed to keep the footage of that day to prove I left James in the DMZ in North Korea. I had a fantastic time in DPRK and would recommend people to go and see the country for themselves. I would also like to stress that Henrik played no part in my breaking "all" of the laws in North Korea!

Do you ever feel you have missed out on certain aspects of life while away from home as you travel so much?

I miss my many dogs and cats when I am away from The Gambia, but I deliberately moved to Africa as soon as I finished university, as I wanted nothing to do with the life that was waiting for me in the UK. I don't envy anyone's lifestyle that I have ever met, and I feel like my life is blessed by being able to live in Africa. I truly love The Gambia and the people of this amazing little nation, and I am never sad for a trip to end, as I know I am coming home to Africa and all that I love in the world. I have still never found a place in all my travels where I feel so at home and at peace as I do in The Gambia. There is so much on offer there, and I feel like I have found my Nirvana.

What advice would you give to others who would like to travel to every country?

Move fast and forget about sitting on beaches getting a suntan. Unless you have unlimited time and finances, setting a goal to visit every country is a commitment far beyond most people's expectations. By the time I have finished a four-week journey, I am exhausted and tend to sleep for days when I return home, catching up on what I have missed out on by traveling so much. Before I set myself the task of trying to complete the Travelers' Century Club (TCC) list, I used to travel at a much more relaxed pace, but if you are serious about actually seeing the whole world you have to run, not walk.

For someone who has been almost everywhere, what still gets you excited about packing your bags again?

The thought of seeing new lands and cultures always gets me excited, even if I am returning to a continent I have visited before. The world is changing at such a fast rate that I feel like I am racing against the clock sometimes to see destinations before they change too much. I have so much fun planning a new journey; I think that is a big part of the travel process for me. Looking at maps and seeing the best route to take through a region is as good as actually packing my bag and getting on a plane.

Looking ahead, what travel plans and goals are you still pursuing, and what is on your "Bucket List"?

I look forward to completing hard to reach territories more than finishing the entire UN country list. I was booked on the last Wake Island trip in December 2015, which was canceled just two weeks before the travel date. Wake Island is one of the hardest to reach destinations. I was very sad when the tour was canceled, and really hope that they run a tour again in the near future. I also have a passion for train journeys, and will do Trans-Siberia Railway when I have more time. I also plan to travel the length of the Amazon River one day. Once I have completed the Travelers' Century Club list, I will concentrate on expeditions to remote areas. I also look forward to traveling at a slower pace than I am at the moment, but that will be a few years away.

Jorge Sanchez, Spain

(At Salar de Uyuni in Bolivia)

Where did you grow up, and what was your early life like?

I was born in a village close to Barcelona, Spain. I was happy during my childhood, but after discovering at an early age the beauties of the world, thanks to my father's encyclopedia, in which I saw pictures of exotic tribes in Africa, high waterfalls and canyons in America, strange wild animals in Asia and other wonders that I had never seen before, even on TV, I wondered to myself: why isn't everybody traveling to discover these marvels? It was a shock to me to see the indifference of the people around me in my village each day having the same routine. I thought that they all should be on the road, traveling. So when I was seven years old, I made the firm decision to become a traveler when I reached adult age.

What was the first international trip you took, and what do you remember most about it?

My first travel abroad was when I was 18. I traveled by bus to Andorra, worked there for three months and with that money could afford to travel more around Europe, hitchhiking. After Andorra I spent several months in Paris, to learn French. I realized that languages would be very convenient for my travel purposes, so I decided to study the six that are official in the United Nations (Spanish, French, English, Russian, Chinese and Arabic). When I needed money I easily found jobs for a few weeks in Genoa selling cheese in the markets, in a reception of a hotel in Brussels carrying suitcases to the rooms of the customers, or preparing cakes in a restaurant of the Isle of Wight, in England. What I remember most of that first journey is that traveling was possible working on the road, in the countries that you are visiting.

When did you go from traveling casually to making this a full-time goal, and what motivated you to travel to every country?

When I finished the compulsory Army, I tried to integrate myself into the routine of a sedentary life in my country, Spain. I found a job and traveled once a year to some random country, during my holidays. But that was not enough to satisfy myself, so soon I left everything to travel full time, finding occasional jobs on the road, in countries rich in money such as Japan, Australia, Canada, USA or Europe, washing dishes in restaurants or any unspecialized job. Thanks to the money saved I could afford to keep on traveling. When I had little money left, I again looked for a job, and so on. Then, when I was 40, I counted my countries visited and found out that I had well surpassed one hundred, and then I resolved to visit them all, a goal that I reached when I was 49, with Somalia being the last country.

What have you done in your life to gain the freedom and finances to pursue as much travel as you have?

I have always worked to finance my travels since I was 18 years old. I have washed dishes in many restaurants, and I have picked fruits in several countries for a salary. Even up until now I have been helping in factories, cleaning the floor or the installations. I know that most people start working hard when they are young, save money, and when they are retired or have gathered a small fortune thanks to their many years of hard work, they start traveling intensively. My case has been just the opposite, I have traveled intensively since my youth, never caring about the future and spending all the money earned on my travels, just living the day, traveling. So, presently I have a bank account that is almost empty, and I am in my sixties, and today I can't even afford to buy a round trip ticket by plane to Argentina, for instance. But I have extracted the knowledge of the travels during my younger years and have incorporated it into my soul, forming myself as a person with universal values, so I have learned from my travels all that I might now know. If you start traveling when you are old, when retired, it is not the same because your inner self is already formed and the travels only give you dead information, but not knowledge. It is when you are young that the travels are useful, and then the Earth becomes your university.

Has there ever been a time where you considered abandoning your travel goals?

Yes, sometimes I have considered giving up traveling, on several occasions when I was left without money at all, sleeping in a park, and hungry, in an exotic country, without even being able to buy a ticket back to Barcelona, in my dear Spain. But something always happened that made me change my mind; I found a job, earned some money and kept on traveling, forgetting about abandoning my travel plans.

What do you consider to be your two favorite travel experiences, and why?

Walking on foot the Camino de Santiago, from the border with France (Saint-Jean-Pied-de-Port) to Santiago de Compostela in Spain, reached my soul. That is my favorite travel experience, internally and externally. The second one is when I finished my first around the world journey. I could not believe it. I had always considered that I needed to be rich to make such a journey. But little by little, month after month, country by country, working now and then when in need of money, I was able to accomplish that exploit, and the first around the world journey is like your first love – you never forget it.

What are the main things you seek to experience when you travel (culture, cities, nature, animals, adventure activities, etc.)?

I like to visit religious places and also local markets or bazaars when I travel. I think that in these two places you get to know the idiosyncrasy of the people of the country where you are traveling.

Looking back from when you started traveling to where you are now, in what ways, if any, has travel changed you?

The travels have changed me completely. My travels have formed me. I have not been in the university since I started to travel when I was 18 years old; the world has been my university and has formed me with the values that I have been able to learn thanks to my travels. I am a product of my travels, and I owe all to them.

Do you speak any foreign languages, and if so, which have been the most useful for you besides English?

I have tried to learn the six official languages of the United Nations, with more or less success, with my unavoidable Spanish accent. The most useful language, excluding English, is Spanish, which is the second most spoken mother language of the world (after Chinese, but Spanish is more spoken as mother language than English, which is the third). French is also helpful, especially in Africa. Arabic is not so useful and can be substituted by French or English since in all of the Arabic countries their inhabitants understand those two European languages. Russian is compulsory if you travel in deep Russia and the countries that in the past belonged to the Soviet Union. Chinese is also a must if you visit a long time in that enormous and fascinating country.

What was the longest extended trip you have ever taken, when was it and where all did you go?

My longest continuous trip was my first around the world journey, from the first of April 1982 until the 25th December 1984, or exactly 1001 days. It was an around the world trip in which I got to know 46 countries of the United Nations, apart from other territories. I touched all the five continents. I started in Europe boarding in Moscow the Tran-Siberian train until Vladivostok (in USSR times), then I boarded a ferry to Yokohama. After that I entered China and visited many countries of the Far East, then I flew to Australia, New Zealand, several Pacific islands, then the USA, Canada, great Antilles Islands, Mexico and Central America, flight to Europe, East Berlin, Yugoslavia, Mount Athos, Israel, and finally, I traversed the North Africa countries, from Egypt to Morocco. Then I crossed the Strait of Gibraltar and came back to Spain to celebrate Christmas with my parents.

What two countries have exceeded your expectations and which ones left you feeling underwhelmed, and why?

India is a country which I had expected that would like, but I ended up loving it with all my soul, as it surpassed my expectations beyond imagination. India is more than a country, it is a universe. I love its culture, religions, nature, people, and also food. Siberia in Russia is another such place that subjugated me since the first time that I traveled there, for its nature and the several tribes that still preserve their traditions, such as the Yakutsk, Evenki, Buryats, Chukchi, etc.

On the other hand, I had more expectations of Argentina. It is a wonderful country; I am not saying that is not interesting. It is interesting, but being so large I had expected more than Iguazu Falls, Perito Moreno Glacier, and some other tourists attractions – not many more, by the way. I get the same feeling with the countries of Scandinavia, plus Finland. Apart from breathtaking fjords in Norway, plus the beauty of Stockholm, nothing else excited me when traveling in those three countries. Perhaps that (the fjords plus Stockholm) is more than enough, but I expected much more out of them.

When you travel, do you prefer to go with others or solo, and why?

I prefer to travel alone, although from time to time I have traveled for a few days together with another traveler because we have had the same destination. When I travel alone, I find it easier to make friends with the locals, which is one of my goals while traveling. If I have a travel companion, the locals are afraid to bother you and are not so accessible.

What has been your most uncomfortable mode of transportation?

I love trains. The worst transport for me is on a bus on a long journey when is overcrowded, with people standing, and you have not been given a seat by the window. And that has happened to me several times in countries like Mongolia and Chad. You have the sensation that the bus will never arrive at your destination.

What is the strangest thing you've seen/experienced while traveling?

Perhaps the strangest thing that I saw was a wedding between two children of no more than 15 years old each. It was in the Philippines, in Sitangkai Island.

What are the best and worst meals you have ever eaten while traveling, and where was it?

The best food for me is Indian. I love it, even if sometimes (in fact very often) it is very spicy. The worst food that I was offered was dog, in North Korea. I always refused it and instead I was given onion soup. And that same situation was repeated almost every day during my stay in North Korea. I was in that country in 1997. I think that the food conditions are better for the tourists now.

Out of the thousands of places you've stayed around the world, what have been your best and worst accommodations?

I have not been in thousands of places, perhaps in hundreds. The best accommodation every time is when the airplane has canceled a flight, and I have been given in compensation a good room in a 4-star hotel, including a copious dinner and breakfast. The worst was in Gangtok, Sikkim. I still remember it, and it was just a wooden box with the measures of a man a little bit greater than I, and I felt like I was in a coffin. But it was cheap, just a few rupees, less than 1 US Dollar.

What is your favorite "off the beaten path" destination, and why?

I love the hidden valleys in the Himalaya Mountains, in the area of Zanskar or the border between Ladakh and Tibet. You feel free walking in those places; you feel like an adventurer that is about to discover something new.

What were your most challenging countries to visit, and why?

It was hard to get to Somalia, and unfortunately, I could not visit Mogadishu, and I only stopped at its airport twice, for a few hours each time, while flying round trip to Hargeisa in Somaliland, a place that was open for travelers. In my opinion, the Democratic Republic of the Congo is another challenging country where I would like to go back in the future. I only know, apart from its capital Kinshasa, the region of Katanga, where based in Lubumbashi I explored the area around for a week. In the Democratic Republic of Congo, there is still pure adventure, noble people, surprises, and unusual customs.

Of which travel accomplishments are you most proud?

I am very proud of my journey by train along Siberia, from Moscow to Vladivostok stopping for a day visit in the main interesting cities along the way, such as Kazan, Yekaterinburg, Omsk, Novosibirsk, Irkutsk, Ulan-Ude, Chita, Blagoveshchensk, Khabarovsk, and finally Vladivostok.

I also remember my journey on a fishing boat from Cape Town to Tristan da Cunha in 2007. A one-way journey takes about ten days, but one never knows when you will be taken back to Cape Town, so I had to wait two weeks in Tristan until the boat caught enough lobsters. Life on board with the fishermen was great and my stay in Tristan da Cunha was also. That was an unforgettable journey.

If you could travel back in time, to which era and place would you go, and why?

I would like to travel back in the Spanish times when they colonized America and the Philippines. I would love to travel on the yearly sailing of the Galeón de Manila (Manila Galleon), from Acapulco to Philippines (or vice versa). Over 250 years the Pacific Ocean was a Spanish Lake and the Galeón de Manila was the greatest trans-Atlantic vessel of its time. During those 250 years, in spite of the frequent attacks of English pirates, only four galleons fell under those sinister and criminal people (those English pirates today would have been considered terrorists, captured by the international nations and hung without pity).

Can you describe any particular situation where you felt completely out of your comfort zone?

Perhaps when I fell ill in Ivory Coast owing to malaria and had to be hospitalized by my Spanish companions. I thought that I would die. After some days, I recuperated my conscience and little by little my health. The doctors told me that I had been between life and death during those three days and nights.

In 2001, in Conakry, Guinea, after having just been through a shakedown by corrupt officials at the port of arrival, I walked downtown to drink coffee. Three little black men, like dwarfs, measuring about 70 centimeters each, dressed in very colorful dresses, like clowns, smiled at me, and the tallest one of them offered me his hand to shake it. I thought, 'Oh, what wonderful people! This gentleness compensates for the robberies at the port. I will shake his hand to show him that I am not a racist, but a traveler and consider everybody to be my friend.' And when I gave him my hand, he held it strongly, and I could not get rid of his hand. Then, his two companions, located under my legs, searched my body trying to find the place where I had my wallet. I kept fighting with them for several minutes, and nobody helped me, the people passed by, looked at us, but no one intervened. Finally, a Cuban, who had helped me at the pier earlier, saw me and gave several kicks to the asses of the gnomes, until they let me go without robbing me of anything. They ran away like devils, laughing. Grateful, I invited the Cuban sailor to a glass of Havana Club rum in an elegant cafeteria.

What are your three favorite cities in the world, and why?

I love Jerusalem. I feel at home in that city. It is beautiful and intimate. I feel the same with Santiago de Compostela, in Spain. Perhaps the fact that I am Catholic makes me chose those two holy cities. The third one is Kolkata. I know that many people dislike this city, but for me it is natural, it is human, it is as life is. I could live in Kolkata forever.

What is the ideal amount of time you prefer to travel on each trip before you are ready to go home and take a break?

In the past, I used to travel one year on average, before returning home, but presently I can't. I miss my family, so the maximum of time that I can afford to be abroad is 80 days.

In your opinion, where are the most beautiful places on Earth?

I would say in Asia. I have not found prettier countries than Nepal, Indonesia, and the Philippines.

If you had an unlimited budget and space and time were no object, what would your perfect travel day look like (for example: start your morning in Bora Bora; afternoon on a safari in Kenya; night in Australia, etc.)?

I would start the day having a breakfast of café au lait with a delicious French croissant in a terrace of the Champs-Élysées, Paris. Then I would head to Bodhgaya, in Bihar, India, to assist a Buddhist ceremony in the Japanese monastery. In the afternoon, I would go with friends in a motorboat to fish in the Coral Sea Islands, in Australia. I would have a dinner of asado in an Argentinean restaurant in the lovely street/museum of Caminito, Buenos Aires, together with a bottle of red wine from Chile. And at night, I would fly to Granada to assist a flamenco show in front of the Alhambra. To sleep, I would choose a tent near Ouarzazate, in the Moroccan Sahara Desert, and would sleep on a carpet looking at the sky, counting the shooting stars. That would be a perfect day for me.

Which three countries would you recommend for adventurous travelers to visit, and why?

I would recommend for a real adventure, plus beauty and exotic situations, three countries on three different continents. The Democratic Republic of Congo in Africa, Colombia in the Americas, and Pakistan in Asia.

These three countries offer the occasion to demonstrate if somebody is a real traveler or just a travel aficionado.

In the Democratic Republic of Congo, the real traveler takes a boat from Kinshasa to Kisangani (or vice versa) along the Congo River. Then travels overland to Lubumbashi visiting the jungle with wild animals like gorillas, and stays with the natives in small villages, conversing in Swahili, and walking when necessary or asking for rides in trucks. He never takes airplanes.

In Colombia, the real traveler explores the Darien jungle, crossing it with the help of a machete, starting on foot from Turbo, walking and occasionally taking boats via the Islas de San Blas. But never taking airplanes. The real traveler also crosses to Brazil in the most adventurous way, from Mitu to São Gabriel da Cachoeira, and treks to the sources of the Magdalena River, studying the ruins of Tierra Adentro and San Agustin on the road.

In Pakistan, the real traveler will not fail to visit the Kafir Kalash valleys and the exotic Chitral, and will cross the Khyber Pass and take the train to Balochistan, apart from getting to the remote villages of the Ismailites close to the borders with India and China.

Apart from these three countries, if somebody wants to leave his condition of being a travel aficionado and to become a real traveler, a connoisseur of our lovely planet Earth and not to fool himself, he has to pay the price for it. For me that person has to meet these seven requirements:

1 – To make in his younger years (from 20 to 40) an around the world journey, lasting at least one year, calling in the five continents (Europe, Asia, Africa, America, and Oceania). Being self-sufficient, learning with virility to survive on the road, and working when necessary.

2 – Learning at a good level (reading and writing) at least 4 out of the 6 official United Nations languages (Arabic, Chinese, English, French, Russian, Spanish), and to have a fair spoken knowledge of the other two.

3 – To spend a minimum of 20 years net of his life on the road.

4 – To sleep at least one night in every one of the 193 countries registered in the United Nations.

5 – To spend at least a whole year in a great region of our planet, for instance, South America, India and the Far East,

Central Africa, etc., and getting to know in depth the cultures of the people living there.

6 – To cross the following four continents overland, without taking planes, as a real traveler, only using trains, buses, and boats. For instance: Europe from Ekaterinburg (in the Ural Mountains) to Portugal; Asia from Turkey to Vietnam; America from Alaska to Tierra del Fuego; Africa from Oran to Swaziland. If you cross the Pacific Ocean in cargo or sailing boat, even better.

7 – To visit a minimum of 100 inhabited islands in Oceania.

If you had just one travel story to share with someone, what would it be?

I have many, but now I only remember one very funny one that happened to me a few years ago, while in Copenhagen. As usual, I was very short of money and arrived late in the night from Oslo to the port of Copenhagen. I was hungry, but nothing cheap was open to buy a kebab in a Turkish shop, and I could not go to any hotel, which is very expensive in that city, so I walked and found a garden and slept inside my sleeping bag. In the middle of the night I woke up because it was very cold, then I saw many statues. I looked at the plaque on one of them and was written in Danish "Gud Pan" (God Pan). It was a statue of the Greek mythology. Pan in Spanish is bread. And I was so hungry and in a state between sleep and wakefulness that my mind started to associate hungry with bread (hambre y pan in Spanish), so in my mind I was thinking: Hambre, Pan, Hambre, Pan... and my mouth was watering. I was in the point to bite the feet of the statue. But fortunately, before that, I completely woke up and stopped my reaction on time. After that episode, I tried to sleep a little bit more. In the morning, I started to hitchhike in the direction to Spain.

I was in Miami in December 2002 and saw in a travel agency a cheap ticket to Bermuda. I decided to go there the next day. I spent several days in those islands. But I have to tell you some inconveniences that I experienced the first day. After passing through immigration, the police suspected that I was not a tourist (maybe because I was alone, and most tourists go in groups or as couples). Then they sent me to the hospital in Hamilton for x-rays suspecting that I had something illegal with me in my body. Five hours I had to wait in the airport and two more in Hamilton hospital for examination. After the police saw that I was a normal tourist and had nothing strange in my body, they allowed me to go to my hotel. Well, I did not complain. It was their duty. Just I lost one day of my trip but enjoyed the rest. But to my surprise when I got back home in Spain, I got an invoice from the police wanting me to pay $381 for the x-rays! Of course, I did not pay anything. It was incredible.

Do you ever feel you have missed out on certain aspects of life while away from home as you travel so much?

No. I have had a normal life; I have experienced all of human nature. The only difference with those who are not travelers is that I have spent most of my time on the road, while they, those who are not travelers, have lived most of their time in the city where they work and live. I have fulfilled my duty with society. I have worked legally in Spain, between travels, the minimum of years required to get a pension (15 years), thus I have given to Caesar what is Caesar's and in due time (when I will be 65 years old) I will start receiving my well-deserved retirement pension. I have also tried to give God what belongs to God, trying to develop my soul thanks to what I have studied in several monasteries where I have lived for a while as a monk. I have a family, I am in love with my wife, I have a small son.

Perhaps the only disappointing thing in my life that I sometimes regret is that I could have spent more time with my parents had I not traveled so much. But I was always in touch with them, by mail or by telephone, even in their last moments, when I was by their beds without traveling. Anyway, we were four brothers and sisters, and only I traveled, so my parents have always had the company of their children, at least three of them. Sometimes you have to sacrifice the family ties for a while to follow your essence, and my essence required me to travel to get to know the whole world to develop myself. I feel that the day when I will pass away, I will be at peace with myself.

What advice would you give to others who would like to travel to every country?

I would advise them never to resign to that project. It is possible to accomplish it, and they do not need to be rich, just be ready to accept any job along the way to help you to keep on traveling.

For someone who has been almost everywhere, what still gets you excited about packing your bags again?

I travel with only one bag, which is small and never exceeding 3 kilos of weight. I feel excited when I prepare my bag because I know that I will travel to an unknown place that will provide me knowledge about a new tribe which I do not have much information about. And consequently, I will receive many new impressions to feed my mind and my soul, and to complete the puzzle of the understanding of life.

Looking ahead, what travel plans and goals are you still pursuing, and what is on your "Bucket List"?

I would like to visit my last five islands in the Pacific Ocean to feel satisfied with my travels in Oceania. These five islands/archipelagos are Trobriand, Rotuma, the northern islands of the Cook archipelago, plus Austral and Gambier archipelagos in French Polynesia. I am presently planning an around the world journey (which will be my seventh and last one) for that travel purpose. There are more travel projects on my bucket list, but I am aware that I will never fulfill them since I am too short of money and can't afford them.

Paulo Mansur Raymundo, Brazil

(Paulo, in center, at the Kutlug Timur Minaret in Kunya Urgench, Turkmenistan)

Where did you grow up, and what was your early life like?

I was born and raised in Salvador, Brazil. My Christian Lebanese father was an accountant and my Syrian mother a piano teacher. We did not have much money; my father bought our first car, a Volkswagen Beetle, when he was 60 years old. My grandmother told me bedtime travel and adventurous stories about Ibn Battuta and Antar. I usually spent many hours looking at photos taken decades earlier by my father in Lebanon. I often asked myself: what would people be like in those places? What would their customs be? What about their foods? My best friends were my three neighbors: two Spanish boys originally from Barcelona, and a half Dutch half-French boy, whose father would project home made 16-mm silent movies of his trips to the Netherlands leaving me always flabbergasted. To visit those far away places was my lifetime dream.

During my early teen years, I started collecting stamps and money (bank notes) from every country that I could and found so exquisite to think that people would use that money in their daily lives. I also used to listen to shortwave radio stations transmitting in Portuguese from Zurich, Stockholm, Cairo, Beijing and Moscow. I loved when they talked about what life was like in those countries. I even wrote to them asking for postcards. Then an aunt of mine went on an organized tour of Western Europe and sent me postcards from every city that she went to. Not long after that, in 1970, my grandmother decided to travel independently to Egypt to visit her sister, whom she had never met! She was 74 years old and could only speak Portuguese and Arabic, however, she managed to change airplanes twice each way without a problem. Come 1975 and my father went to Lebanon for three weeks. Those travels were driving me crazy, and I was never included in any of them. We were living in an apartment with the window facing the Atlantic Ocean and I could see cargo ships arriving and departing every day, while daydreaming that one day I would be part of the crew and travel to every port of the West African coast, to listen to live exotic music that by then I could only afford to listen to my short wave radio tuned to *Voice of America*.

What was the first international trip you took, and what do you remember most about it?

It was very hard. I went to Argentina for a three-month professional assignment and could not understand a word of Spanish. Although some people think that Spanish and Portuguese (my mother tongue) are very similar, it took me one month to start understanding Spanish. And the weather was hell, I had never been to any place where the temperature was below +19° Celsius (66° Fahrenheit) and in the Argentine Patagonia it was -20°C (-4° Fahrenheit); it seemed another planet to me.

When did you go from traveling casually to making this a full-time goal, and what motivated you to travel to every country?

I had traveled by bus to only eight states in Brazil until I was 23 years old when I then took an airplane for the first time in my life. It was very adventurous to be the only passenger in a single engine airplane being taken for maintenance in Rio de Janeiro, where I had a job interview with Schlumberger, the world's leading supplier of technology to the oil industry. The direct flight took six hours, whereas it should have normally taken under two hours. While waiting for my job interview I saw for the first time an issue of *National Geographic* magazine and I was mesmerized at how many beautiful places could exist, all within my reach, provided that I could excel in my career. I considered myself an extremely high-energy and self-motivated person with exceptional problem-solving, communication, leadership and interpersonal skills, so why not seek challenges around the globe? I could live the dream to give some real contribution to society as a whole, the dream to represent my country and take the name of my family to far away lands, the dream of doing something that had never been done, all of this while traveling. I could hardly imagine that a full-day job interview would change my life forever. A few weeks later I received a phone call from them and was told that although I was coming from a not-so prestigious university, I had been the only engineer hired among a few dozen candidates who had graduated from ITA, the Brazilian version of MIT, and I had to fly immediately to Patagonia to spend three months at the Schlumberger Training Center.

In 1980, I was assigned to Trinidad and Tobago, where I took every opportunity to visit as many Caribbean islands/countries as I could on my days off. I started scuba diving in the then "unknown" island of Bonaire with Captain Don, the pioneer of Coral Reef Conservation who had opened one of the first dive operations in the Caribbean.

One year later all of a sudden I was given a 27-hour notice that I had to move to the United Arab Emirates (UAE), and so I did. I was promoted again, and I sometimes had to work continuously for up to 88 hours without any break, but even so I felt in heaven having a 15-day trip paid back home every 2.5 months. Instead of going home, I always spent that allowance exploring neighboring countries. Traveling was much harder at that time, when a letter would take as long as three months to get home; a phone call had to be booked a day ahead of time and you had to stay put for that day until the operator called you back. On my first annual vacation, I bought a 42-day round-the-world (RTW) ticket with unlimited stopovers for only US$1,999 and visited many Pacific islands that I had never heard of. At an airport bookstore I bought the *South Pacific Handbook* by David Stanley and saw that my trip to that region was only scratching the surface because there was a lot more to see than I had originally thought.

The first time I counted how many countries I had visited was in 1992 when the girlfriend asked me and I was surprised to find out that I had already been to over 100 countries; in 1994 I then became a member of the Travelers' Century Club (TCC). Due to my work in oil exploration, I had the honor to be elected Member of the Explorers Club in 1996. I kept traveling mainly to the USA for the next eight years visiting universities, research centers, driving coast to coast many times and visiting large and small cities, national parks, astronomical observatories often being invited to stay overnight to observe, and running road races whenever I could find one from 5km to a marathon. Racking up a number of countries or destinations did not inspire me; it was only a side effect of my search for knowledge and adventure.

On September 11, 2001, I was watching *CNN* when the World Trade Center was hit and it sort of woke me up and showed me that our beautiful world could completely change in a matter of minutes. I realized how life was even shorter than I thought. So I resumed traveling to new countries in 2002 whenever I could. Joining the Most Traveled People (MTP) community of travelers from its beginning in mid-2005 also motivated me to explore each country in much further detail and opened my mind to new places that I did not know anything about.

Therefore, traveling to every country in the world was never a full-time goal. It became just one among many other goals only in 2007 after my year-long overland solo trip through Africa, which was very hard but still easier than I had expected, probably because I was over-prepared for the worst to happen at any time during that trip; so visiting the 193 UN countries would be definitely doable. With my limited time for traveling, I spent the following five years slowly visiting UN countries that I had missed and revisiting a few other countries, also visiting TCC and MTP places that I had missed on previous trips to Argentina, China, India, the USA, Canada, Mexico, and Western Europe. Traveling to every UN country was not an obsession, so in the meantime, I visited TCC and MTP places like Antarctica, Easter Island, St. Pierre & Miquelon, Prince Edward Island, Rodrigues Island, and Sikkim. By that time, I had already been to around 100 countries at least twice. Then on December 03, 2012 I finally arrived in Libya, my 193rd country.

What have you done in your life to gain the freedom and finances to pursue as much travel as you have?

Freedom: I am an independent consultant to oil service companies. I live a very busy life and have been working really hard since I was in my early 20's, usually between 14 and 18 hours per day. I plan my life so that I can take at least two months off for traveling every year, where I free myself from material concerns and seek rich life experiences.

Finances: I do not smoke, and I rarely drink; those two things alone would cost me more than one intercontinental air ticket every year. I do not go to fancy restaurants, and I do not spend on expensive clothing, jewelry, cars – it's been two years since I sold my car, which was 17 years old. I am a budget traveler and my biggest expense in most trips is the air ticket, which I often purchase either taking advantage of promotional fares, flying with Internet-based budget airlines, or redeeming free frequent flyer mileage points. My second biggest expense is accommodation; I usually stay in 3-star hotels, and depending on the country I stay in, hostels with clean private rooms, guest houses and homestays. When not traveling on business, I avoid other expenses by always planning my own itinerary, booking my air tickets, getting my visas, and almost never booking any accommodation unless it is an immigration requirement. I travel independently to most countries without using the services of a guide, except when a travel agent is a prerequisite like Bhutan and North Korea for tours, Libya for the visa, the Stans for letters of invitation, and so on.

Has there ever been a time where you considered abandoning your travel goals?

Never. Most of the time my only travel goal was to be on the road, in other words, the journey itself; the destination was just an excuse. As recently as 2009, I was in China and already had a visa and a ticket for my first ever visit to Mongolia, but I was enjoying China so much that I was flexible enough to say "Mongolia can wait until 2011" and I kept traveling through China. The same goes for Israel, which I only visited in 2011, although I did not even need a visa for Israel and I had been nearby so many times.

Traveling has not been my only interest in life; I also like running, scuba diving and snorkeling, astronomy (in 2002 I became the first Brazilian ever to discover a comet), yoga, photography, science, anthropology, psychology, genealogy, and I still have to work!

What do you consider to be your two favorite travel experiences, and why?

There are so many, and each trip is special and unique with unforgettable experiences. I will mention two random ones:

While having days off from work in Abu Dhabi in 1983, I picked my travel destination by chance opening the ABC, which was a thick catalog of flights used by the airline industry. And so I went to Burma (Myanmar) without knowing anything about the country. The airplane from Bangkok landed in Rangoon around midnight and as usual, I had not booked any accommodation. There were no taxis, so I accepted an offer from four locals who did not speak English to get a ride to town, where they found a hotel for me. They spent the week showing me around their country without asking anything in return.

Traveling overland the South American Pacific Coast. It is so close to home and yet so different.

What are the main things you seek to experience when you travel (culture, cities, nature, animals, adventure activities, etc.)?

I seek a diversity of things: meeting locals, visiting remote temples, remote tribes, and isolated tropical islands. I enjoy not only big cities but also small coastal towns. I like taking local public transportation, the thrill of getting lost in unknown places, and I could spend hours people watching everywhere. I am interested in sightseeing, adventure, seeking new experiences, tasting local food, especially seafood. I like to come back to places where I have already been and explore them in greater detail. At each visit, I rediscover new facets of that culture and of myself.

I seek as a traveler to interact with foreign cultures and expose myself to different values as a way of self-knowledge. To research the genealogy of my ancestors and visit members of my family that spread all over the world long ago. To visit the greatest astronomical observatories everywhere. To see the underwater world in most countries. To visit the main universities and learning centers in the world. To see the marvels of our times visiting the observation decks of the highest skyscrapers. To visit UNESCO World Heritage Sites and national parks, and to enjoy life as much as I can, being always respectful to the local culture.

Looking back from when you started traveling to where you are now, in what ways, if any, has travel changed you?

Travel has changed me in every way I can think of. I would not be who I am today, neither as a professional nor as a person, had I not traveled. Directly supervising engineers and scientists from 58 UN countries at different times and places opened my eyes to so many things. When I see my old non-traveling friends, they seem to have been trapped in time living inside a bubble. I have seen firsthand over and over again that it is so easy to be happy. Traveling independently allows me to absorb an amount of self-knowledge that can not be bought. I have experienced situations that can not be experienced by reading a book, watching a movie, or by attending an intensive course. The more I travel the more I realize how small we are on this planet. This relentless thirst trying to have a glimpse of the meaning of our existence has given me as a bonus the satisfaction of conducting my life with rhythm and humbleness, quality and happiness, harmonizing priorities, goals and results.

Wherever I am on this planet, I find pleasure and happiness in being able to sip a simple glass of water...

In hearing the sound of waves breaking on any beach in an endless rhythm...

In looking out the window and finding beauty in every sunset as if it was all for me...

In looking up at the skies in a starry night and seeing most of the same constellations, making me feel at home wherever I am in the world...

Do you speak any foreign languages, and if so, which have been the most useful for you besides English?

English is my foreign language. I had Basic English language classes at a primary school in Brazil; I did not get exposed to foreign languages living 3,000km away from the nearest border. I moved abroad when I was 23 and had to learn English the hard way listening to audio tapes and practicing with colleagues who were originally from the USA and Canada. Five years later I simultaneously attended English, Spanish, French, German, Russian, Arabic, and Mandarin language classes at night for two semesters; it's been 30 years now, and the ones that I do not use are kind of hibernating in my memory. Without a doubt, the most useful languages besides English are French in West Africa, and Spanish in South and Central America.

What was the longest extended trip you have ever taken, when was it and where all did you go?

It was my 7th trip to Africa in 2006/2007; I spent one-year traveling solo overland clockwise from Egypt to South Africa and back up to Morocco. In several countries, I pretended to be a missionary just to protect my cash, which was $8,300 US at the start of the trip. My luggage weighed seven kilograms, one-third of which was all sorts of medicines, just in case I needed anything. I traveled by local buses and shared taxis most of the time, also riding cargo trucks in Sudan, Botswana, Zimbabwe, Zambia, Malawi and

Mozambique, taking canoes to cross borders, riding camels in Niger and Burkina Faso, hitch-hiking in Mauritania and Western Sahara.

What two countries have exceeded your expectations and which ones left you feeling underwhelmed, and why?

There are so many countries that exceeded my expectations... it would be unfair to name only two.

Syria (1981-2002 on four trips), because the incredibly hospitable people, its history and monuments.

China (2004-2012 on seven trips) always exceeds my expectations. There is so much history, amazing temples, and landmarks. And the people are very helpful even if you do not speak the language.

I would add to that list Egypt, Iran, Yemen, Uzbekistan, Ethiopia, Mozambique, Bolivia, Peru, Mexico, and Switzerland, just to name a few.

I felt underwhelmed in North Korea in 2009. Having always traveled independently, I had to join a group of around 200 Chinese tourists and I was the only foreigner, which I liked. However, I was accompanied all the time by a local guide and had to delete at least 30% of my photos. The worst part was that I could not interact with the locals. In my travels, I want to be part of the action, not a spectator.

When you travel, do you prefer to go with others or solo, and why?

I like to go solo and meet others along the way. Others often join me for part of the trip or only for a few days. I am very energetic and like to savor every minute of my life to its fullest. I like to immerse myself in the local culture, but I am happy traveling with anyone who would have a different lifestyle, like he/she spending the day reading a novel while I am out doing something else.

What has been your most uncomfortable mode of transportation?

Crossing the Sahara Desert in Sudan in the back of a pickup car for eight days in a row, together with six locals. Taking intercity buses in India isn't anything near comfortable either.

What is the strangest thing you've seen/experienced while traveling?

While attending a week-long Petroleum Engineering seminar in Egypt in 1981, it was a national holiday, and I went to watch the annual victory parade to celebrate Egypt's crossing of the Suez Canal. Unexpectedly, I became an eyewitness to the assassination of President Anwar Sadat from a distance when automatic weapon bullets started being fired all over the place by a few soldiers who were taking part in the parade and we had to look for shelter. I ran back to my hotel, the Mena House, while the military jets kept flying and celebrating the holiday unaware of what had happened on the ground. I turned on the TV in my room and kept watching the Reuters channel, which had news via text messages coming from reporters all over the world. It took some time until news started to arrive from Washington D.C. saying something like "There are rumors that President Anwar Sadat of Egypt has been attacked during a military parade in Cairo. More details soon." Two days later the seminar was cancelled and my colleagues and I had to leave Egypt, as our hotel would be occupied by President Ronald Reagan, Jimmy Carter, Gerald Ford and P.M. Margaret Thatcher, who were coming for the funeral.

What are the best and worst meals you have ever eaten while traveling, and where was it?

I rarely eat at upscale or gourmet places; I'd rather eat where the locals go. The best meals:

1. Tabouleh, hummus and fried kibbe (home made in Tartus, Syria)
2. Fish tika with naan, butter garlic king mackerel fillet, masala naan and lamb minced naan (at Rainbow Restaurant in Jaipur, India)
3. Fried calamari (at Fatima's Backpackers in Tofo, Mozambique)
4. Ceviche de camaron (at Bismarkcito Restaurant in La Paz, Mexico)
5. Rockefeller oyster, shrimp fillet and queen oyster (at Mariscos Progreso in Guadalajara, Mexico)
6. Pulpo al ajo (in Veracruz and Oaxaca, both in Mexico)
7. Fried rice with shrimp (in Bangkok, Thailand)
8. Ensopado de camarão (at Donana Restaurant in Salvador, Brazil)
9. Sopa de concha (in Roatan, Honduras)

It is hard to choose the worst, as I love eating everywhere. Perhaps the worst that I have had were:

1. Fruitbat soup (in Palau)
2. Pizza (in Venice, Italy), although I love pizza
3. Camel milk (in Hargeisa, Somaliland)

Out of the thousands of places you've stayed around the world, what have been your best and worst accommodations?

I have stayed in many luxurious chain hotels on business trips, but the best place I have stayed while traveling independently was sleeping on a mattress rented for $2 over the sand of the Sahara desert near Abri in Sudan. I woke up at 2:30 a.m. and the sky was something indescribable; the Milky Way was so intense that I felt I was inside a spaceship. I kept seeing shooting stars all night and tried hard not to fall asleep again until 4:30 a.m.

The worst: a US $3 campement bed in Dakhla, Western Sahara was a really depressing place to sleep, full of mosquitoes. Also, a US $20 hotel where I spent three nights in Monrovia, Liberia.

What is your favorite "off the beaten path" destination, and why?

Tofo, Mozambique in 2006-2009. Inexpensive accommodation, nice village people and great atmosphere, delicious and inexpensive fresh seafood, world-class scuba diving and snorkeling with whale sharks and manta rays guaranteed on every trip, amazing 20km stretch of white-sand beach, dark and romantic starry nights. You only have to be aware of malaria.

What were your most challenging countries to visit, and why?

Sub-Saharan West and Central African countries because border crossings and bribery. Libya because the visa. In 2007, I stayed with a distant relative of mine in Nouakchott, Mauritania. He had been living there for the last four decades, and he invited over for dinner the Libyan Ambassador, who happened to be his long time best friend. There were just the three of us and after dinner I asked him if he could issue me a tourist visa for Libya. He told me that I should get it in my home country, period. Finally, in 2012, I did get a business visa for Libya through an American travel agent and completed the list of 193 UN countries.

Of which travel accomplishments are you most proud?

Nothing very sophisticated, neither real accomplishments, compared to groundbreaking scientific discoveries. My professional and personal life, most of my skills and my moral values are a direct consequence of my travels. I am proud of having been invited to have my biography listed in reference volumes like *Who's Who in the World*® and *Who's Who in Science and Engineering*®. I am very proud of having been able to live each minute of my life to its fullest. In a more mundane way, I am proud of:

1. Always organizing the trip myself and traveling solo, only with hand luggage (5-7 Kg) regardless of the duration of my trip, without gadgets, sometimes not even with a camera.
2. My aforementioned year-long solo overland trip to Africa in 2006 and 2007.
3. Traveling extensively throughout Asia in 1982 and 1983 without seeing any tourists in countries like Burma (Myanmar) and Taiwan.
4. Doing my first safari in Kenya in 1983 was unforgettable.
5. Traveling six months by train throughout Europe in 1986, including Iron Curtain era Czechoslovakia, Hungary, Yugoslavia and Bulgaria, countries where I did not see any tourists at all.
6. Traveling six months in 2004 with the girlfriend on my 5th RTW trip, mainly through the South Pacific. We made side-trips within side-trips within the RTW to visit a few remote islands.

7. Traveling five months overland in 2009 crossing Central Asia, parts of China and parts of India.
8. Mentioning figures may seem that traveling is a competitive activity, which it is not. However, I am proud of a few travel related lifetime accomplishments because each figure brings back an equal number of memories, like having logged 341 scuba dives in 98 TCC countries, and technical visits to 15 of the 16 largest optical astronomical telescopes in the world.

If you could travel back in time, to which era and place would you go, and why?

I would travel back in time to circa 60,000 BC to join the migration of Homo sapiens from Africa to the Middle East/Europe/Asia. I would like to experience being one of them and feel what it was like traveling with them for a few weeks. I am sure I would be able to communicate. I would tell them how important they were to the future of humankind and how worthless was their suffering.

Travel to 2570 BC to witness how the Great Pyramid of Giza was being built, because how they did it is still a huge mystery. I would then travel a few years forward in time to attend Pharaoh Khufu's funeral.

Travel to circa 280 BC to visit the other six wonders of the ancient world because they no longer exist.

At different times, I would try to be a direct follower of Jesus Christ, of Siddhartha Gautama, and of Prophet Muhammad. What teachings have been distorted after so many centuries? Who were they really?

I would also join Marco Polo and Ibn Battuta in part of their travels, to learn what real traveling overland was like.

Can you describe any particular situation where you felt completely out of your comfort zone?

I feel partially out of my comfort zone in my own country Brazil. It is an every man for himself world, with scams, fake smiles, and fake happiness everywhere. The lack of civility and most basic regard for others is disturbing. Not to mention the 200+ homicides per day, which is nearly one Boeing aircraft crashing every day without any survivors only because authorities could care less.

While traveling it is rare to feel completely out of my comfort zone. I should add that I have never been robbed outside Brazil, never been involved in accidents, and I have never caught malaria either. The only serious sickness was catching chicken pox while traveling through Norway and Sweden in 1986; and an intestinal infection in 1992 after eating a hamburger in Costa Rica, when I then took that opportunity to spend a week without eating any solid food because I wanted to lose some weight – and at the same time I made the bacteria starve to death.

What are your three favorite cities in the world, and why?

1. New York because of its vibe, it is the center of the business world, it is dynamic, it never sleeps. It has restaurants from every corner of the globe. Americans share my values and my dreams. I have visited the USA more than 70 times and there is a lot to do and see.

2. Dubai because I lived in the UAE from 1981 to 1984 when there was almost nothing there and it reminds me of my youth.

3. London because the atmosphere and the culture. There are so many universities and museums, and so much history.

What is the ideal amount of time you prefer to travel on each trip before you are ready to go home and take a break?

Between one and two months is ideal nowadays.

In your opinion, where are the most beautiful places on Earth?

1) Iguaçu Falls

2) The Atacama Desert, in Chile, for the starry skies

3) The underwater world in the Pacific and Indian Oceans

4) Antarctica

5) The monuments of Egypt, Ethiopia and Uzbekistan

6) The temples of Thailand, Burma (Myanmar) and Cambodia

7) The Bolivian Highland

8) A few beaches on the Northeastern Brazilian Coast

9) The national parks of the USA

10) The lakes and flowers of Switzerland

11) The fjords of Norway

12) A few West African markets, for the colorfully dressed people

If you had an unlimited budget and space and time were no object, what would your perfect travel day look like (for example: start your morning in Bora Bora; afternoon on a safari in Kenya; night in Australia, etc.)?

Wake up in Iran before sunrise and listen to the call for prayers from nearby mosques. Watch the sun rise in Tofo, Mozambique, while hundreds of humpback whales migrate before my eyes; then eat fried calamari for breakfast, before snorkeling with whale sharks and scuba diving with manta rays. Spend the rest of the morning in Rio or the Brazilian

Northeast, running at the beach and people watching; then have lunch at an all-you-can-eat buffet. Start the afternoon exploring the temples of Southeast Asia. Continue the afternoon taking candid photos at the market in Djenné, Mali. Go to India and spend an hour in Bodh Gaya, and then do a quick stop at the Golden Temple in Amritsar. Go to China and spend a little time in the Labrang Monastery in Xiahe, and then go to Kumbum Monastery in Xining. Watch the gorgeous sunset in the Arabian Desert. Start the evening feeling the atmosphere in a hutong in Beijing. Have Maine lobster for dinner on a luxury cruise ship in the Caribbean. End the evening stargazing in the Atacama Desert holding hands with my girlfriend.

Which three countries would you recommend for adventurous travelers to visit, and why?

It depends on the type of traveler that you are and what the word adventure means to you. You may find adventure at any time and any place, all you need to do is be aware of every opportunity that may arise and may disappear at the blink of your eyes; you may not have another opportunity in the next 50 years.

For instance, when I was in Erbil, Kurdistan-Iraq in August 2009 I spent two nights with a Kurdish couple whom I had met on the bus from Iran, and they invited me to stay over in their house. When I left them in the early morning hours I knew that it would be a long day because I had to board taxis and buses to cross a land border, and arrive in time for two domestic flights within Turkey. I had a technical visit to Tubitak National Observatory which had been arranged months in advance for the next morning, and I did not want to miss it.

So from Erbil I took a brand new Toyota Corolla shared taxi to the Turkish border driving through Dohuk and Zaho, and arriving at the Ibrahim Khalil border post at 11:40 a.m. to find both sides closed for lunch. When they reopened, I crossed the border and took the Turkish bus to Diyarbakir. The driver assured me that I would arrive before 7 p.m. to the airport where I had my first flight departing at 7:55 p.m. After a 10-minute drive, the bus driver stopped for lunch and resumed driving after 35 minutes. We traveled another 10 minutes and the air conditioning stopped working so they called another bus. After a while I boarded the replacement bus, but at 4:20 p.m. we had a flat tire. The bus kept going at 40km/hour until 6:00 p.m. when I came to the conclusion that I would miss my flight. I then decided to leave the bus in the middle of the road and took an old taxi for the remaining 100km offering to pay US$50 for it.

When there were still 30km to go, the car in front of us ran over a pebble which was thrown in my taxi's windshield, and it shattered the glass completely. Fortunately, no glass fell in our eyes, but both arms and hands were filled with small pieces of glass. I insisted through hand gestures that the driver continued driving, and he agreed, but the wind was very strong, so I gave him my sunglasses, although it was already dark. I sat in the taxi's back seat with my hands protecting my eyes from remaining pieces of glass that could fly from what was left of the windshield. A few minutes later it began to rain heavily in the desert, and I wondered how many more obstacles destiny would put in front of me that day, as I had not seen rain or a cloud for over one month! Or perhaps I was misinterpreting what was happening, and I should stop trying because that could be a sign that I should not board my flights? Why so many things were going wrong one after the other? The both of us started laughing out loud while we got more and more wet due to the rain entering the car through the place where there should be a windshield, and the driver wearing sunglasses at night made it look even funnier.

The taxi arrived at the airport at 7:35 p.m.; I quickly gave him US$100 and wished him good luck, and ran to the check-in counter, which had just been closed. Thanks to my having only hand luggage the lady checked me in and I ran again to the gate which was about to close. They were extremely gentle in letting me in all wet and sweaty with blood on my fingers, with no questions asked. I was laughing out loud while every passenger on the plane was staring at me! I felt as if I were James Bond or Indiana Jones! My AnadoluJet flight to Ankara left on time at 7:55 p.m. and I could happily connect to another flight to Antalya for my scheduled visit to Tubitak National Observatory the next morning. In the observatory I was greeted by the director who asked me "Have you been enjoying the beaches of Antalya for many days?" and I said "Not really, I arrived from Iraq a little after midnight and am flying to Dubai this afternoon to catch connecting flights to South Africa and then to Mozambique". He said, "I beg your pardon?!" while exchanging looks with his astronomers, then I smiled and said "Nevermind, it's a long story..." with the same James Bond feeling that I had when I entered the airplane the night before. Those are the adventures which we do not have the time to take photos, but still, are intense and registered in our memories forever.

If you had just one travel story to share with someone, what would it be?

Sorry, but it would be impossible to share just one story. Depending on the person's interests I would tell different stories:

To those who like airplanes and airports I would tell:

- How much I enjoy people watching in airports, trying to guess where each person is originally from just by the way they behave.

- The joy of having flown over 2,000 hours by helicopter as a passenger, including a Russian helicopter in Sierra Leone, which crashed four weeks later killing all 22 passengers after the firefighter who had the keys for his truck took 40 minutes to arrive to the scene.

- To those who think that it is hard to go unnoticed as a visitor in another country I would tell:

- Stories of how in Apia I was mistaken as being a visitor from Savai (both in Samoa); in Samoa as being from Tonga; in London as being a Londoner; in Cairo as being a Egyptian; in Manila as being from the Philippines; in Solomon Islands as being from Papua New Guinea and from New Caledonia; in Lesotho as being from Brazzaville; in Zambia as being from Botswana and from Zimbabwe; in Botswana as being from South Africa; in Indonesia as being from India; in Fiji as being from India, Solomon Islands, Australia and Germany...

To those interested in scuba diving I would tell a few stories:

- Touching the Eurasian continental plate and the American continental plate at the same time while diving in Iceland; they are drifting apart about 2 cm per year, the Eurasian tectonic plate stretches across the North Sea, Europe, and Russia to the Sea of Japan, the North American plate stretches across the bottom of the Atlantic Ocean and North America to the San Andreas Fault.

- Crossing the Equator underwater while diving in Cape Verde.

- Taking DNA samples from whale sharks for a friend's Ph.D. thesis while diving in Mozambique.

- Thinking that I heard a symphony of classic music while I was in awe diving with 60+ hammerhead sharks in the Galapagos.

- Night diving in Sipadan and being amazed seeing giant parrot fish sleeping in their caves.

- Asking the boat captain in Tonga to wait a little more so that we could look closer to some beautiful fish before coming back onboard while he was having a panic attack because his boat was sinking.

- Having had the opportunity of being one-on-one technical diving student of the two-time world-record holder and yet very humble Mark Andrews in Dahab, Egypt, and diving with him to The Arc, which by then had claimed over 120 lives of divers trying to go underneath it.

- Having my dive boat drift away while I was underwater in Papua New Guinea and having to wait for several hours for rescue after I swam to an uninhabited island.

To those interested in Astronomy I would tell:

- How I took the last known photo of Russian space station MIR before it disintegrated above the South Pacific in 2001. Within hours, the photo became viral throughout the world and was featured in NBC News and many NASA websites. *Newsweek* magazine chose the photo to be published on a double page and their editors were on deadline and needed to receive a 50MB file. We agreed on conditions and price. However, I could not find a professional negative scanner in town in the middle of the night. I even tried to purchase an air ticket to New York, but the flight would arrive too late to deliver the image on time for publication. After eight international phone calls, we gave up, and both sides were very sorry. Even so, I felt as if I had won the Oscar and received a $$$ check from *Newsweek* just for the beauty of the image.

- About my quest to visit all the largest optical astronomical telescopes in the world, and how hard it has been to arrange technical visits to each observatory, even being an Emeritus Member of the American Astronomical Society.

To those who travel with large suitcases or huge backpacks I would tell:

- Stories of how much easier it has always been to travel extremely light, and how much more exciting it gets when you do it yourself from the very early stages of planning, and you arrive in a place expecting the unexpected.

- To Brazilians, in general, I would tell:

- Many stories showing that traveling is not all about luxury, splurging, staying in five-star hotels, and shopping compulsively.

To those interested in genealogy and history I would tell:

- That traveling has been dormant in my genes for a long time... having done my genome sequencing a few years ago, my Y-chromosome results identified me as a member of Haplogroup R1a1, M17 (Subclade R1a1a, M198). Therefore, I would start sharing my travel story roughly 60,000 years ago during the temporary retreat of Ice Age, when our ancestors crossed from Africa into the Arabian Peninsula. They slowly traveled by foot following the animals they hunted until around 45,000 years ago when they reached what is now modern-day Iran. About 5,000 years later they had moved to the north of the mountainous Hindu Kush and onto the game-rich steppes of present-day Kazakhstan, Uzbekistan, and southern Siberia. After spending considerable time in Central Asia, around 35,000 years ago they began to head west towards Europe, where they interbred with Neanderthals, as I have 2.7% of Neanderthal genome myself. Around 20,000 years ago the expanding ice sheets forced them to travel south to Spain, Italy, and the Balkans. As the ice retreated and temperatures became warmer, around 12,000 years ago they started traveling towards present-day Ukraine and southern Russia. Over 2,000 years ago they had already reached northern Lebanon, where they settled. Fast forward to 1866 when our forefathers, Christian villagers still in the same area, fought the Battle of Bnachii in Lebanon and defeated the Turkish invaders, even outnumbered in 1 to 6. Then in the early 20th Century my Lebanese grandparent bought a ship ticket to America bringing his family away from Muslim persecution, and unknowingly was given a ticket to South America. Here is where my Lebanese father met my Syrian mother and I was born. Since then I have lived in 12 different countries. Although our family spread throughout the world, I have had the pleasure of having visited close and distant relatives in almost every place where they can be found; this is a result of my own direct genealogy research in over 130 countries through numerous archives, libraries and through oral interviews in the last 37 years. I would end that one long story saying that, had I not traveled, I would be just another engineer working 9 to 5 thinking that the world is what we see on the news, with no clue about who I am. I am so grateful to live the life that I have... A life that is what it is thanks to all my travels and all the people whom I had the opportunity and privilege to meet during my travels.

Do you ever feel you have missed out on certain aspects of life while away from home as you travel so much?

I feel that it is the other way around, people who do not travel much miss out on many aspects of life. When you go back home you realize that you moved forward while everything at home remained the same and most people did not change at all.

What advice would you give to others who would like to travel to every country?

Stop with excuses and start traveling now, not when you "have more time", or "have more money", or "find someone to travel with". Carry only hand luggage and travel overland as much as you can without flying between countries. Enjoy the journey as much as the destination. While traveling do not waste time with gadgets or staying connected online for more than a few minutes per day if necessary; immerse in the local culture safely and discover yourself under different circumstances. Focus on quality rather than on quantity, and do not count how many countries you have visited until you have traveled for at least 15 years. Experience as much as you can from each place and meet as many people as you can, otherwise you will end up with just a number, and no memories to share nor stories to tell.

For someone who has been almost everywhere, what still gets you excited about packing your bags again?

Just being on the road gets me excited, regardless of the destination. I always expect the unexpected. The few days before I depart I am a bit afraid of what will go wrong and at the same time I look forward to having things go wrong, so that I can feel out of my comfort zone and overcome those challenges. Every trip is a fresh start with new adventures and new challenges, even if your destination is a familiar place, because it has changed and you have changed too since your last visit.

I also get excited about what new places I will "discover". I usually avoid knowing too many details about the place before I get there. I get excited about what new people will I meet, and about what I will learn about myself that will be useful for the rest of my life.

Looking ahead, what travel plans and goals are you still pursuing, and what is on your "Bucket List"?

I do not have a Bucket List. I have no intention of completing neither the TCC nor the MTP lists; if I eventually do, it will have been only as a result of my love for traveling and exploring.

There are countries that I would like to keep going back many times: China, Indonesia, Thailand, Egypt, Lebanon, Ethiopia, and Mozambique are just a few. There are also many countries that I would like to go back once because I visited them at the very beginning of my travel life and would like to see how they changed and how I changed.

There are still several islands and archipelagos that I would like to visit: South Georgia, Tristan da Cunha, Ascension Island, Diego Garcia (British Indian Ocean Territories: BIOT), Saint Helena, Pitcairn, Tokelau, Christmas Island, Lord Howe Island, and Norfolk Island.

Hopefully, in July 2016, I will spend a week on the Trans-Siberian Railway and then travel overland for one month through several republics and oblasts of Russia.

Bart Hackley, U.S.A.

(Prolific world traveler, Olympic Bronze Medal swim champion, Guinness World Record holder, Six Time Ironman Triathlon Finisher, competitive eater, and "Future Space Traveler" – Bart Hackley, on the cover of *Los Angeles Times Magazine*, 1989)

Where did you grow up, and what was your early life like?

I grew up in Southern California. My parents were from Illinois. During World War II, my Dad, an officer in the Navy, traveled west by vehicle for eventual ship duty on a naval destroyer. I was conceived in Columbus, Ohio, and born in downtown Los Angeles. My Dad did not first see me until I was halfway through my first year of life after my parents started our family life in the Los Angeles area after the war. My early life up to college was fairly mundane. My travels, although not extensive, were limited to the United States and Canada. My family didn't have a surplus of funds for travel and my dad, a CPA, worked long hours through much of the year. I studied, participated in numerous sports, and worked several jobs. I was fortunate enough to go to college in Tucson at the University of Arizona. I had a great four years and added Mexico (sixty miles south of Tucson) to my now growing list of countries to THREE (3). I had very interesting fraternity brothers (many came from wealthy families) and traveled one summer across the USA with a few of them. I grew up with the nickname "Skip" because my dad was a naval officer on a ship and we both shared the same first name. In college, my nickname was "Lenny Bazoo" derived from a handwritten scribble on a toilet wall in some small U.S. town in the middle of nowhere.

What was the first international trip you took, and what do you remember most about it?

Besides Canada and Mexico, which meet the definition of international, I flew to Europe (Germany) round trip from Los Angeles. I am fortunate to have a wonderful wife and best friend of approximately 48 years. In our early years of marriage, we packed up our two kids (then aged 3 and 1), and flew on a low-cost, chartered aircraft for Army veterans to Europe. The flight had to stop en route in Gander, Newfoundland, to fuel. In those years, planes couldn't fly directly from the West Coast to Europe without refueling. This was around 1972. We picked up a VW in Frankfurt and drove to the Costa del Sol in Spain and rented a condominium for a month. I was so jet lagged at Frankfurt airport that I thanked the rental car attendant in Spanish. That was the longest continuous vacation I ever took during my 30 plus years as a self-employed CPA and real estate developer. Visiting European countries and Morocco (local ferry from Spain) was a real eye-opener for me. We were so tired of driving that we jumped on a ferry to Marseille in the lowest class for a portion of the return trip. The ship's crew felt sorry for us with children and upgraded us one class when I offered some money. It was my first lesson in "bribery", which I have used extensively and successfully in my travels. I was a participant in a travel symposium a few years back when the subject of "bribery" was discussed extensively. I quickly did the math and estimated close to one hundred thousand dollars ($100,000) in lifetime bribes I had distributed throughout the world!

When did you go from traveling casually to making this a full-time goal, and what motivated you to travel to every country?

In 1997, at the age of 53, I learned of the largest travel club in the world, the Travelers' Century Club (TCC). They had a provisional membership of 75 countries visited, so I became a member of the club. I had accumulated about half of these first 75 countries in the Caribbean (where my wife and I traveled yearly mostly by cruise ship with friends we had met around the world). I soon became an Officer and Board Member of TCC and traveled with some of the members to interesting places around the world. I lectured for a time on travel and its benefits. I have completed many goals in life, and during the years of 1997 and 2011 (when I completed the entire TCC list) there were times when I did not believe I could complete the list. The completion of the goal was a labor of love that I thoroughly enjoyed.

What have you done in your life to gain the freedom and finances to pursue as much travel as you have?

I began full-time work as an accountant the day after I graduated from college at the age of 21. I was very focused financially with a goal to become a millionaire by the time I was 30. Besides receiving a CPA license in a few years, I also obtained an MBA in International Business and had one additional year towards a doctorate in law (JD). I worked very long hours (sometimes 24 hours straight) in the accounting field (I was always a partner in a CPA firm, including one firm that eventually became the largest in the world) and used excess funds developing real estate and other investments. My wife and I, for a time, were owners of a travel agency which provided travel benefits! I exceeded my financial goals and was comfortable financially when I retired in my early 50's. It was very important for me to follow my long time slogan: Work hard to play hard! Now the hard work of previous years is parlayed into freedom from NO client demands. I am a huge believer of removing all evidence of stress from your life. So the first 50 years were stressful and, hopefully, the second 50 years will be stress-free so that I can reach my goal of living to be 100!

Has there ever been a time where you considered abandoning your travel goals?

Never. I hope that old age will not limit those continuing goals!

What do you consider to be your two favorite travel experiences, and why?

I cannot quantify two favorite travel experiences. I have loved every travel experience I have ever taken. Some of the trips in many Central African countries were demanding (I would typically fly into an area and visit approximately five neighboring countries per trip by vehicle).

What are the main things you seek to experience when you travel (culture, cities, nature, animals, adventure activities, etc.)?

I have been asked literally a thousand times if I have written a book about my extraordinary life and its related experiences. I even hired a "best-selling author" to help me put the book together. I think part of the problem was that I am a "selfish" traveler. I rarely take a photograph. My photos are all in my head which is a great place for them to be until you try to write a book. So I now have a computer full of hundreds of extensive notes on subjects and locations that I thought would make an interesting book. Some day I hope to, at least, put the stories and photos (some from websites) into a "table top book" for my family and guests.

Looking back from when you started traveling to where you are now, in what ways, if any, has travel changed you?

My stories have captivated my friends, relatives, and acquaintances. I still do not consider myself a good storyteller, but I am getting better at it through public speaking, etc.

Do you speak any foreign languages, and if so, which have been the most useful for you besides English?

I speak 2½ years of Spanish schooling worth! Spanish, being a Romance language, has helped when I am in other Romance countries. There are similarities!

What was the longest extended trip you have ever taken, when was it and where all did you go?

A tie between my first European trip (above) and my second trip to Antarctica.

My first trip to Antarctica was on a cruise ship, and we visited the Antarctica Peninsula. That cruise ship experience gave us 65-foot waves, furniture flying everywhere, and a very seasick ship (I have, fortunately, never been seasick but expect it to occur someday). My second trip to Antarctica was supposed to be a short six-day trip to visit the South Pole in December for "summer" weather and 24-hour sunlight. It was an extremely expensive trip and included a 4-hour flight from Punta Arenas, Chile, accommodations (tent on snow/ice), food, and airfare to the South Pole. We landed in western Antarctica at Patriot Hills in the Ellsworth Mountains. The landing site is a natural blue ice runway. Patriot Hills is near the largest mountain (Vinson Massif at 4897 meters) on the highest continent on Earth. Patriot Hills is the only private camp operating in Antarctica, and many famous guests have made their way through the camp at one time or another. The first woman to ski across the entire continent had been at the camp before I was there. I spent the night in my outdoor tent, and we then continued to the South Pole, via a Cessna single engine aircraft, and 600 miles to the southeast. It was a big thrill to visit the South Pole (at approximately 9,000 feet of elevation) as we landed on skis on the blue ice. We spent the entire day flying both ways and visiting the South Pole buildings and area. The South Pole, along with the North Pole (I was able to get within three degrees of the North Pole on a later excursion) have the earth's most shallow atmosphere. You are only receiving half your normal oxygen supply. Back at Patriot Hills we waited, and we waited, and we waited for a month for our transport back to Punta Arenas. An advertised six-day trip turned into thirty days. I missed Christmas and New Years with my family. The story was that it cost the owners $250,000 (16 years ago) to fly the chartered aircraft from Chile to Antarctica, and they wanted to be sure, with the weather conditions, that they could make the flight round-trip. They kept my wife informed by telephone that I was having a fantastic time, which was hardly true. I would call daily to Punta Arenas to tell the operators that the runway was clear and ready for their arrival. So my daily routine was to eat (the chef had recently cooked for Chez Panisse Restaurant in Berkeley and done BBC cooking shows), read, and cross country skied using the flags from the airport as visual guides. We had a two year supply of food in the storage locker (a large hole dug into the ice). Antarctica is the driest continent on earth and similar to the Sahara Desert. The winds just blow all the time. Slowly, daily, the camp increased in size from a few people in the beginning to probably over 100 individuals when we finally returned to Punta Arenas. The new campers were arriving from other parts of Antarctica via skis and ski-mobiles. Many had climbed the largest mountain on the continent so that they could be a part of the "Seven Summits" contingent (those that had climbed the tallest mountain on each continent). I became close to individuals from a Chinese television documentary company based in Hong Kong. They were to film, starting in Antarctica, for a year, various excursion sites around the world for Chinese television. One individual was a talented artist, we played several games, and we learned to communicate effortlessly even though I speak zero Chinese, and they knew no English!

What two countries have exceeded your expectations and which ones left you feeling underwhelmed, and why?

Australia and South Africa exceeded my expectations. If I did not have a family in Southern California, I wouldn't hesitate to live in Australia (Sydney) and South Africa (Cape Town). If you look at latitudes Sydney, Cape Town, and Southern California are all similar latitudes disregarding north or south.

The countries in the middle of Africa would be on the top of any underwhelming list for me. I don't need to name them as there are a dozen or so. They are poor economically, somewhat mundane geographically, dangerous if you are not careful, and difficult to navigate.

When you travel, do you prefer to go with others or solo, and why?

If I had to make a choice I would choose solo. I do not mind traveling with others as long as they are interested in accomplishing the same travel tasks and are not a pain in the ass! Due to my ability to accomplish goals, it is reasonable to do this solo thus disregarding other travelers wishes to accomplish their goals, which may be different.

What has been your most uncomfortable mode of transportation?

Run, bike, and swimming. I am a triathlete who has completed in over 500 triathlons in my lifetime. There is only a handful of us with that accomplishment. I also hold the *Guinness Book of World Records* for completing 123 sanctioned triathlons in a year. When I set that record, I was constantly moving to get to the next race site. There were times when I raced Thursday, Friday, Saturday, Sunday, Monday, and Tuesday going to a new location each day. I was in many countries and U.S. states to accomplish that goal. One day in March, I couldn't find any races except in New Zealand. So I flew there and raced in cyclone conditions and returned to the U.S. – all in a few days. Another time I packed up my bike from a Saturday race in Florida and flew to Puerto Rico and drove to the other side of the island arriving at 2 am. Slept in my car for three hours and then "built" my bicycle in the dark for an early triathlon race start, as bikes need to be partially disassembled for airlines. I am a prolific walker and have walked every day (usually at least three miles) in every country in the world. I have also traveled across the southern U.S. states on my bicycle while I was working full-time in California. We traveled from the Pacific Ocean (San Diego) to the Atlantic Ocean (Florida) and took one day off each week. I would fly home at each stop (Phoenix, El Paso, San Antonio, New Orleans) to work the day at home before flying back to continue the trip. During my 50th year, I swam, biked, and ran in each U.S. state, having a "close" encounter with an alligator in one state.

What is the strangest thing you've seen/experienced while traveling?

I was flying from Kenya to Djibouti. We had a scheduled stop in Mogadishu, Somalia, and the plane landed on a dirt landing strip somewhere near Mogadishu. All passengers got off the airplane except me. The airplane crew also stayed on board. While we waited for the new passengers for the continuing flight, I was able to ask the airplane crew what the commotion pertained to that I was viewing outside my window. They asked if I had noticed the passenger sitting across from me in the aisle seat. I said yes. It turned out that he was a warlord. It also turned out that the dirt strip that we were parked on was his land. It also turned out that the airline had paid him $500 for landing rights. Mogadishu Airport did not exist at that time. In fact, Somalia didn't exist. It is the only country that I have been to without a functioning government. The several dozen warlords were fighting with each other for control of the country. It was an anxious time for me to watch the people (non-uniformed soldiers?) demonstrating with the warlord that had just occupied the same row as me! Guns everywhere. Shooting into the sky like fireworks!

What are the best and worst meals you have ever eaten while traveling, and where was it?

The best meals were at Michelin-starred restaurants around the world in Paris, Hong Kong, New York, etc. In Hong Kong, I had a chicken breast cooked in a pig's bladder by a world famous French chef. The worst meals were in Lampedusa and Mongolia. In Lampedusa, my room included a meal and they brought to the restaurant something that appeared to be an eel. It was elongated, bony, and had nearly no meat on it. It was disgusting, but I was hungry. In Mongolia, the train stopped for a break while traveling from Siberia to Beijing. I had met another traveler on the train, and we headed into the train station restaurant to get a quick snack. We did not have Mongolian currency and certainly didn't speak the language. We ate something that resembled a "hot dog" and was disgusting. I have no idea what animal it was but, again, I needed to eat.

I enjoy eating and consume a lot of calories daily due to my daily penchant for exercise. While training for the many Ironman Triathlons I competed in, it was not unusual for me to consume at least 10,000 calories daily. And I am also a competitive eater having entered into two "hot dog" eating contests (one was the Nathans' Famous Hot Dog Contest, where I came in second in a qualifier).

As a side to the Mongolia stop, my new friend and I came outside to enter the train after our "meal" and to our dismay, the train had disappeared. Our luggage, passports, etc., were on board. We eventually located the train hidden from our view as they were moving it to change tracks and number of cars. A scaring incident indeed!

Out of the thousands of places you've stayed around the world, what have been your best and worst accommodations?

The best accommodations was a unit we owned on *The World*. *The World* is a cruise ship owned by approximately 100 owners, and it sails around the world. Its itinerary is set by the owners and we shared a two bedroom unit with a kitchen with another couple in a partnership. We owned it for approximately two years and made enough on the unit appreciation to pay for our travel during that time. The worst accommodations were the many nights I spent in airports around the world sleeping on the floor or uncomfortable chairs. Cold, dreary and uncomfortable!

What is your favorite "off the beaten path" destination, and why?

Greenland. When clear and sunny the world just stops in this environment. Greenland is an investment in life experiences. We docked *The World* in a pristine harbor out in the middle of nowhere. We then rounded up all the willing passengers and boarded inflatable Zodiacs for a great experience in viewing the icebergs up close. Maybe eight to ten Zodiacs all with approximately eight to ten passengers headed away from the ship. I would guess we were ten miles away from the ship when someone suggested that we should have champagne delivered to us from the ship. We had a walkie talkie, so we radioed the ship and ordered multiple bottles of champagne. In a while staff brought the bottles (and glasses) to us on silver trays and gloved hands. We saluted the ship, and the captain used his ship's horn to acknowledge us. The sound bounced around the large harbor. We were the only people in the entire area. The cost of the multiple bottles of champagne were paid by one of the wealthier unit owners!

What were your most challenging countries to visit, and why?

The many isolated islands of the world. Pitcairn, St Helena, Tristan da Cunha, Iwo Jima, Cuba, Lord Howe Island, and Midway Island to name a few of many. All of the above, and many others not listed took very special arrangements and long-term planning.

Of which travel accomplishments are you most proud?

My travel accomplishment of visiting every country on the Travelers' Century Club country list (which was 321 countries when I completed it in 2011) is the one I am most proud of. While pursuing this goal, I honestly thought I would not be able to complete the entire list. I have never been a "quitter" in all my other accomplishments/goals and this one was no different. I am a competitor, and although it was a large competition (as evidenced by the small number of individuals who have completed the entire list during the clubs 50+ years of existence), I kept up my cadence and completed the task.

Do you remember encountering particular people that left a lasting impression with you?

Interesting question of my encounters with particular people during my travels and lasting impressions. I went to Cuba during the Pan American Games specifically to meet with Fidel Castro. My goal was to encourage him to support the inclusion of the sport of triathlon in the upcoming Olympic Games. The sport was not part of the games, and I was an unofficial "lobbyist" for the US Olympic Committee/USA Triathlon Association/International Olympic Committee. Fidel Castro, having a teenage son, was keenly interested and became a supporter. It was fun to interact with him at a basic level (informal talks and some recreational sports) during those few hours we were together! This is one instance among many.

Another sporting encounter was during the Atlanta Olympics. I had a famous multiple Academy Award winning songwriter CPA client, and they supported the Olympics with a donation that allowed a disabled individual to run a segment with the Olympic Torch as it made its way to Atlanta for the start of the Games. The client was famous in Georgia, having grown up there. I was very involved with the chosen disabled individual, and we ran together simultaneously holding the torch – what a thrill!

A third encounter had to be my years of traveling on the cruise ship *The World*. *The World*, with its approximate 100 "Type A" owners of all the suites on the ship, was an experience for my wife and I. We had a "shiek" owner, a professional baseball team owner, a lady astronaut owner, and a whole bunch of rich individuals from around the world as owners. The typical owner was 50 years old, and he had recently sold his company for $50 million dollars. He wanted to travel the world in luxury (many bedrooms, a full kitchen, etc., for each suite). He lasted as an owner (before selling at a profit) for maybe, four years, since the ship traveled, on an owner voted itinerary, around the world every two years. The owner personalities were outrageous and very difficult for my wife and I to enjoy.

If you could travel back in time, to which era and place would you go, and why?

Cuba. I would have loved to be invisible in 1959 and living on the island. A second choice would be to board the Concorde again (I was fortunate to travel on the aircraft from New York to Barbados).

Can you describe any particular situation where you felt completely out of your comfort zone?

Iraq. I drove east across Jordan for several hours to reach the country during our heavy U.S. war involvement. I stepped across the Iraq border, found a bush and relieved myself, stepped back into Jordan and headed west. The Iraqi border officials would not allow me to enter Iraq on that particular day. Starting a mile or so from the border of Iraq, while still in Jordan, there was heavy military presence. Tanks, troops, trucks, artillery, etc. I do not know whether a cross-border strike was imminent or possibly if it was a safe place for the troops to form in mass before crossing the border for an intense battle. If I could have continued into Iraq, I would have been in the way of warfare, so it didn't really bother me that they denied me entry into Iraq. I knew that someday I would return to Iraq during, hopefully, peaceful times in order to explore the ancient treasures the country holds.

What are your three favorite cities in the world, and why?

Amsterdam, Sydney, and Cape Town. I have already talked about my love for Sydney and Cape Town. Amsterdam, although I would not live there due to the climate, is, in my opinion, one of the world's truly great large cities. It is so interesting and beautiful!

What is the ideal amount of time you prefer to travel on each trip before you are ready to go home and take a break?

My ideal time would be around ten days. Usually, enough time to rid me of jet lag.

In your opinion, where are the most beautiful places on Earth?

Jamaica and the sub-Himalayan region covering Kashmir, Bhutan, and Nepal. For my definition of beauty, the region must have all of these: rivers, mountains, abundant animals (such as monkeys), sandy beaches (from lakes, rivers, or oceans), lakes, lush greenery, waterfalls. I notice I do not include oceans (I guess because I live on an island in the Pacific Ocean). Yet, the people of Jamaica, would not be high on my list for social behavior and attitude!

If you had an unlimited budget and space and time were no object, what would your perfect travel day look like (for example: start your morning in Bora Bora; afternoon on a safari in Kenya; night in Australia, etc.)?

I would board the airplanes that I see advertised where every seat is first class. They take you on a first class set itinerary around the world to exotic locations (that I have probably already visited). The prices are astronomical ($150,000+ per person) but would be a great luxury for me.

Being a CPA, this is one luxury that I will probably be a hundred years old before I splurge!

Which three countries would you recommend for adventurous travelers to visit, and why?

1) Vietnam: absolutely gorgeous and packed with history.

2) Israel: the religious history is phenomenal. But, I have a question... Christ was baptized in the Jordan River. Was he baptized in Israel, Jordan, or both?

3) Iceland – but don't take any drugs into the country as a tour participant did. It took him a month to get out of jail and the country.

Do you ever feel you have missed out on certain aspects of life while away from home as you travel so much?

Absolutely not. I didn't know my wife was unhappy with me while I was so absorbed with my conquest to complete 123 triathlons for a Guinness World Record. She later admitted that it was a difficult time. My wife and I take each grandchild when they reach 10-years-old to anywhere in the world that they want to go. It is such a great education for young children. In fact, I think it was the great golfer (and world traveler) Gary Player that said travel is the best education you can give anyone.

What advice would you give to others who would like to travel to every country?

Do it while you are young. I am constantly lecturing younger golf partners or anyone that will listen that you cannot wait, during your lifetime, to travel. Do it while you are more mobile and can savor the memories more in younger years than in older years. Don't make excuses that you do not have the money, or the time, or your career, etc. You will not regret it. It is one of the smartest things I have done in my lifetime. What a thrill to see the aurora borealis (northern lights), to experience Ramadan, or to watch from our ship as the Tongans rebel against the monarchy by burning 80% of their capital city! Or, to travel by raft down the Colorado River days after 9/11 and wondering if the Dam above would explode! Or, to scuba dive all over the world. Or, to run an organized marathon on a small island (St. Helena) in the middle of the Atlantic Ocean, or on the Big Island of Hawaii while Kilauea Volcano is erupting. Or, to meet the 50+ Pitcairn Island descendants from Bounty mutineers (nearly all with the last name of Christian). Or, to wonder why the Shwedagon Pagoda in Myanmar or Rila Monastery in Bulgaria are not one of the Seven Wonders of the World, instead of the Taj Mahal. Or, to walk the Falkland Islands, through land mines, to see penguins. Or, to see the three million birds sitting two feet apart from each other on Midway Island. Or, to be arrested in Chad after illegally entering from Cameroon at night on the Chari River with its deadly rhinos. Or, to climb Mount Kilimanjaro. Or, to be crowned "The World's Greatest Travelers" along with my longtime friend when we won Great Escape 2008, The Global Scavenger Hunt (our prize was a free trip on the 2009 Global Scavenger Hunt where they re-wrote the rules because of our commanding victory).

For someone who has been almost everywhere, what still gets you excited about packing your bags again?

Travel always seems to boil down to the basics of:

1. Meeting people around the globe. You need to meet them in their habitat, not in your habitat. See how they live and, hopefully, enjoy life.

2. How do these people survive in their habitat? What do they eat and drink? You never can completely duplicate those foods here at home. Learn how they cook and their recipes.

3. Animals and how they survive in their natural habitat.
4. Actual sites around the world that pictures cannot duplicate.

These are exciting things to look forward in travel. But, soon a new frontier will open up to the public. Commercial space flight and I hope to be one of those travelers (probably in my 80's due to many setbacks). I recently returned from Russia after spending an entire day at the Yuri Gagarin Cosmonaut Training Center (named after the first man to fly into space) in Star City outside of Moscow. One of my granddaughters and my wife accompanied me as I took extensive one-on-one classes that evolved around the International Space Center (a ground mock up of the one orbiting earth), the wearing and use of Space Suits (both inside and outside the spacecraft of which I am now a proud owner of one), and the tasting of various dried foods they consume while living in space. The training center is directly involved in all cosmonaut/astronaut training today. Every space traveler eventually goes through this training center as we witnessed several cosmonaut/astronauts throughout the day in training. I can't wait to pack my bags for that trip!

Looking ahead, what travel plans and goals are you still pursuing, and what is on your "Bucket List"?

Now in my 70's, having visited every country in the world, and having visited a large portion of the world's surface I find my "Bucket List" very short. Without a doubt #1 on the list would be to visit "Space" if commercial flights are ever approved, and a distant second would be to travel first-class on an organized (around the world) itinerary with a customized jet travel program. My future travel plans involve my family. My wife and I take each grandchild, when they turn 10, to any place in the world that they wish to visit for a week. Of our five grandchildren. Three have reached that threshold and have visited Paris, London, and the Mediterranean Sea respectively. I am also revisiting interesting places with my wife (examples are Myanmar last month or Cuba this year) since she did not accompany me on some of the interesting trips I took years ago! We are starting to gather information for our 50th wedding anniversary in 2017. Our goal is to include all of our family on an "expedition". Possibly Africa to visit the "Big Five", or the Galapagos Islands (Darwinism), or Australia (Sydney, climbing its bridge, or the Kimberley remotely in the far northwest). My wife and I enjoy cruising the oceans of the world and have numerous itineraries booked in the next several years.

Jack Goldstein, Colombia

(Inside the exclusion zone,
near the reactor in Chernobyl, 2010)

Where did you grow up, and what was your early life like?

I was born in 1969 in Bogotá, Colombia to a traditionalist and highly cultured family of Eastern European immigrant Jewish parents. As such, I was brought up under a heavy influence of World and Jewish history – a family tree where no two generations were born in the same place and with a very dramatic recent past. I lived sheltered within a small community and with a strong feeling of being part of a minority in an overwhelmingly Catholic, third world country, still backward, where FARC guerrillas and Pablo Escobar's war on society were the norm, and the mentality of people was not yet open to the wider world. But even so, life was great and happy.

The sense of being different was always important. Since very young, I grew up with a strong inclination toward world affairs, politics, cultures and with sufficient exposure to world travel, especially at a time and place where it was not the norm. It was very clear to me from the beginning that there was a lot more outside my small world, and I had to see it.

I distinctly remember sitting on my dad's lap and reading maps, skimming through the *Encyclopedia Britannica*, and learning from him about world history every night before going to bed. To him, I owe a huge head start in life. Consequently, I was also a top student, always seduced by maps and stats, showing early on a great desire to explore, ask, and accept challenges. I always disliked being part of the norm. I chose not root for the same football teams as my peers. I had to be different even within a minority. The obvious path was to go out and conquer the world, count the places, the days, and the distance traveled.

In my childhood I grew up reading Jules Verne and imagined navigating miles underwater, going around the world in eighty days, traveling to places and cultures that were inaccessible. Television fed images of exotic animals in documentaries; newscasts would report wars in distant lands, and only the Football World Cup would allow me to feel it was feasible to unite the world. Growing up in Colombia, TV shows like Naturalia or the travel documentaries of Hector Mora got me near hidden places of the world, although arriving there was beyond my earliest imagination.

What was the first international trip you took, and what do you remember most about it?

Before my 4th birthday, in 1973, I traveled with my mom and sister during the two-month summer holidays to Hungary to visit our grandparents. On our way back, we met dad in Madrid and spent about a week traveling in

Spain. This would become the norm for the first years of my life. Two months courtesy of my grandparents, followed by a different European country or countries for a couple of weeks.

From '73, I remember how my mother would prepare us for the trip and tell us stories about Budapest, the country house outside the city with the little clay elf by a tree that would give us candy. She told us about family history and how Hungary was so different from Colombia. And I remember how expectant I was of the trip. At the time, the flight meant stopping in Caracas, San Juan and Madrid for another change of planes and on to Zurich and then again to Budapest. I can remember meeting friends of the family at the airport in Caracas and the snacks they gave us, the wait at the airport in Madrid, climbing the ladder on the final ledge. From Hungary, I vividly remember the elf, and my birthday party, my first military parade, and understanding that those were communist troops. I remember watching Hungarian TV with Russian coverage about the wars in Vietnam and Angola. And I remember how surprised I was to see the small size of my grandparents' apartment and the explanation of why post-War Communist Hungary had made it that way. I remember meeting my dad in Madrid for the last week of the trip, and the Casa Sueca hotel where we stayed, and how I could find Sweden on the map because my dad taught me the map of the world before I could read and write. And I remember Toledo and Avila, and just about everything on that trip. And since then, I remember how I always felt the best reward after an academic year was to be able to travel in the summer.

Thus, my first love became travel and I knew then it held the keys to understanding the world and relate to all the stories my dad would tell me every night before going to bed. Without a doubt, when people ask me what the appropriate time to start traveling is, I say the younger, the better.

When did you go from traveling casually to making this a full-time goal, and what motivated you to travel to every country?

I was always a traveler and my friends always saw me as such. I had the fortune of entering the world of traveling at a very early age. Every summer I would visit my maternal grandparents in Budapest. We would spend two months together with the family and always, before the start of the school year, we would go to some other place in Europe. Maybe this marked me from an early age as different; Hungarian, rather than English, was my second language. Life behind the Iron Curtain was the first 'other world' that I knew, and not the beaches of Cartagena or the parks in Orlando. I got accustomed to watching the news of the Vietnam and Angola wars under the Soviet prism and not the American. Getting to Hungary over 40 years ago was a long journey, one that implied changing planes many times in different countries – the weather, the way people dressed and the language would change at every stopover. In each destination, I learned one more history, heard a different language; tasted new flavors, learned about a new hero or anti-hero, about a new God. And everything, absolutely everything, would become a new adventure.

I read maps and drew dreamed-of itineraries. I was not yet 10 when I realized through the *Guinness Book of World Records* that there were people truly dedicated to seeing the entire world and that it was indeed achievable. I remember reading about a Bengali fellow who had been to about 154 countries. When I turned 15 and had been to 15 countries, I realized that life was not long enough to continue at such a slow pace. Today, I owe the Bengali gentleman a big "thank you" for his unsolicited encouragement, but I can happily say he is no longer the bar I measure myself against.

When I finished high school, I had already traveled to many European countries and some places in the Americas. For my high school graduation, my father allowed me to choose the destination I wanted to go on vacation. His surprise couldn't have been greater when I told him we'd go to South Africa. It was with that whimsical moment followed by that trip that I opened a new page in my travels, now to remote and exotic destinations.

What have you done in your life to gain the freedom and finances to pursue as much travel as you have?

I grew up in a middle-upper class family so, admittedly, that served as a good starting point. I have always been self-employed, running my own businesses (first as a flower grower and exporter and then as a hotel manager, the Lancaster House, which in a sense is a way of feeling on the road even when I am not traveling).

Given my adventurous nature, I have often been able to arrange affordable alternatives to exotic and bizarre destinations. I am not much into grand resorts or pricey packaged tours, so I feel I get more miles for my bucks then many travelers.

These reasons, plus the fact that for most of my adult life I have been single, have provided me the flexibility and ease to travel at will.

Has there ever been a time where you considered abandoning your travel goals?

Never. Travel defines my nature. It is one of the most profound beliefs in me and raison d Être, my earliest driving force in life. Not being able to travel again would be just like putting me to solitary confinement for life. It is my way to compensate for the troubles of daily life. I have a closet full of catalogs, maps, and dreamed-of itineraries waiting for their right moment to come. Never in my life can I recall not having a travel plan ahead.

What do you consider to be your two favorite travel experiences, and why?

To me, road trips make the cut because they are intense. Driving hundreds of kilometers per day make you a witness to how the landscape changes little by little, or dramatically, like upon crossing a border – Morphology, scenery, culture, politics, religions, traditions, ethnicities. These trips allow you to imagine how you "paintbrush" through the map, while you get a better understanding of humanity, and how geography and history explain one another. I imagine placing pins on the places visited and try to connect the dots as I sink in the cultures and places visited before moving on to the next one. Plus, these trips give you a greater chance to interact with locals or come across fellow travelers and exchange experiences.

Highlights include camping in Mauritania, driving from Kathmandu to Lhasa, two road trips in Russia (an 8,000km loop south of Moscow down the Volga to the Caspian, across the Caucasus and Black Sea and back along the Ukrainian border, and then a 13,000km loop around western Siberia from the Urals to the Arctic Circle and down to the Altai and Tuva and as far east as the Yenisei). Also various trips in Midwest, Southwest, Northeast and Southeast of the USA, where 1,000km's per day is easily achievable and extremely diverse. But two others stand out.

First was western Mongolia in the summer of 2004, right after my divorce, a moment when I needed to find peace of mind. With two friends (Natalie and her boyfriend – I had met her once upon a time in Timbuktu and then bumped into her a year later in Luang Prabang), we flew from Ulaanbaatar to Hovd where we were met our guide, who incidentally had helped write the first *Lonely Planet* guide to Mongolia. He brought with him another driver, a cook, and a mechanic, a crew of four for the three of us. We drove down along the Altai Mountains, often camping literally in the middle of nowhere, or spending the nights in random nomad's yurts enjoying their unique throat singing. We then crossed the Gobi desert, driving along the Chinese border toward the Singing Dunes and finally returned two weeks later to the capital in time for the very unique Naadam Festival.

The intense beauty and diversity of the barren landscape were enhanced by the fact that, at least then, Mongolia had no fences, no paved roads (and hardly any dirt roads!), no trees to offer shade, hardly any landscape obstacles to provide you with bathroom privacy, and a proud nomadic population. The most beautiful of desert sceneries is adorned by a few tranquil streams, hordes of small Mongolian horses or fury Bactrian camels, white tents and thousands of popping prairie dogs. The sun and a compass were our guides as no good maps existed, and often we would have to "detour" when going from point A to B because we would discover major canyons, gorges, craters, or sand banks that would make the trip impossible. A first ever – we saw just one group of tourists in 15 days.

The other one was Eastern Europe: A week with family in Budapest and then solo from the Baltics to Balkans – 12 countries and three autonomous republics or places that don't exist. A part of the world of unrivaled intense history, shtetls, death camps, Chernobyl, crazy Balkans, ethnic cleansing, outstanding guides, diverse cultures, long hours, plenty of exciting border crossings, good music, and soulful walks along city promenades. A trip I started with my dearest people and brought me closer to my roots, in deep contact with world affairs, and a great sense of self-assurance. A trip that from beginning to end was simply perfect to the soul, mind and camera.

What are the main things you seek to experience when you travel (culture, cities, nature, animals, adventure activities, etc.)?

First and foremost, I look for adventure, a good story, a unique destination, and an unusual itinerary. I look forward to detaching from mundane reality. I love meeting locals or fellow travelers. In my trips, I love to connect the dots on the map and come back with a greater knowledge and with thousands of good pictures. I still print them out and assemble them into an album together with maps, tickets, stickers, bills, stamps and brochures. In essence, I look for moments of awe.

"How does Buddhism explain the creation of the world?" I asked this question to Tientzin, our guide, while visiting one of the rooms of the Lamaist monastery in Gyantse, Tibet. Each person, each human group, will formulate its own answer to every question and circumstance of life. More so, questions that could be fundamental for me end up being not so vexing for others. His surprising answer explained much and nothing at the same time, but it was assertive enough to help broaden my horizons. In those brief moments that Tientzin took to begin his answer, I was able to capture the greatness of humanity's immense pluralism, the fascinating feat of being able to explain one same fact in so many different ways. "I don't know how Buddhism explains the creation of the world, but I can gladly explain the creation of Tibet". That was all I allowed him to say. I opted to smile, and with great interior peace, decided to continue my way down the temple without worrying about more answers. Possibly, Tientzin never understood my reaction nor how much he had said without even answering. I had learned more by staying in a place of ignorance than by inquiring for more details. Those are the priceless moments of traveling. That's why I love to travel. For my guide, even though he had lived under communist occupation for over fifty years, his reason for living was to find nirvana. His raison d'être is in un-attaching himself from the human condition, avoid questions and desires, even if his road becomes difficult (a contradiction in itself for my taste). In synthesis, there we were, the two of us, living in the same time and space, both happy, both spending time together, both seeing this world in different ways. Everything is relative.

To me, traveling is the best way to learn about history, geography, philosophy and religions, politics and conflicts; it is the funnest way to spend our free time. I can hardly understand a beach holiday, and it is difficult for me to repeat destinations even if the trip was great. The adventure is in the destination itself and in getting there, in the lack of comfort, in the sensation of isolation and remoteness, and in each of the anecdotes with which I come back. Each trip opens new horizons and raises new challenges; the world never ends. My goal began wanting to know each and every country in the world, but later became a quest for regions and roads, a desire to set foot in every time zone, travel down Route 66 or the roads traveled by Marco Polo or Livingstone, and be able to place a pin on the map to many UNESCO monuments.

We, extreme travelers, can be weird, petulant, and incomprehensible for many. Jailings, malaria, shipwrecks and other scares make part of the emotions that motivate us to continue traveling and are not reasons to stop doing it.

Lastly, I believe that we, extreme travelers, celebrate the greatness of humanity in each adventure, we celebrate the capacity to colonize jungles and snow peaks, to adapt to deserts and tundras, to combat and not give up before the unforgiving nature. I always marvel at the colors, flavors and scents, be they pleasant or repulsive. We appreciate the good and the bad of each culture, religion, and society, and don't deny any destination. Trips open our senses, makes us more critical of our circumstances, redesign our lives, and teach us to share with the stranger, the friend, and the enemy, and learn to see the heads and tails of each coin.

It is traveling that defines me and dictates the way forward.

Looking back from when you started traveling to where you are now, in what ways, if any, has travel changed you?

It has had a dramatic effect on me. I am now more open, adventurous, liberal, skeptic yet opinionated. I am spiritually richer. I have learned about religions and politics and enjoy very much when I can compare cultures and situations, draw parallels, explain and relate. I celebrate humanity and its accomplishments without falling prey to parochial preconceptions. But I also got to value my heritage and culture with more solid arguments. I have seen and experienced world conflicts from both sides of the spectrum and learned to look for balance.

To me, there is no bad trip. Einstein once said that the more man expands his circle of knowledge, the more he expands the boundaries of what he doesn't know. Traveling for me has that fascination: a well-formulated question, more than expecting a certain answer, leads to more questions. The desire to know a country, a culture, a language or a way to interpret a fact, or life itself, fills my yearning to visit another country, more cultures, and languages, and to compare in order to better understand.

The formulation of the questions is the real motor for knowledge, of the desire to become better, to find the road to follow and to obtain that what validates our existence. Traveling has been and will continue being the carousel of fun that has taught and shaped my vision of the world. I'm immersed in a cycle that takes me on a search for answers I know I'll never find because in the journey I keep on formulating more questions, and I'll keep on changing my mind. The circumstances and the traditions I grew up with, the education I received, my successes and failures, loves and broken hearts, have also strengthened my particular way of seeing things and interacting with my world. Traveling allows me to give a universal context to so many things that concern and happen to me. I don't think about failing in the attempt to learn. I live with intensity and try doing things 'well' and enjoy immensely while doing it. For me, this is what life is about, at least my life.

I am happily fulfilled knowing I have walked the path I chose when I was young, and I have gone beyond those earlier childhood expectations. So it a nutshell, it has made me happier.

Do you speak any foreign languages, and if so, which have been the most useful for you besides English?

To start, I am a native Spanish speaker. English, by far the most useful language to travel, came much later in life.

Hungarian was my first foreign language. I started learning it at age three listening to my mom and grandparents speak. It is a good language to learn if you find yourself in Hungary or in need to communicate a secret to my mom. It serves as a good mental exercise as its grammar rules are very different than most other languages. Otherwise, it is of no use even if you believe it is close to Finnish, Estonian, Khanti or Mordovian.

Then came Hebrew, which I learned in school and improved it while spending a semester of high school in Israel. Certainly, it is much more useful for business and travel as many backpackers are Israeli. It serves me well in order to connect with my history and my tribesmen anywhere in the world.

English came fourth, in late elementary school, and eventually became my second language. On and off, I have lived for many years in the USA, and it is also where I finished college.

To a lesser degree, I speak some Yiddish, which I learned while at U. Penn, simply because I wanted to surprise my father who grew up with Yiddish (not Polish) and just like most in his generation, did nothing to pass on the language. Although with a "funny accent" Yiddish has been good to me mostly to read menus while in Germany.

I took perhaps five classes in French, so when I have had the need to communicate, I have mixed it with Spanish, rolled my tongue and twisted my lips in an elegant manner, and thus have been able to overcome more than one situation in various places in West Africa, although never in France.

I can also read Cyrillic and would love to make Russian my next language. But until then, the only way to safely travel the remainder of Russian is to do it with my good friend, Myisha Rybotchkin, the quintessential guide to road trips across Russia.

Finally, if I could do it all over again, I would learn a bit of Russian, Arabic, Mandarin, Japanese, French, Portuguese, Hindi, Farsi, Swahili, just enough to be able to converse with the people in every place I visit.

What was the longest extended trip you have ever taken, when was it and where all did you go?

I have yet to allow myself a sabbatical and take off for a long, long time. Perhaps one day Sandy and I will be able to look the other way and hop on a cruise around the world. I look forward to the day when time and money will not be an issue, and we could go away for two months at a time, three times a year.

Until then, and to date, and other than the summer holidays in Hungary during my childhood, the longest trip for me was 30 days across Eastern Europe, from the Baltics to the Balkans, in the summer of 2011.

I had been numerous times before in that part of the world, and it is part of my family's history, my mentality, and sensibilities. It's an area riddled with drama and horror, very dense and passionate history, a myriad or peoples and traditions yearning to write a new chapter in their futures. That summer, with my mother, sister and her husband, we took Ethan and Tamara (my nephew and niece) to visit Budapest and show them that very meaningful part of our past and our souls. We needed to share with them the places, flavors and people that mean so much to us. After a great week with them, I packed and went my way.

First, I flew to Riga, Latvia to enjoy its medieval and Art Nouveau districts. Then it was on to Lithuania where I visited, among others, the Hill of Crosses, Trakai and its peculiar Karaite community and, of course, the very baroque Vilnius, which will remain dear to me. Then came Poland, a day and a half visiting mostly Jewish sites: the neighborhood where my dad was born, the towns of my grandparents, even getting to see their original house. I got to do genealogical research in more than one place and ended up in Treblinka, where most of the Goldstein's saw their last days alive, all extremely emotional moments for me.

From there, I flew across the twilight zone and landed a century before in bizarre Belarus, where totalitarianism remains alive and kicking. Next jump was Ukraine, which seemed futuristic compared to its northern neighbor. Kiev was superb and will also remain dear to me, with special visits to see Stalin's secret tunnels and Chernobyl's disaster zone. Backward Moldova was the next stop showcasing the most spectacular cave wine cellars, and side trips to the unrecognized communist republic of Transnistria and the time forgotten autonomous republic of Gagaúzia. Going south, I reached legendary Transylvania and very impressive Bucharest. Then it was turn for a short stop in Sofia, Bulgaria, where the highlight was treating myself on my birthday to a day at the Kempinski, relaxing, sipping whiskey non-stop and chatting online with friends. From there, I drove via Rila Monastery into Macedonia to visit the northern part of the country which I had missed out on once before due a horrible snow storm, where the visit to Skopje will remain memorable.

I continued to Kosovo where I had firsthand impression of ethnic cleansing, vibrant hatred and KFOR presence. Then it was across into the operatic Republic of Montenegro and the beautiful Adriatic coastline. From Tivat, I flew to Belgrade, arguably one of the nicest surprises – a vibrant, happy city, with trendy people and a complex recent past. The last leg of the trip was to drive across Vojvodina and back again into Hungary.

I couldn't have asked for better guides. Each one of them was unique, superb, and full of life. I was always in the company of someone with deep knowledge of history, passionate about his or her country. I visited the best and the worst in Jewish history, in my family's history and world history. I saw armies pointing at each other, cultures clashing and mixing; I delved in centuries of art and war and shed many tears of joy and sorrow. And I had with me at all times my iPod. To date, whenever I use it, I go back in time and remember the feelings I had in each of the places I visited then, as I was listening to my music.

What two countries have exceeded your expectations and which ones left you feeling underwhelmed, and why?

Very tough to narrow it down.

Overwhelmed, clearly with the people of Myanmar and Japan. The first are by and far the nicest, most amicable people, always smiling and eager to help, going beyond their ways to show the beauty of their culture and country – something that would seem impossible under a military dictatorship. The latter, because they are the ultimate society: polite, advanced beyond imagination, peaceful, clean and extremely professional.

As far as places that have exceeded my expectations, I will go out on a limb and say the USA for its wide diversity and vast territory. It is so much more than just the two coasts, making it a highly underrated tourist destination. Others on my list would include Abkhazia, Malta, and Slovakia

Underwhelmed? That is a hard one to answer because my approach to travel makes me savor the ugly, the dirty, and the chaotic just as much as the beautiful. But if I ever felt shortchanged, it was in Greece. The cradle of western civilization back in 1982 was far from being tourist friendly. A never-ending collection of rude and unprepared guides, crazy drivers, badly kept archaeological treasures and terrible restaurants.

When you travel, do you prefer to go with others or solo, and why?

There is a type of trip for every moment in life just as there is a proper type of company depending on the destination or the moment in life.

My first of many trips were with the immediate family. Later in life I traveled with close friends, Juan and Andres, and their families. Not to sound like an Arab sheik, but there was also a time when I traveled with my two wives (each separated by legal divorces, of course.) There have been magical moments in solo trips which happened simply because I either had no one to travel with or because I needed the brake from life's headaches. Going forward, I also look to the day I take my nephew on a grand tour upon his high school graduation.

What I do not plan for is group tours, especially those that make you follow a guide with an umbrella and stick to a tight schedule. However, in some places, this was the only way to go about it, like when we drove from Kathmandu to

Lhasa, which turned out to be a great experience with a group of very nice people, some of whom I still remain in contact with.

But now my future is with Sandy, my perfect companion, my soul mate, a travel agent and TV travel show producer; a person with an endless desire to travel and no holds barred. I have now found the best companion to travel the rest of the world and for the rest of my life.

What has been your most uncomfortable mode of transportation?

That would have to be a small boat along the Orinoco River for ten continuous days in July of 1994.

After an embarrassingly early exit from the World Cup of Colombia's national team, and having concluded the worst, most stressful work experience ever (successfully defending my case against the US Department of Commerce on charges of dumping roses in the U.S. market), I needed to go far away. The answer was to escape for ten days with a group of 10 college friends, and travel along the Colombian-Venezuelan border on a camping-river "cruise", and hour and a half by plane from home, but eons away.

I contacted a guide who eventually turned out not to know the terrain. We had hired a cook, a weird Spanish guide who'd been living in the jungle for a while, and a motorist. We took with us camping gear, hammocks, gasoline cans and some food. A big surprise came when on the day of our trip our guide showed up completely drunk and with a dozen inflatable live savers. Only then did we understand the type of boat we would have – a rustic pirogue with two overboard engines and wooden benches hammered across to allow the 15 of us to sit.

The motorist was a heavy-built Puinave Indian, who took two weeks off from work from one of the local cocaine producing labs. Luckily, the boat was mostly fully covered with a tin roof that protected us from the tropical sun and gave just enough space in the front for only two people to be standing at any given time. "Bathroom breaks" were for the most part exercises in un-rhythmic gymnastics while the boat kept on sailing down the river.

One evening, and running late to our destination, a big thunderstorm caught us. Big waves were rocking the boat. Adding to the drama, our motorist started to recite out loud the Holy Father in a combination of holy and very unholy words. Eventually, we saw a providential light in the distance and approached it to find refuge for the night.

While helping to tie the boat to a tree, the engine got flooded and broke down. One in the group panicked and shouted, "the engine is broken!" And so, in the middle of the night and with the waves rocking our boat, the people still on board jumped off, and we had to help them get ashore. The following day, after a long hike along the gorgeous Tuparro park, we came back to see that one of the engines was "missing". That was the day we were scheduled to return and go upstream 12 hours straight, but not before I broke my ribs playing football (soccer) against the local team of barefoot Indians. Twelve hours of pain, going at half speed in our little raft.

Still, and precisely because of the boat, that trip ranks as one of the most remarkable, exotic and off the beaten path excursions ever.

What is the strangest thing you've seen/experienced while traveling?

That would be a piss-stop plus coffee at a mountain-top restaurant in Montenegro, just after crossing the Kosovo border.

Montenegro is arguably one of the most ridiculous countries in the world, and the perfect setting for the weirdest moment I can remember. It hardly has a population to sustain itself and has an economy based on Adriatic tourism and Russian mafia. It is an EU-NATO country with more Russian spies and big shots per square inch than Moscow, and a clown-for-president more likely to rule in Central Africa, himself a relic from the late 1980s Communist bloc. The national motto claims to make it the first "ecologic" country in the world granting it the chutzpah to charge a €5 "eco-fee" to enter this "amusement park" of a country, which ironically happens to be the dirtiest place in Europe together with neighboring Kosovo and Albania. It boasts to have two capital cities and an empty high-rise residential building claiming to be the second home of Pamela Anderson. Simply put, Montenegro is a big joke.

So, with my guide, we sat on the terrace and ordered two cups of coffee. Shortly after, a police car with its sirens flashing parked next to our car. Two officers stepped out and proceeded to open the back seat door. Out came a thug in handcuffs, straight out of a Russian mafia movie. The policemen then took the handcuffs off and allowed this capo to walk in and go to the bathroom while they waited outside. After the bathroom break, this scarred criminal proceeded to sit by the table next to ours and order his coffee. He drank calmly and without haste. After a half hour or so, he walked down the stairs and toward the policemen who were smoking and idling by the car. They put his handcuffs back on, sat him in the back and drove off into an eco-friendly mountain range.

But I must mention two other instances of feeling strange, places where ironically I turned out to be the strange thing.

In 1993, I went to the Amazon and camped two hours upstream from Leticia. Before going to bed on the first night, I asked the camp manager what had been the strangest thing he had witnessed in the jungle, hoping to hear stories of jaguars and anacondas. But the joke was on me as, after a few seconds, he replied that once he hosted a group of people that would only eat certain heavenly ordained foods that were prepared in very particular ways, and who would pray in the mornings with strange leather things wrapped around their arms and heads. All I could do was laugh at the irony, as our bags were filled with kosher food and tfilins (the Jewish prayer phylacteries).

The other one was in a small village, a few kilometers from Comrat, the capital of the autonomous republic of Gagauzia, in southern Moldova, shortly before having shared pizza with the President himself. There is a small ethnological museum, in typical Soviet style, with an old collection of misplaced pictures, yellowish newspaper clippings, dusty costumes and explanations in unfriendly languages. Before I was able to ask for permission to take pictures, both the local museum guide and the always present fat lady director guided me inside the administration office and took pictures of the two of them with me. They then asked me to sign the guest book. It was July, and I was the first non-Moldovan to visit that year.

Two instances that show life's relativity: when we go out to find the exotic and realize the exotic is actually you.

What are the best and worst meals you have ever eaten while traveling, and where was it?

This is one where I can't truly contribute as I maintain a certain degree of Kashrut (adherence to kosher dietary laws), so I never expose myself to eating creepy, crawling animals. Cans of tuna or dry and vacuum sealed kosher beef jerky are often found in my bags.

Having said that, and precisely because of the above, one of my favorite places is India, with its abundance of vegetarian dishes and spices. A close second would be Peru with its superb variety of ceviches and a fusion of Creole and oriental flavors. But if I am to choose a specific dish it would be Arctic Char in Iceland. And then there are the boring places for me simply because they offer a lot of meat-based cuisines. For vegetarians, places like Morocco, Mongolia, and even Germany can be hellish. Eating injera with bare hands in Ethiopia was not my cup of tea, but the worst have to be yak butter tea in Tibet and a full week of wild bitter cassava bread and smoked fish along the Orinoco River.

Out of the thousands of places you've stayed around the world, what have been your best and worst accommodations?

As far as the best is concerned, well, I am not into luxury and resorts, but places that stand out would be Dresden's Kempinski, Rajasthan's Mogul castle hotels, and the Okura in Tokyo.

On the other hand, worst accommodations need a disclaimer: they can also be a lot of fun.

Runner-ups include: Camping in Guyana's Karanambu, which was actually quite good but the sight of two dozen bats walking on the net over your bed was quite spooky. Vienna's fancy Hotel Bristol without A/C in the peak of summer is the worse given the price paid. Then there is the unmarked trucker's cottage somewhere in the mountains in Khakassia, with the single light bulb to carry between bedroom and bathroom, its messy decor and those lovely half-naked drunk intruders looking for vodka. And finally, the many unfinished hotels in Mali built with leftovers from Chinese factories, where nothing would match.

But the gold medal to the worst has to be Miramar. Not the one in Florida but that "big, ample house, built on a rock and overlooking the mighty Orinoco", as our guide described it. Indeed, Miramar was big, was built on a rock, and the river was right there. Having said that, it was an odd-looking wood structure, with a very ample living/dining area showcasing a pool table and indoor "tejo" courts (typical Colombian game where you aim to hit a powder with a cement weight), and to top it all, about a dozen suspicious-looking cabins. The filth was out of this world, and way too many pigs, hogs, dogs, chicken, and cats were roaming around and feeding themselves in the most disgusting way possible. The place was run by a small and obnoxious gentleman wearing only his shorts and showing enough proof he had not showered in a long time. When night came, we proceeded to hang our hammocks, two to a cabin. The length was not enough to tighten the ropes, so we slept in awkward positions and woke up one over the other and in pain. It turns out; Miramar was a brothel run by the Cali Cartel and for the pleasure of their cocaine lab employees. It was such a godforsaken place, the prostitutes actually fled.

What is your favorite "off the beaten path" destination, and why?

To the not-so-crazy traveler, off-the-beaten-path (OFTB) may mean something else. It could be Cuba, Burma, or Ethiopia. But I believe we have different standards. Personally, I am not into remote islands or isolated rocks which could certainly classify as such. To me, OTBP means that getting there is in itself an adventure, and once there, there is hardly a tourist to be found. Under this definition, I would have to include road trips across the many Russian provinces, and places I mentioned before like the Orinoco and western Mongolia, and the places that don't exist, like Transnistria or Abkhazia.

My favorite moment would in Banc d'Arguin, Mauritania, while on a solo trip. It is a place where the dunes of the Sahara meet the turquoise, quiet and tepid waters of the Atlantic, near a flat rocky plateau that serves as a magical viewpoint. This place has thick green vegetation, a multitude of birds, fish jumping from the ocean and the occasional dolphin. To add to its beauty, a few tents and fishing boats Maldives-style enhance the landscape. Getting there was the final ledge of a six-day loop that took me deep into the Sahara to see holy Muslim sites, rock paintings, craters, old Portuguese ruins and the flat beaches where the Paris-Dakar rally once went. The night before, I was lucky enough to find a tent with a satellite dish to watch the Africa Cup of Nations Final.

Initially, my luggage had not arrived from Madrid where I was attending FITUR, a tourism trade show. I arrived in Nouakchott at 2:00 am and the plan was to sleep a few hours and take off for the desert at 8:00 am. And that we did. That meant that all I had with me was a suit and tie straight from the trade show, and shiny black leather shoes. That and my small carry-on with a laptop, a DVD player, a cell phone and a toothbrush. Along the way, I bought a scarf and a change of clothes, and that is how I went on my trip. It was so OTBP that nowhere in those many days on the road did I find a place to recharge my electronics. My lack of knowledge of Arabic or Hausa meant that I could only communicate with the hundred words I know in French, which were not necessarily the same my guide knew.

So that night, I found myself in the most spectacular of places, truly away from everything, not having seen a tourist in days, and practically all by myself. No phones, no laptop, no DVD player, no iPod, no flashlight to read. Nothing to remind me of the 21st century. The sun went down early, around 6:00 pm, so before falling asleep, I had about six hours, all to myself, in the desert, under the stars and the occasional shooting star, surrounded by dunes and the ocean. A magical, almost religious moment that shed light into how big religions once must have started.

What were your most challenging countries to visit, and why?

Visas make Central Asia tough and expensive, and reclusive Turkmenistan is in a league of its own. My dear friend Guillermo was not allowed in because all he had was a

Colombian passport and had only applied for the visa three months before.

Russia outside of the main cities, Golden Ring or Trans-Siberian, would be impossible if it were not for Myisha, the king of Russian roads. Language is a huge barrier, and there is hardly a chance to rent cars, road maps don't always make sense, and hotels, motels or cottages are not necessarily obvious to find.

Lower Omo Valley in Ethiopia and its lack of bridges was a major frustration.

But the biggest frustration is that there are still many wonderful places in my native Colombia I have not had the courage to visit. But the day will come.

Of which travel accomplishments are you most proud?

I'd say being a part of this book is a great accomplishment, although not a trip in itself. I have not aimed for isolated rocks in the ocean nor climbed the highest peaks. I may have been to places where, other than my travel companions, I have not met any other people that have been there. Certainly, I should not be the one to boast top rankings in any list. So my accomplishments are perhaps best rated by the degree of personal fulfillment they brought me. These would be the trips to trace family origins, in part because of the work done prior to the trip, the level of difficulty in finding the exact places, and mostly because of the deep emotions they stirred in me: finding my grandfather's wooden house in Siennica, Poland, and my mom's extended family's turf in the Carpathians and Ukrainian Galicia. A long list of streets, houses, lands, documents, and even people that connected me to my family's origins.

Do you remember encountering particular people that left a lasting impression with you?

Arguably, people contribute with some of the greatest moments in a trip. Some people you meet along the way become friends-for-life. Some remain dear in your memories, and some unnamed characters can leave you with the greatest moments of awe. Many are fellow travelers with whom I crossed paths at some point, like Natalie Grabczak whom I met in Timbuktu and bumped into again in Laos and then traveled together to Ethiopia and Mongolia; Ed Gingrass with whom I traveled through Central Asia; John Burke in Southern Russia and Abkhazia; and Karel and Barb Noordover in Tibet and Nepal. There is also Larry Leventhal, who I have not yet met, but having corresponded so much and shared so many travel tips he is by now a good friend. And of course, Leon Hochman, somebody I know since childhood but only 40 years later did we find out we had the same passion for travel and have been on some trips together. Some remarkable people were among my stand-out guides like Ilan Dellagi in Greenland, Daniel Vanderpuye and Doris Holmes in Ghana, Aljona Shukhina in Kiev, Tientzin in Tibet and Mikhayl Rybotchkin through half of Russia.

And then there are those unique "aha!" moments in life with the locals, that happen unexpectedly and leave a mark in your heart and mind, like the one in Tibet with Tientzin I shared before. Among those spectacular moments, I would mention being woken up to the most soulful Christmas Carols by village kids in Mole Park in northern Ghana, 2000; joining a Javanese wedding celebration in a village in Surinam, 2013; sharing a day of history and traditions in Ladino with Ranko Jajcanin (a.k.a Eliezer Papo) in Sarajevo, 1988; drinking beer with park rangers in Masai Mara, Kenya in 1998; bumping into a lively Don Cossack village fair near Rostov, 2012; chatting the night away about Balkan politics with the hotel receptionist in Skopje, 2010; discussing

Middle East politics with a former Syrian rebel in Petra, 2015; sharing a flight with two dozen Algerian guerrillas in-route to do military training behind the iron curtain, Hungary 1985; celebrating the Passover Seder together with 1,000 Israeli backpackers in Katmandu, 2000; celebrating the end of Passover in the most spectacular of jungle huts in Karanambu, Guyana, 2013; sharing kosher South African biltong with the only tourists we found in the Gobi, and enjoying throat singing inside a random yurt near Hovd, Mongolia, 2004; watching the Africa Cup final inside a tent with the entire Hausa tribe somewhere near Atar, Mauritania, 2010; joining various families for picnic at the Yangon Zoo, 2002; helping a 12 year old girl calculate the cubic root of various four-digit figures (sans calculator) under a palm tree in the jungle beaches of remote Capurganá, Colombia, 1995; listening to the Cuban lady in Trinidad explain why she was not happy that her daughter wanted to study medicine, 2010; drinking coffee in Merv with the gentleman on a bicycle trip from Paris to Beijing, Turkmenistan, 2008; and listening to the Sandinista guerrilla commander tell stories about the revolution, Leon, 2009.

They are all people I bow to as they all have had an indelible mark on me and will forever remain dear as they have left me with wonderful, lifelong memories.

If you could travel back in time, to which era and place would you go, and why?

I would be a Rhadanite and travel back and forth the various routes along the Silk Road. It must have been magical to reach walled cities, meet the local chief or King, trade spices, and gems, go on caravans, use translators and messengers. Every place would have been truly, truly legendary and unbelievable.

Can you describe any particular situation where you felt completely out of your comfort zone?

Borders are often troublesome. I was detained by a drunken policeman in Livingstone, Zambia on charges of spying for the Apartheid government of South Africa. I was also detained by the FSB (formerly known as KGB) at Gal border between Abkhazia and Georgia during Abkhaz Independence Day and brought before the chief guerrilla commander. Crossing from Ukraine into Poland was a chaotic nightmare worsened when we were almost forced to smuggle out people in our car. Back and forth between Guyana and Suriname was another uncomfortable rip-off, malaria in Ghana was a treat, meeting Guatemalan guerrillas was a thrill, but the title goes to getting stranded in Laguna Colorada in Bolivia.

In December of 1999 I was with my sister in the Atacama Desert in northern Chile and decided to go for the day to Bolivia's Laguna Colorada, one of the nicest places on earth. At the border, we were transferred together with a Spanish lady to a 4x4 driven by a coca-chewing moron. It was a most wonderful trip until we got stuck in a sand dune near the lake. Obviously, we expected the driver to take his tools and get us out. But he had no tools and no radio and against our advice, he kept on stepping on the gas and sinking us deeper in the sand. We tried digging the car out, but to no avail. Time was slowly passing, and not a soul was in sight. All I could do was think that in a few hours night would fall and at close to 15,000 feet above the sea temperature would surely drop to a cool -20F. We were without food and proper clothes, so our worries became existential.

Eventually, I decided to leave my sister behind with the Spanish lady and the never-ending, coca-chewing idiot and venture into the desert with only a baseball cap and two bottles of water. I figured that perhaps another car would come along the same path we came from, passing by the side of a volcano. After two long hours, I finally saw in the distance a column of sand rise into the sky. A car I thought! I started to run desperately towards it and blessed the heavens the moment I saw that the car was also driving toward me. But the car came and went and did not stop even as I was frantically waving at him and yelling for help in good Spanish. I cursed at him, but soon realized I had seen something strange in that car: side view mirrors at the front of the hood, steering wheel on the right side, and prices written on the front window. I figured it had to be a smuggled Japanese car brought in from Antofagasta and taken to reassemble and sold in the black market in La Paz or Santa Cruz. I also figured that if there was one car, there could be more up ahead. So this time, I pull out a $20 and some minutes later I saw another column of sand in the distance. I started running toward it, now with my two hands firmly holding the $20 bill. This time around the car stopped, picked me up, and the driver told me about the smugglers route. For $20 he graciously took me on yet another spectacular trip to the nearest mining town where I was able to buy enough wood and road equipment and for another $10 he took me back to find my sister and our car. It is incredible how difficult it was to find them even with so many clues in the landscape. Shortly before nightfall we were able to dig ourselves out and drive back.

What are your three favorite cities in the world, and why?

I would classify them into two groups based on size.

Among large cities, I would rank Berlin, New York, and Rome. The first, because I had a great guide, Yeshay Jakubowski, who had a story for every window and brick and taught me to like everything I saw. It is full of history and culture, and the people are particularly nice for a city that size. New York is Manhattan, the quintessential city. Rome, because it was my dad's passion and my first intense introduction to world history.

Among the smaller size cities, I would choose the very charming and idyllic La Valetta, the ever passionate and multicultural Jerusalem, and the extremely ridiculous Skopje.

What is the ideal amount of time you prefer to travel on each trip before you are ready to go home and take a break?

Three weeks if I am on a demanding trip, covering long distances and exposed to heavy culture shocks. It is the right amount of time once I pass the moment I can't remember which day of the week or what the date on the calendar is, and passed the moment I start feeling disconnected from reality.

In your opinion, where are the most beautiful places on Earth?

In no particular order, the Altai of western Mongolia; the deserts of the US Southwest; The Atacama and Salar deserts; the Gran Sabana in Venezuela; Greenland; central Iceland; the road from Kathmandu to Lhasa; flying over the Amazon jungle or San Blas Islands in Panama; Ngorongoro Crater in Tanzania; the Irish countryside; Parc du Banc d'Arguin in Mauritania; Bagan in Myanmar; the coastline of Cape Province; Angkor Wat; Wadi Rum in Jordan; Dogon/Timbuktu areas in Mali; the eastern Adriatic coastline; little towns in Italy, and the colors of India.

If you had an unlimited budget and space and time were no object, what would your perfect travel day look like (for example: start your morning in Bora Bora; afternoon on a safari in Kenya; night in Australia, etc.)?

I would imagine a trip to places I have not yet been to, and a combination of the type of places that trigger in me the deepest feelings. Therefore, it would entail going to a desert, a jungle river, a mountain range, a political place and a far away destination, somewhere where I can truly disconnect.

I would thus wake up in Antarctica and stare at the ice changing colors, and the penguins go about their lives. I would then have brunch while sailing up the Congo River, and later enjoy tea under a tent with nomads further north in the Tibesti desert somewhere in Tchad. Dinner would be while enjoying the mountain views and village life in Kashmir and then end the day attending Arirang ceremonies in Pyongyang.

Which three countries would you recommend for adventurous travelers to visit, and why?

Colombia, the new shining star for tourism in the Americas, a country with mountains, jungles, deserts, beautiful people, two oceans, archeology, flowers, coffee, and quaint colonial towns, still very untapped to the really adventurous.

Russia's collection of oblasts, okrugs, republics, krais, and autonomies, simply because they are unreported, unexplored, distant, extreme, full of unique cultures, ethnicities and religions in a country that is both third world and super power. And at best, they are all in Russian. They cover a vast chunk of the earth's surface and people hardly ever visit and hardly see any documentaries about them.

And finally, western Mongolia, simply because few people go there, and it is inspirational. No roads, no trees, no shade, no fences, beautiful pastel colors, unique animals, nomads. It is as unique and picturesque as a place can get.

If you had just one travel story to share with someone, what would it be?

Oh yes! There is one story.

I was tired, bored and working late one evening when I decided to take a break and Google up new adventures and trips. I thought about the Arctic and tried to look for balloon expeditions offering BBQ's at the North Pole or weird cruises sailing through bizarre passages. For over an hour I was looking at pictures of Inuit people, seals, polar bears, icebreakers, and icebergs when suddenly I received a friend's request on Facebook. There she was: this gorgeous blonde, with the most fascinating smile, pictured in a sunny Antarctic day, surrounded by thousands of penguins, a cruise ship in the background, and a lot of ice. Plus, she had a microphone in her hands, so I figured she had to be a professional doing her work, of all places, in Antarctica! What a happy coincidence.

Immediately, I clicked back and started chatting with her. There was so much we had in common, and the conversation could not have livelier. Turns out, she owns a travel agency in Panama, Columbia Tours, and produces *Bon Voyage*, her own cable TV travel show. She shared with me links to various documentaries she not only produced but also hosted. I watched her climb snow covered mountains in my native Colombia, and walk the streets of my dearest Budapest as we continued to chat for a good two hours. It was simply magical. She was new to Facebook and was looking at profiles of friends and family. On one hand, I am friend's with a cousin of hers, so we only had two degrees of separation. And on the other hand, once-upon-a-time when I registered my account, I decided that the only thing I would write about my interests was "travel, travel, and then more travel." Six years later, that description caught her eye and thus I became one lucky dude.

We continued chatting for hours every day and eventually moved on to Skype. Things were flowing just beautifully. We engaged in all types of conversations and would find more and more things in common, likes and dislikes. Of course, from time to time I would ask random questions in order to get relevant, and "useful" information to then be able to charm her little by little. Flowers, chocolates, all the good stuff, delivered from across cyberspace. Even though she was in Panama and I was only an hour away in Bogotá, we were not able to find the opportunity to meet. It was, however, the perfect long distance relationship. But one day I popped the question (no, not that one, at least not yet.) "And where would you like to travel next?" She said, Africa. I remained cool and did not blink. I had to surprise her later and avoid the tacky and pushy "Guess what?!"

As luck would have it, a month later I was scheduled to fly to Berlin in order to attend ITB, arguably the best Travel Trade show in the world. And as I often do, I planned to take ten days off just before the show and booked a solo road trip through to Senegal, The Gambia and Guinea-Bissau with a jump over the waters to a couple of the Cape Verde Islands. That night, before I went to bed, and after I knew she would be sound asleep, I sent her a short and sweet email. It only read "just in case" and along I attached my itinerary and waited for her to open her inbox the following morning. With the adrenaline flying high on both sides, she gave me a yes, and immediately we started sorting out the ordeals of getting in Panama last minute visas to those countries. Long story short, a few weeks later, we had our first blind date at the airport in Dakar. The rest is just the most beautiful love story ever.

We enjoyed hiking up the volcano in Fogo, crossing the mighty Gambia River at midnight, taking the boat to Gorée Island and visiting the voodoo village in Bissau. The adventure of meeting Guinea-Bissau's Prime Minister's nephew who mistook me for a Colombian drug kingpin and proposed to do "good business" remains one of the scariest moment of any of my trips. And everything was great, and everything worked out beautifully, and we fell in love and since then, all our trips are together, and they are the best trips. So yes, this is the trip that stands out as my favorite travel story.

Do you ever feel you have missed out on certain aspects of life while away from home as you travel so much?

Not at all. I am sure that had I been a father, perhaps I would not have traveled so much. But that is a different proposition.

What advice would you give to others who would like to travel to every country?

I would say "You can do it!" Take advantage of every business trip and take a few days off, jump over to the nearest weird place that otherwise you would not have planned a specific trip to. Every place is worth a visit but not necessarily worth a specifically planned trip, so stretch your schedule and go the extra mile.

I would advise not to look at political maps so much and not be focused so much on individual countries. Roads can be drawn differently than political borders and (visas aside) one can cover more countries this way. I would advise looking at what is next door to where you want to go. If I were too concerned with just Russia, I would not have visited Abkhazia. Now that I am going to the Canary Islands I will jump across to Western Sahara.

For someone who has been almost everywhere, what still gets you excited about packing your bags again?

The thrill of a new adventure. The knowledge that I will broaden my views of humanity's greatness. The delicious feeling of placing new pins on my map and updating my lists on MTP and thebesttraveled.com. The fact that I will come back with new ideas of itineraries and destinations.

There is also a sense of rush that motivates future trips, as many of the most exotic places are precisely the ones that are changing more rapidly, whether due to climate change, technology, demography or wars.

Looking ahead, what travel plans and goals are you still pursuing, and what is on your "Bucket List"?

In the process of going everywhere, I am aware that the more I know and visit the more I feel I have places yet to visit. The list will never deplete.

I need to get fast to the places that will change the most in the near future. I am leaving Australia for when I old, but I can't put off that easily a trip to remote places in Africa. The rush is only accentuated when I realize the sadness I feel to know I did not get to see Bamiyan in its glory, and perhaps will not get to visit Palmyra, Aleppo, or Nineveh.

However, in the immediate future, I would like to be able to say I can connect the dots between Lisbon and Vladivostok and in the process, cover all the Russian oblasts of which I have visited almost half. Get to Alaska, my one remaining US state, and to four Caribbean islands, as well as San Marino and (strangely enough), Northern Ireland, Wales and Scotland in order to check off the lists on those and, as my good friend Leon would say, eradicate those problems. As far as stats go, I would love to reach and remain to be within the Top 100 on the MTP and thebestravelled.com lists.

Random destinations topping my list and with no list-related "urgencies", are Antarctica, Kashmir, northern and southern Caucasus, certain road trips across France and southern Italy, Madagascar with my nephew, and if ever peace comes back a great trans-Saharan journey.

And finally, I would love to make Sandy happy and take her to her dream destinations to see big game in Botswana, Namibia, Tanzania, Rwanda and Uganda. After all, she is the best possible companion.

Kolja Spöri, Monaco

(Kolja Spöri is the "Gentleman Adventurer" – traveling in style to dangerous places – pictured at a Turkish refugee camp near the Syrian war town of Kobane, during a tour along the ISIS frontline, November 2014)

Where did you grow up, and what was your early life like?

In my first 10 years I was stuck in the foggy Swabian Alps, near the source of the Danube, in Germany. Life brightened up when my parents were posted to Istanbul, which I consider the greatest city in world history. From my bedroom I could see the Bosphorus, Golden Horn and Sea of Marmara. At the German High School, we had more than three months summer breaks. In addition to windsurfing extensively, my parents dragged me to every antique rock in the region, from Troy to the Soviet-Armenian and the Syrian border. Those formative years sparked my lifelong interest in travel and history. And probably my joy of danger zones, because in the early 80s, Turkey was in a civil war. I remember a bombing at school, curfews and severe shortages under the military regime. As a kid, it didn't feel threatening. I had a happy childhood. We were then also stationed in Madrid and Astana, Kazakhstan.

What was the first international trip you took, and what do you remember most about it?

To be honest, I don't remember it. It was probably Austria and Switzerland at age 1. My first travel memory is from Italy, maybe 6-years-old. A highway station behind the Brenner Pass, and the sound of the passing cars, especially the trucks. I am still fascinated by all sounds associated with motion. The sound of the race cars at the Monaco Grand Prix goes so deep under the skin, it is so archaic, it must be DNA-flashbacks from ancient battlefields, or Saint Michael slaying the dragon.

When did you go from traveling casually to making this a full-time goal, and what motivated you to travel to every country?

I still work more than I travel, and I wouldn't want to become a permanent vagabond. The country collecting is somewhere in between a useful system and a crazy addiction. I caught the virus in 2002 from a British couple travel-traveling on board the MS *World Discoverer* from Tahiti via Pitcairn to Easter Island. They introduced me to the idea of counting my countries (103 at the time) and the Travelers' Century Club (TCC). My focus is now on the United Nations Plus list where I am at 200 out of 206 countries.

What have you done in your life to gain the freedom and finances to pursue as much travel as you have?

Freedom is a state of mind. Finances follow the mind. In my case, I already financed my studies as a journalist by covering what I loved most: sports and travel. Then, after my MBA, my first and only slave employment was as head of sports marketing for Hugo Boss, traveling to almost every Formula 1 Grand Prix, Indy Car race, PGA Golf and Tennis Davis Cup tournament around the world. I guess I was a privileged slave. Then I started my own company where I was doing consulting, organizing, and brokering sponsorships. My major sports deals were bringing Compaq into Formula 1, BMW to Larry Ellison's Oracle Racing, and the Turkish F1 Grand Prix in Istanbul. For some time I was a major shareholder in television production companies in Cologne and Monaco, but they were not really lucrative. While I am still teaching about "The Business of Formula 1" at the University of Lausanne, my focus is now on Private Equity and High Net Worth Industries, such as Luxury Goods, Private Banking, Personal Security. At the end of the day, it's about bringing people together, and adding value to all parties, including myself.

Has there ever been a time where you considered abandoning your travel goals?

My travel thrills and motivations have certainly changed over time, but only to become better, more fulfilling. I would never think of abandoning them altogether.

What do you consider to be your two favorite travel experiences, and why?

Driving 20,000 kilometers from Monaco to Magadan, Siberia, in an old Mercedes M-Class, zigzagging through all of Russia, the whole of Trans-Siberia, including the infamous Road of Bones in winter, at temperatures between -50°C and -62°C, several nights continuously without sleep, like through an ice tunnel or a time warp, east, east, east, always afraid that the car might break down and leave us prey to conditions like on planet Mars, that was my most memorable trip ever. The other top-trip was participating in the North Pole Marathon in 2014 and meeting the amazing organizer Richard Donovan who has run seven marathons on seven continents, including Antarctica, in less than 5 days, using only scheduled commercial flights in between. That's the beauty of expeditions like to the North Pole: you meet people who are even more crazy and certainly more capable than yourself.

What are the main things you seek to experience when you travel (culture, cities, nature, animals, adventure activities, etc.)?

My perfect travel moment is sitting in the lobby of a historic landmark hotel, smoking my Romeo & Julieta cigar, in one of the few free countries where this is still allowed, and a local big hitter walks in, we strike up a conversation, he introduces me to the real story of his country, and the power structure behind it, and I will have learned something outside of the copy books and the mainstream media, and often I have a new friend for life. I think it was Erich Kästner who said, "Only fools travel to see museums, the men of wisdom meet in taverns."

Looking back from when you started traveling to where you are now, in what ways, if any, has travel changed you?

I have no more fear. I travel much quicker. I have much better antennas to feel the local vibrations. I feel the ease of belonging there in almost any situation, and I don't see differences between races or nations anymore. The differences between classes are however pretty much the same everywhere.

Do you speak any foreign languages, and if so, which have been the most useful for you besides English?

My father speaks about ten languages and my uncle was head of the big translation department at the European Union in Brussels. So it probably runs in the family. But I speak only fluent English and French, good Turkish (which means decent Azeri as well), Spanish quite OK, Italian so-so, some Russian words on the street, but unfortunately I didn't keep much Mandarin from an early language course, or Bahasa from my half year internship in a Chinese bank in Kuala Lumpur. I regret that I don't speak better Russian, or indeed no Arab. My Turkish really became useful for business in Russia, because many minorities there speak some sort of Turkic, especially in the Caucasus, in Tatarstan and Yakutia anyway, but even among the many guest workers in the Siberian oil cities above the polar circle.

What was the longest extended trip you have ever taken, when was it and where all did you go?

As a student, I took a sabbatical in 1992, and did a sponsor-financed "surf around the world" trip for half a year, windsurfing in the waves of the most famous beaches, including Margaret River in Western Australia, Byron Bay in Queensland, Ho'okipa in Hawaii, and some PR-stunts in front of the Sydney Opera, the Golden Gate Bridge or the Statue of Liberty in New York.

What two countries have exceeded your expectations and which ones left you feeling underwhelmed, and why?

All those countries that our Western propaganda portrays as rogue or evil have exceeded my expectations, in particular Sudan and Iran, but even North Korea. At the other end of the spectrum, I absolutely dislike the communist crab-in-the-bucket culture in Norway that they call The Law of Janteloven. And I boycott the rogue police regime of the United States. It has been a long time since we could associate freedom with the 'American Way of Life', propagated by *Easy Rider*, Route 66, *Endless Summer*, 'California Dreamin'' or 'Come to Marlboro Country' slogans. Nowadays, freedom exists predominantly in the East. Communism and the surveillance state rise dangerously in the West. Times have changed.

When you travel, do you prefer to go with others or solo, and why?

When I travel solo, I tend to feel lonely. Traveling with my wife is the best of all worlds. She's been to more than 100 countries with me, and we even did relatively tough trips together like driving in a Range Rover all the way from Munich to Nigeria, on the West Sahara route, selling the car in the end. Many of my tougher trips were with my best buddy, Harald, from Austria. He also loves danger zones, fears nothing, never sleeps, and with his clients for luxury watches and safe rooms, including some famous Forbes-listed names, we have had some interesting encounters, and access to off-limit areas and presidential mansions.

What has been your most uncomfortable mode of transportation?

The Trans-Siberian train. I really don't think that trains should transport anything else than cattle or commodities. And I once took a flight on Ryanair. Compared with this, the occasional matatu in Africa or marshrutka in Central Asia looked rather comfortable. I'm a gentleman traveler. Whenever possible, I travel in my own car, or in a private taxi.

What is the strangest thing you've seen/experienced while traveling?

The City of the Dead in Mizdakhan on the Uzbek-Turkmen border. A monstrous cemetery. As if Genghis Khan is still lurking round the corner. What a strange vibe this place has, and almost no info to be found.

Another strange experience was negotiating my way onto the United Nation's daily jet, from Lokichoggio near Lake Turkana to Juba, the new capital of South Sudan. Against all my convictions, I paid US $200 to a local Christian missionary and thus qualified to board the aircraft as an official on duty. Together with my buddy, Harald, we were the only passengers on the beautiful brand new 40 leather seats of this Avro jet, which obviously transports nothing more than hot air on most days, thanks to the taxpayers of the world. For us it definitely felt like a private jet.

What are the best and worst meals you have ever eaten while traveling, and where was it?

I don't like talking about food. Travelers who talk about local food - or worse, the end of the digestion process/the local toilets - have never earned my full attention when they did so.

Out of the thousands of places you've stayed around the world, what have been your best and worst accommodations?

As a student, I slept in a brothel in Caracas, on mosquito-infected sugar cane fields in the Caribbean, and in a run-down Gaijin House in Tokyo. Nowadays, collecting the worlds most charismatic hotels is my hobby and I have been privileged to stay in several Amanresorts, Wilderness Safari lodges and &Beyond in Southern Africa, Oberois in Rajasthan, the Huka Lodge in New Zealand, The Dhara Devi in Chiang Mai, Orient-Express Hotels (now unfortunately renamed Belmond), or almost every famous Grand Hotel in capital cities. Many trips were just for the sake of seeing a particular hotel. I particularly like the social intensity of the last stronghold in a conflict zone, for example the Mamba Point in Monrovia, the Ihusi Hotel in Goma, the Club du Lac Tanganyika in Bujumbura or the Esplanada in Dili, East Timor. My two worldwide favorite hébergements combine a certain luxury embedded in danger: the Airways Hotel in Port Moresby and the Hotel Oloffson in Port-au-Prince. I run a travel blog about charismatic hotels called Luxury Rogue. My most clicked blogpost is called "*Spy - War - Dangerzone Hotels*".

What is your favorite "off-the-beaten-path" destination, and why?

Definitely Chechnya. I became friends with the Kadyrov family and therefore was able to visit this war-torn republic when it was still more dangerous. The people are proud and special, operating on a different energy level. On my first visit, I felt like walking into a lion's den and coming out not only unharmed but as a friend of the lion king, sharing many of their traits. I am happy to see that now there is peace in Chechnya, an excellent skyscraper hotel called Grozny, and tourists flock in and reverse their prejudices.

What were your most challenging countries to visit, and why?

The only challenge I can think of is visa procedures. Angola, Turkmenistan, and Saudi Arabia were particularly difficult. But usually there is always loopholes, like the Sudanese embassy in Cairo, the Iranian consulate in Munich, and in addition, I have an excellent visa agent in Berlin. Libya once rejected me despite holding a visa because of my "unusual travel patterns." I later drove into that country at the peak of the Arabian Spring uprising, with a bulletproof vest, from Cairo to Benghazi, the rebels didn't yet have their own visa regime, and finally firing shots with their sub-machine guns in front of the Tibesti Hotel.

Of which travel accomplishments are you most proud?

I am proud of the Extreme Traveler International Congress (ETIC) which I organized first in Munich and then in Grozny, bringing together outstanding personalities like Charles Veley, Jorge Sanchez, Don Parrish, Patrick Maselis, Karimatti Valtari, Wolfgang Stoephasius, Nina Sedano, and several others. Currently, I am trying to organize the next get-together in Gaza, but despite excellent contacts in the region, I am struggling to get permission by the occupying power. Shame. The abbreviation ETIC signals that we are non-political. Travel in itself is an ethical undertaking, based on universal values, by simply bringing people together and building bridges.

I am also a bit proud of my book, Ich war überall (I've Been Everywhere). I think it was one of the very first books about systematic traveling, and I was lucky to get an offer by a German publisher who I met by coincidence in the lobby of the Hotel Vier Jahreszeiten Kempinski in Munich. To sit down and write down memories for half a year required more patience and discipline than I expected.

Do you remember encountering particular people that left a lasting impression with you?

I am particularly motivated by meeting interesting people on my trips, and I think I am talented at it. One of my most treasured encounters was befriending a retired Foreign Légionnaire on Mangareva Island, part of the French Gambiers in the South Pacific. This veteran of many wars and book author about close quarter combat had his final posting as a security guard on the atomic test fields of the Mururoa Atoll and then turned to cultivating black pearls in this remote little paradise. He gave his biggest black pearl as a gift to my wife.

In Port Moresby, Papua New Guinea, and in Bamako, Mali, my wife and I befriended a local art dealer, the latter doubling as Minister of Antiques, which helped grow my wife's collection of native masks and sculptures. The Dogon masks in Mali have a fascinating history, being buried by the high priest, the Hogon, and dug out for ceremonies in intervals of 1 year, 7 years and even 60 years. To have a private Dogon dance just for the two of us was truly memorable.

I've also met warlords like Prince Johnson in Liberia and Donald Rumsfeld in the elevator of the Sheraton Batumi, Adjaria. Other chance encounters, even with very friendly conversations, included Richard Branson at the Regent Hotel Singapore, Adnan Kashoggi at the St. Regis in Rome, and Kim 'Dotcom' Schmitz at the Bayrischer Hof in Munich. Madonna and Guy Ritchie at the Oberoi Udaivilas in Rajasthan were less approachable.

Through my job, I was fortunate to travel with racing drivers, Hollywood actors, pop singers, and having private dinners with several heads of state, including Prince Albert, Michail Gorbachov, and Helmut Kohl. My overall highlight was French-German world explainer Peter Scholl-Latour, a war journalist and traveler to all countries, who sadly passed away last year.

If you could travel back in time, to which era and place would you go, and why?

I would have loved the combination of aesthetics and adversity in the British colonial times, from Africa to India. However I probably would have fought on the other side, like Eduard Schnitzer, the 19th-century adventurer, anthropologist and German spy, also known as Emin Pasha, after whom the best hotel in Kampala, Uganda and soon in Juba, South Sudan is named.

I've also found myself daydreaming in the lobby of the Winter Palace Hotel in Luxor about Howard Carter and the moment he opened Tutankhamun's tomb, after so much hardship, fundraising and patience. Just seeing the golden glory of that archeological treasure in the Egyptian Museum in Cairo brought tears to my eyes.

Can you describe any particular situation where you felt completely out of your comfort zone?

I have a special interest in so-called danger zones or political hot-spots. When there is news of a conflict, I often pack my gear and travel right there. It's not about seeing blood at the frontline, getting a kick out of war, or seeing the carnage after natural disasters, not at all. I keep a respectful distance. But I want to be close enough to understand the reality, which is usually completely different from our mainstream media coverage. A good example is the whole ISIS situation which I examined on a drive last winter from Chechnya over the Georgian Military Highway into Armenia, Karabakh, Iran and northern Iraq, and then 500 kilometers along the Sykes-Picot border between Turkey and Syria. Honestly, I don't easily feel outside my comfort zone. I deal with situations where and when they arise. Once, when we drove a self-organized charity truck to the refugee camps in Dadaab at the Somali-Kenyan border, the road was blocked by a pick-up with shifta bandits or even Al Shabaab fighters. It helped that I had already been untypically fast on the sand track, so instead of slowing down I managed to curve around and speed ahead in a huge dust-cloud which probably saved us. I have also once been physically attacked by a Moroccan youth in Tangier in 1997, but I was able to defend myself. In Gabon I was detained for 24 hours by corrupt border police, and the Uzbeks guards at the Afghan border gave me a rather unpleasant body search. Knocking on wood, I was spared more serious encounters so far.

What are your three favorite cities in the world, and why?

Istanbul, Venice, and Udaipur, because of their beauty, history and mystique.

What is the ideal amount of time you prefer to travel on each trip before you are ready to go home and take a break?

Nowadays, I prefer speed travel. Ideally within a week, or a maximum of two. Sleeping in the airplane, or driving all night in the car. Sleep is overvalued. With discipline, one can see much more in a shorter time. The feeling is more intense. And there is less of falling into a void afterwards, less of a post-trip depression.

In your opinion, where are the most beautiful places on Earth?

The Okavango Delta in Botswana comes to mind. Also the Ngorongoro Crater; the Kivus region in the DR Congo; the Pantanal in Brazil; Torres del Paine in Chile; the Maldives; Bora Bora, and many other islands in the South Pacific, with the Isle des Pins (Isle of Pines) in New Caledonia possibly being my favorite. I am also attracted to the polar regions and the crisp cold of Siberia. But even the Alps are of amazing beauty, in particular, Tegernsee, Berchtesgaden, Wilder Kaiser or Lauterbrunnen Valley, although I needed many years to realize that I had such a unique gem right in front of my nose.

If you had an unlimited budget and space and time were no object, what would your perfect travel day look like (for example: start your morning in Bora Bora; afternoon on a safari in Kenya; night in Australia, etc.)?

I would stare all day long from the International Space Station to Mother Earth, like a guppy in an aquarium.

Which three countries would you recommend for adventurous travelers to visit, and why?

The corner of Rwanda, Uganda, and the DR Congo to smell the mountain gorillas. The Pamir Highway along Tajikistan, Afghanistan and Kyrgyzstan to breathe the thin air. And the deepest oblasts of Russian Siberia to hear absolute silence and to feel really cold.

If you had just one travel story to share with someone, what would it be?

One road trip completely changed my life, but it is hard to share the experience with the uninitiated. The European Road E50 from Volgograd to Verdun combines two ancient navels of the world that stand for well-known and for lesser known history. By driving along the Volga-Don canal and the so-called steppe highway, from the Caucasus over the Crimea, through the Intermarium, and cities like Sataniv, Burshtyn, Halic, Hotzenplotz, then up the Danube corridor past the Lechfeld and the Gugel to the Rhine with its SchUM-Cities, then finally reaching that god forbidden war magnet, I slowly understood the meaning of Europe as 'Home of the Avars', Tsaritsyn as 'Home of the Saracens' and the Caspian 'Khazar' Sea as 'Home of the Ashkenazi'. There exists a thousands of years old interaction between Turkic, Slavic, Gothic-Germanic and Jewish peoples, but much of it is hidden in plain sight. Travel has been the eye opener for me.

Do you ever feel you have missed out on certain aspects of life while away from home as you travel so much?

Not at all. On the contrary, I have found all aspects of life while traveling. Like everything in life, one needs to maintain a healthy balance.

What advice would you give to others who would like to travel to every country?

Sign up at mosttraveledpeople.com and thebesttravelled.com and meet some of the other travelers for inspiration and advice as early as possible.

For someone who has been almost everywhere, what still gets you excited about packing your bags again?

Packing itself gets me excited. I'm a minimum luggage or even zero luggage advocate. I've reduced my Tumi bag to a size that fits under the airline seat. A special coat sometimes doubles as a luggage container. Merino underwear and shirts can be worn for several days without smelling. Galoshes multiply the roadworthiness with just one pair of shoes. Although I reduce my luggage to the max, I always wear a jacket with hanky and look like a gentleman. I keep cut-proof leather gloves for any occasion, my key chain conceals a tool that isn't confiscated at airport checks, and I have personalized note cards in case I need to leave a message or a gift. At the North Pole Marathon I was the only traveler who made it with hand luggage only, and that was the hardest part of the expedition. I like to think that people with big suitcases aren't travelers, they remain tourists.

Looking ahead, what travel plans and goals are you still pursuing, and what is on your "Bucket List"?

Driving to the northernmost dead end, the "Anabar Road", has never been done, or at least reported, by a Westerner, and after two failed attempts it is still the highest on my bucket list.

Bob Parda, U.S.A.

(Bob Parda and his wife Cathy in Herat, Afghanistan, their last of the 193 UN countries to visit, 2013)

Where did you grow up, and what was your early life like?

I grew up in central Connecticut in a middle-class family with one younger sister. We lived with my maternal grandmother in an old house my great-grandfather had built. The neighborhood was mainly first or second generation immigrants which helped shape my world view. My father was first generation Polish, and my mother mixed but mainly of Irish decent. Our home was basic but comfortable. We had a coal furnace and stove when I was very young, and I remember playing in the coal bin in the basement, much to my mother's chagrin. When I was eight, my Dad was promoted to a sales management position for a large hardware company, and we moved to Detroit where he headed up the small office there. When I turned ten, we again moved this time to the Chicago suburbs where Dad took over another small office. I remained here until I left for college. While moves when young can be somewhat traumatic, I think they prepared me to adjust when I found myself outside my comfort zone. We did not have much money, so we never had any exotic vacations and the only foreign travel were a couple of trips across the border to Niagara Falls and Windsor, Canada, but I found that exciting. As a kid, collecting stamps and then getting my Amateur Radio (Ham) license opened my eyes to the world outside. Since many of my relatives served in WWII, I was fascinated by the military, particularly the Navy where my father was an officer in the reserves and also served in WWII and Korea. Fortunately, I was a good student, and I was offered an appointment to the U.S. Naval Academy (Annapolis), so I joined the Navy to see the world, as the saying goes.

What was the first international trip you took, and what do you remember most about it?

Not counting my day trips to Canada as a kid, my first real foreign travel was on a Midshipman training cruise to Europe between my junior and senior years (1967). Several of my Annapolis classmates plus midshipmen from some of the civilian colleges that were enrolled in NROTC and I boarded an old WWII aircraft carrier, the USS Essex (CVS 9), in Newport, RI. The thrill of seeing the horizon disappear as we sailed out of port, knowing that I would not return for over three months was truly exciting. As part of my training, I filled in on the bridge watch cycle and because I was one of the few people with a ham radio license, I helped man the radio shack where a couple of crew members and I would contact stateside hams each evening so crew members could talk to their loved ones via phone patches. One night we were unable to reach any stateside stations, but another ham with a call sign I did not recognize tried to contact me. As it turned out, he was from Russia. I had studied Russian in school, and the guys in the ham shack goaded me into returning his call (I think they just wanted to see if I could really speak Russian...). Unfortunately, the Naval Security Team in Spain took a dim view of an American aircraft carrier speaking Russian to Moscow hams and sent a team to meet us when we pulled into Bergen, Norway... I don't know if it was payback or it just wasn't my day, but I was assigned as the pier security officer in Bergen later that day. Shortly after I set up shop a crusty old man came up to me and in broken English ordered me to remove all the sailors and our liberty launches or he would have his men hidden in the hills descend and attack us, showing no mercy. My first reaction was utter panic, but fortunately, a couple of the local constabulary came to my rescue, said this guy was one of the local town drunks and that I should pay him no mind. I thought the cruise was going well after that but when we pulled into Hamburg, Germany I had another surprise awaiting me. I had been invited to join the ship's basketball team, not because I had any talent but I was tall (6'5"). Someone had arranged for the ship's team to play the University of Prague (not sure why they were in town) and the match had attracted a lot of local attention since this was the height of the cold war. It was a relatively close game until the last quarter, but then our guys broke it open. We had two or three men on the team that could have played for the Globe Trotters, and they delighted the audience. The coach must have felt pity for me and put me in for the last quarter, and I miraculously scored a few points. After the game, we shook hands. They did not speak any English, but I was able to communicate in my reluctant Russian. Purely by coincidence, when I was out bar hopping with some friends that night, I bumped into the Prague team. They recognized me and invited me over. After one or two beers (perhaps more) we exchanged names and addresses. As luck would have it, they sent me some postcards to the ship in Russian raising more eyebrows. I spent the next six weeks in Garmisch-Partenkirchen, Germany attending the Russian language program set up for our diplomats and attaches with three other midshipmen from the Naval Academy and cadets from West Point and the Air Force Academy. While there, one of my friends and classmates, Denny Blair set up a Soccer match with a German military team who happened to have two players that were on their Olympic squad. Never having seen a soccer match at that point in my life, I was chosen to play goalie. Diving after far too many near "saves" on a gravel court left me looking like a bloodied pin cushion, a game I will never forget...

Upon completion of the school, I bought an old German motorcycle for $30 and traveled across southern Europe for two weeks. Europe was full of American college kids clutching their camera in one hand and Frommer's *Europe on $5 a Day* in the other. Many were overly obnoxious, and I delighted in sending them off in the wrong direction when they stopped and asked me for directions, taking me for a local and marveling at how well I spoke English. I thought I would go them one better and decided to budget only $3 per day, including gas and lodging for the balance of my trip. I felt I was doing good until I met a French college student who hitched a ride with me for a few days. He had 15 French Francs for two weeks, the equivalent of about $0.20 a day! In those days though we could get a bottle of cheap wine, a baguette and can of sardines for less than 3 Francs. When I got to Barcelona I hoped I could sell the bike and pay for a good train ticket to Rota, Spain (near Seville) where I would catch my military flight back to the U.S. Unfortunately, since I kept the German license plates on the bike and did not have proper papers, I could not sell the bike. Some college kids in Barcelona adopted me, showed me the city and fed me. When it was time to leave I "sold" them the bike for 100 Pesetas, the equivalent of $1.60. Considering I had put about 4,000km on the bike, I was happy. I could only afford a third class train ticket for the overnight trip. Not having taken any long trips by rail before, I was not sure what to expect. I found a seat in one of the old cabins that fit eight people on two wooden benches. Shortly before the train was to leave, an elderly woman with a young child and what seemed like everything she owned including a chicken and a 20-liter jug of water plopped herself down on the space next to me. I should have taken the hint when most of my compartment mates immediately left, but by the time I realized what was about to happen, all the spaces in other compartments were full. Within 30 minutes out of the station, the water jug had spilled, making the compartment a wading pool and both the chicken and the child were apparently afraid that if they stopped squawking, they would die. After an eternity, I finally made it to Rota and back to school, logging my first 15 countries and a lifetime of memories.

When did you go from traveling casually to making this a full-time goal, and what motivated you to travel to every country?

Once I was wearing a Navy uniform, travel became part of my daily life. I chose the surface Navy because it offered the most opportunity to visit distant lands. Besides making port calls in places like Hawaii, Hong Kong, Singapore, Sydney, plus numerous ports in the Mediterranean and lots of islands and smaller cities in between, I used my "leave" (vacation) time for as much independent travel as my limited budget would permit. Occasionally I was able to get seats on military aircraft (Space A) to other countries. After I was married in 1974, my wife Cathy joined me wherever possible. We were stationed in Korea for two years (1978-80) where I was attached to the U.S. Embassy. This proved to be a great jumping off point for our travels in Asia. I had previously served in Vietnam during the war (1971-72) for 13 months as an advisor to the Vietnamese Navy as part of Nixon's "Peace with Honor" program, and I had also been sent to Brazil and the Philippines to help train their Navies. When I retired from the Navy in 1991, my wife and I decided to open our tour company, Advantage Travel & Tours. She had already been working in the travel business for eight years as General Manager of another travel company. We knew that travel was something we truly enjoyed and I was anxious to do something together with Cathy since I had spent so much of my career at sea, away from home.

It was many years later that we entertained the thought of actually touring every country. Since we specialized in arranging itineraries to unusual destinations, we had the opportunity to meet and talk to a number of serious travelers. They introduced us to the Travelers' Century Club (TCC) in the mid-1990's. Our initial reaction was negative because travel to us should be a meaningful learning experience, not just an adult scavenger hunt where you checked off some boxes. My opinion changed when I was leading a tour in the late 1990's to Papua New Guinea, and several members of the group belonged to TCC. The outgoing president of TCC, Ken Ziegler, was among the group, and I remember vividly his description of places he had been, and I knew he was a real traveler. He said this was his 5th trip to PNG, but he wanted to join our group to explore the Sepik River.

Cathy and I started tracking our progress on the International Travel News (ITN) and TCC lists, plus later the MTP (Most Traveled People) list, particularly after clients pushed us to offer programs to many remote countries and destinations. It became more of a CV qualification to show potential clients that we walked the talk and knew travel rather than simply a fixed goal. It was not until we were down to just a handful of the UN countries around 2012 that we finally said, "Why not?"

What have you done in your life to gain the freedom and finances to pursue as much travel as you have?

Not being saddled with a college loan to pay off (in fact the Midshipmen at Annapolis received a small paycheck ($14/month) we called our "monthly insult") and knowing that I had a secure future ahead of me where I could project my finances was a big plus. I was able to save some money and invest it in real estate and a few furtive forays into the stock market. While there were tough times, particularly when the markets tumbled and I lost more than I could afford, we came through it OK and were able to budget money for travel. Cathy and I consciously decided to put off having any kids since we traveled so much, both for work and pleasure. We ultimately decided to not have any, which somewhat selfishly gave us more flexibility to travel.

Perhaps the smartest thing I ever did was marry a clever woman like Cathy, who has a remarkable knack for saving money and finding great deals for our personal travel. Once we opened our own business, much of our travel became a write-off since it was directly related to operating our company. Leading tours and exploring new destinations was a real perk since the industry is notoriously underpaid and the great deals travel industry personnel used to be able to get had long since disappeared.

Has there ever been a time where you considered abandoning your travel goals?

I really had not established any goal per se except to travel as much as possible and explore the world. It was part of my lifestyle, first through the Navy and then through our travel company. As long as I have my health and enough money in the bank to keep me going, I see no reason to stop. There are too many temptations out there that I want to see.

What do you consider to be your two favorite travel experiences, and why?

In 1995 Cathy and I were approached by a local San Diego astronomy group sponsored by the Ruben H. Fleet Planetarium and their then resident astronomer, Dennis Mammana, to organize a trip to view a total solar eclipse at Angkor Wat in Cambodia. We had been prominent in promoting Cambodia in the 1990's and were excited about such a trip since Angkor Wat is one of our favorite places. It took several high-level meetings with the Culture, Tourism and Scientific Ministries in Cambodia to get the necessary permits for our group of about 30, mainly amateur astronomers. Angkor Wat is a cultural and religious masterpiece, the only building to be prominently featured on a national flag and this was the first eclipse to darken the hallowed grounds since it was built in the 12th C. To commemorate the event, Dennis and the group decided to donate a motor driven, pedestal mounted telescope (which we later had to bribe Customs officials to release it from shipping) plus an extensive library of reference and textbooks on astronomy to the national university. As it turned out, they had not established any program in astronomy yet, so this was a welcome gift. In gratitude, the government erected a wooden hall within the walls of Angkor Wat and hosted a champagne lunch during the eclipse solely in our honor. As this was my first ever total eclipse, I cannot imagine a more perfect setting. To top it off, the weather was excellent, and we got to witness a magnificent "diamond ring" while the jungle all around us went silent and the monks gathered there were chanting in complete awe.

While any serious traveler could tell lots of stories about their adventures, the second travel experience I would like to relate occurred in 2009. Cathy and I had been waiting for an opportunity to visit Iraq plus Syria, Jordan, and Lebanon. She had previously visited the last three, and I was captivated by her stories and photos as well as my limited knowledge of the history of the region. Iraq had a relative moment of peace (fleeting as it turned out) and the others were also comparatively quiet. We had several of our "regular" travelers, people who we consider part of our traveling family who were also anxious to visit so we arranged the tour. While we had some misgivings about the timing, the American Embassy personnel we met in Baghdad welcomed us with open arms and encouraged us to bring more people. We were the first all American group to visit since 2003, and I felt good about it because we were also making a statement that the U.S. and UN military and diplomatic efforts had made a difference. All four countries have so much to offer in terms of history, archeology, religion, and culture. We cherished the opportunity to visit sites such as Babylon, Samarra, Petra, Anjar, Baalbek and Byblos, particularly in light of some of the damage that have occurred during recent fighting. While the trip was at times difficult (more on this later), we found it immensely satisfying.

What are the main things you seek to experience when you travel (culture, cities, nature, animals, adventure activities, etc.)?

I appreciate nature (particularly wilderness settings) and animals, but I rarely get excited about cities or doing something simply for the thrill of it. Being able to approach an orangutan with her baby in the wilds of a Sumatran rainforest and actually feed her, seeing the mountain gorillas of Rwanda up close and being befriended by thousands of penguins in Antarctica rank high. But I must say that it is experiencing the culture and history of a country that fascinates me the most.

When I plan a trip, I normally focus more on the cultural sites, using the UNESCO World Heritage List as a yardstick rather than simply tick off a country. While I disagree with several of the sites that UNESCO has inscribed, it is still the most comprehensive compilation of culturally important destinations. Archaeological sites intrigue me because so many of them showcase the advanced civilization that made these places possible. I am not a big fan of operas and theatrical performances, although I do like good music and am impressed by some of the concert and opera halls that were constructed centuries ago. I always enjoy good museums since they can tell a story about the history and culture of a place or era that no other medium can. As recent world events have shown, far too many of our cultural treasures are at risk and by seeing them now and hopefully encouraging their protection, future generations can benefit.

Looking back from when you started traveling to where you are now, in what ways, if any, has travel changed you?

It has certainly broadened my mind and my knowledge of the world. I am far more open to accepting different solutions or methods than had I been trapped inside the American cocoon. While this may offend some, it has certainly changed my views toward religion. I was baptized a Catholic in deference to my father's heritage but allowed to choose my own religion once I entered my teen years. I became a devout Lutheran, going to catechism classes, serving as an altar boy (acolyte), attending religious summer camps and ultimately accepting Jesus as my savior. The more I traveled, the harder it was for me to say that there was only one way to live a good life and find salvation. If being a true Christian meant that only by accepting Jesus could you find salvation, I could not condemn those of other faiths to life in hell. It also changed my perspectives on politics. I was able to see why the 'American Way' was not always the best way but through respect for other's opinions, you could find a more meaningful solution. I think travel is one of the best educations you can get.

Do you speak any foreign languages, and if so, which have been the most useful for you besides English?

The only other language I have had formal training in for more than a few weeks is Russian. Unfortunately, due to lack of opportunity to practice, I have lost much of this though recent travels have helped refresh my "reluctant Russian." Serving in Vietnam in 1971/72 as an adviser and having a six-week crash course in the language gave me some facility in the language but much of our training was job focused such as the first phrase we learned, "dung bang" (don't shoot!). As an anecdote on one of my first trips back to Vietnam leading a tour in the early 1990's, I was walking along a street in central Vietnam (Qui Nhon). In those days, about the only westerners that could be found outside the major cities were Russians. A young man rode past on a bicycle, reached out and hit me. I shouted after him and asked why he did that. Surprised that I could speak Vietnamese, he said that he hated Russians (although they were a big help to the government then, they offended many locals). I further infuriated him by speaking a bit of Russian. Then I laughed and told him again in Vietnamese that I was American. After the shock had worn off, he came back, hugged me, gathered up some of his friends and they all wanted a picture with the "American." It's moments like that you are glad you can speak at least a little of another tongue.

By nature of living near the Mexican border in San Diego, I have picked up a little Spanish and also some words in Korean while I served at our Embassy in Seoul from 1978 to 1980. I would love to speak more Chinese, but I am tone deaf, and tonal languages like Chinese and Thai are a real challenge (somehow I was able to learn some Vietnamese). My wife speaks five dialects of Chinese in addition to Vietnamese but has proclaimed me hopeless when it comes to mastering those languages. I was able to recognize several hundred "Chinese" characters which helped in Chinese, Japanese, and

Korean, where the meaning is essentially the same, but the pronunciation is totally different.

What was the longest extended trip you have ever taken, when was it and where all did you go?

I guess it depends on how you define "trip." During my Navy career, I had several cruises of six to seven months duration visiting many remarkable places. This does not count the 13 months I spent in Vietnam, the 25 months in Korea or the first overseas trip I took in 1967 I recounted in the second question. If you focus on my recent travel history during the last ten years, my 30-day expeditionary cruise with 65 other intrepid passengers to various islands, including Bouvet Island plus time before and after this trip (about 35 days total) would top the list. We flew to Ushuaia, the jumping off port for most Antarctic adventures, sailed through the Drake Passage visiting the South Shetland, South Orkney, and the South Sandwich Islands and continuing to the most remote island on earth, Bouvet Island. From there we headed north along the mid-Atlantic Ridge passing Gough Island, briefly stopping at one of the small islands in the Tristan da Cunha group (the most remote inhabited islands in the world) since the main island was under quarantine due to a viral outbreak, visited St Helena and departed the ship on Ascension Island. After spending a few days on the island, we flew to London and spent a day there before flying back to California. What made this trip seem particularly long was the fact that due to the gale and hurricane force winds we met, high seas and epidemic at Tristan, Cathy and I (like most people on board) only got off the ship for about 18 hours during the entire cruise.

What two countries have exceeded your expectations and which ones left you feeling underwhelmed, and why?

On a people to people basis, I would have to say Vietnam and Iran. Despite a long history of animosity between our respective governments, the people have given Cathy and I (and our clients) extremely warm receptions and have shown undeniable affection for America and her people. I wish our governments could learn from this. The candidates for underwhelmed on the people side reside mainly within Africa. While not outwardly hostile, they appear indifferent, expecting more than we are prepared to give. From a cultural standpoint, I am always impressed with China, India, and Russia. Ethiopia, Cambodia and most of Europe are not far behind. I do not understand why Myanmar, which has so much in the way of cultural treasures, has had little recognition by UNESCO. The Galapagos, while not a country, disappoints me since it is now overly saturated with tourism in what was once a very pristine natural setting and risks spoiling its historic advantage.

When you travel, do you prefer to go with others or solo, and why?

My preference is to travel with my wife, Cathy, who is my soul mate and protector (she warded off at least two pick pocket attempts on me despite my size and her rather diminutive stature - 5'4"). Besides being far more organized than I am and very street smart, she shares my love of travel. She does question some of the places I want to visit, but without her support and assistance in organizing our travel, I would not be as successful in my quest to explore the unusual. There have been many occasions where traveling with groups made the most sense, driven mainly by cost considerations, but we were fortunate that we could select most of our traveling companions. A different dynamic enters into the picture when we escort a group, because the degree of responsibility changes, but we are almost always among friends who share similar interests.

What has been your most uncomfortable mode of transportation?

I have always taken pleasure going to sea whether it was in the Navy or on a personal trip. For 15 years I owned a full keel 41 ft ocean-going ketch which I had built with hopes of sailing around the world. Life intervened, and I had to settle for much shorter cruises, ultimately selling the boat after Cathy promised to honor my love of the open ocean by taking several romantic cruises and incorporating cruises into several of our tour programs.

Remote islands have always fascinated me and several clients were pushing us to visit Tokelau in the Pacific, part of an ambitious Circle Pacific program we were arranging. We found what promised to be the perfect voyage aboard a 12 passenger motor "research" catamaran named the M/V *Bounty Bay*. Following numerous emails and phone calls with the owner, Dr. Graham Wragg (aka Scally Wragg among some on Pitcairn Island - not a term of endearment...), plus researching the web and finding a couple of positive articles about the vessel and the work Wragg had done, I chartered the boat. I did not know it at the time, but this vessel is infamous within the community of serious travelers.

We had arranged for *Bounty Bay* to pick up my group on Wallis Island, sail to Tokelau and spend two days exploring the atolls and then sail to Apia via Swains Island. I requested special provisioning for our group and was assured all permits had been arranged. The boat showed up late in Wallis, failed to get proper clearance and then had to find a part needed for the vessel despite having just come from a shipyard for repairs. At first glance, the ship looked OK (it did have a fresh coat of paint...), but once I was aboard and had a chance to inspect more closely, I was very concerned about the condition. As a senior inspector for ship readiness in the U.S. Navy, plus having owned two boats myself, I had a strong background in inspecting ships of all sizes and types. Hatches did not properly close and were not watertight, the engines leaked oil making the lower decks slippery, one of the two life rafts was well outside its service date and was of questionable utility, plus the windows on the sides of the pilot house cabin were loosely fitted Plexiglas in wooden frames that would have probably buckled if hit with a big wave and because of the slow speed and direction of travel the ship rode very uncomfortably. I had enough confidence in my own seamanship and navigational skills that I made the decision to continue, in part because we did have a working satellite telephone aboard, but judging from the reaction of the rest of my group, it was truly a voyage from hell. To make matters worse, when we finally arrived at Tokelau, we were denied landing because Wragg had not obtained proper clearance so we had to anchor offshore and wait a day. Even on our arrival in Samoa, his reputation must have preceded him because on checking in with the Port Authority at Apia we had to wait several hours for anyone to board the vessel in order to be cleared even though they were not busy. I met with Wragg and offered him what I felt was constructive criticism on how to improve the boat, but after a short while, he stormed out of the meeting. Because I was concerned that the vessel might pose a real safety hazard to those less fortunate than our group, I forwarded my observations to the Captain of the Port in the Cook Islands where the boat was registered and shortly after that the boat was taken out of service for several months (coincidence?).

What is the strangest thing you've seen/experienced while traveling?

Our friend and fellow world traveler, Ed Reynolds, has reported on this in the first edition of this book, but I still laugh when I relive the experience in my mind. In November 2011, we were visiting some islands off the coast of Guinea-Bissau, including Bolama, the first capital of the country. Our local guide had arranged for a boat and crew to take us out to the islands and return to another settlement where we were to tour an NGO project providing employment for the people and meet our bus. Everything was going fine until we headed back to the coast, which was lined with mangrove forests and swamps plus lots of various channels leading to small villages. The boat captain had a GPS and explained that he was very familiar with these waters, but their body language was not good. We made our way into one of the many inlets only to find out it was the wrong one, and we promptly struck a mud bar mixed with mollusks. Since it was a soft grounding, I thought that I along with a few of the men on board could push the boat off, but we were stuck hard. As we pondered what to do, the tide was dropping so fast that the boat was sitting high and dry on the bar within 20 minutes. I had visions of being there until the next tide cycle, but a curious crowd started gathering on shore. Shortly after that, more than a dozen young men and boys in dugout canoes made their way out to our boat. To the delight of the women in our group, most of them were completely naked. I doubt this was the first time this had happened because after some quick negotiations and an appropriate expression of our "gratitude," they were able to move the boat off the bar and we finally made it to the right village.

What are the best and worst meals you have ever eaten while traveling, and where was it?

Probably our most memorable meal was on the beach at a resort in Pointe-Noire, Republic of Congo. Cathy and I had gone for a walk along the beach and came across a small restaurant on the bluff overlooking the ocean. We stopped for a beer and were watching a local fisherman surfcasting. Suddenly his rod was bent almost double, and he was dragging in what looked like a large clump of seaweed.

When the "weed" got closer, we realized that it was a lobster, at least four or five pounds. We had never seen a lobster caught with a rod and reel and were fascinated. Then we got hungry! We asked the owner of the bar to see how much the fisherman wanted for the lobster, and he agreed to sell it for five Euros. We paid the restaurant another five Euros to cook it with trimmings and had the freshest and best-tasting lobster ever.

Speaking of lobster, even though I am originally from New England and love the Maine lobsters there, the spiny variety from Robinson Crusoe Island are amazingly tasty. We have had them done several ways and always enjoyed it. Our favorite cruise fare is at the Red Ginger Restaurants aboard Oceania Cruises (everything is delicious). Other notable meals, partly because they were unexpected, were a set plate meal in the Eiffel Tower, which included the best foie gras we have ever tasted, a seafood hot pot in Honfleur (France) and a foie gras pizza in Bordeaux (as you might suspect, we are not members of PETA).

When you travel to remote destinations, bad meals come with the territory. I can eat almost anything including fried insects, worms, weird bush meat and various organs, including monkey brain. I draw the line at undercooked tripe and okra. Our biggest disappointment was on the *Bounty Bay*, where despite our emphasis on a well-stocked pantry and paying extra, we survived on carrot sandwiches with stale bread, rotten eggs and one frozen fish plus another we caught.

Out of the thousands of places you've stayed in around the world, what have been your best and worst accommodations?

We normally place value and location above luxury, but we have splurged on a few occasions. Perhaps our favorite is the resort on Desroches Island in the Amirante Group, Seychelles. We figured that if it were good enough for

Prince William and Kate for a romantic getaway, it would probably be good enough for us, and we were not disappointed. Our villa, the food, service, and beach were beyond anything we had experienced. Worst is relative. No one likes spending a night in an airport due to flight delays and cancellations or a hotel lobby when you thought you had an early check-in only to have people extend. When I was young and traveled around Europe on the motorcycle, on more than one occasion, I slept in barns, on beaches, and under bushes. If I had to pick a place, though, it would be in India, where the room was equipped with one bare light bulb, an Asian-style squat toilet, and more mosquitoes than I could kill or count.

What is your favorite "off the beaten path" destination, and why?

This depends on what your time reference is. Early in my travels, there were parts of Africa and Asia that time had forgotten. One particular striking memory is my first visit to Singapore in 1968, shortly after their independence when there were militia with semi-automatic weapons at every major intersection and snake charmers with cobras enchanting crowds and cobras at nearly every major corner. Myanmar during the 1990's, well before it was discovered, was magical. The same holds true of Vietnam. However, today, to really get "off the beaten path," I find the polar regions exceptional. Protected by international treaties and limited in their appeal due to expense, you find only a special breed of traveler who will attempt these destinations. I still find parts of Northeast India and Papua New Guinea amazing, although this is rapidly changing. If you were to go far enough into the interior of Africa, there is no doubt that there would be some exceptional experiences, but given safety considerations in today's world, I am reluctant to push that boundary and can only rely on reports of those more adventurous than me.

What were your most challenging countries to visit, and why?

I would have to say Tokelau (although not a country) for reasons I explained elsewhere. Not having any airport and only a periodic ferry that gives preference to locals living on the island and NGO's (understandably), you have to resort to unscrupulous charter operators like the *Bounty Bay* (never again!). Picking a real country, it would probably be Afghanistan or Somalia due to security concerns. This can change and is a moving target. For many people it is Libya, but Cathy and I have been fortunate to visit the wonderful sites there twice. We have been lucky with regard to visas almost everywhere, although I was once denied a visa for Turkmenistan on a subsequent visit when a member of my group, despite numerous warning, stopped in the middle of the bridge separating Turkmenistan from Iran, pulled out his video camera and in plain sight took a panorama of the respective borders.

Of which travel accomplishments are you most proud?

Without question, it is being able to visit all 193 countries with my wife by my side. I know many other people who have visited all the countries, but very few have been able to do it with their spouse or significant other. Cathy and I celebrated 193 (Afghanistan) on her birthday in September 2013 (we reached the goal together). Sharing those moments are truly special. I am also proud of the fact that I am one of only about a dozen people in the world who have visited over half the UNESCO World Heritage Sites, which numbers more than 1,000. Being part of the travel industry has given me the privilege of helping hundreds of other serious travelers' progress towards their personal travel goals.

Do you remember encountering particular people that left a lasting impression with you?

I don't always know the names, but the scenarios are indelible. I recall the French kid I related earlier during my travels in 1967 that was traveling on $0.20/day for two weeks and loving every minute of that. He embodied the spirit of doing it now. Money should not be an impediment. It is ultimately your desire that drives the soul.

In Papua New Guinea I felt I had a soul mate in James, my native guide aboard the vessel *Melanesian Discoverer* on several trips during the late 1990's. He was highly respected among the villages we visited, encouraging the locals to rekindle their native arts and improve their life. Unfortunately, he passed away several years ago.

Perhaps most importantly I remember the countless people who unselfishly helped a young traveler (me) realize his dreams by helping to understand why we are so different yet so much alike.

If you could travel back in time, to which era and place would you go, and why?

I would have loved to have lived during the "Age of Exploration." The 15th and 16th centuries began a remarkable era of discovery when ships and navigational skills were being tested to their fullest. To have sailed with men the likes of Magellan, Vasco da Gama and Columbus would have been exciting. The explosion of man's knowledge of the known world, confirming old legends and creating new ones would be manna from heaven for someone like me who loves the sea and has a passion for navigation. A close second would be to have sailed with Captain James Cook on his first (1768-71) and second (1772-75) voyages of discovery. I would skip his third because of his tragic death and the change in his personality. There are many areas of the world tied to historic moments that I would also like to see, but the lure of the open ocean is strongest.

Can you describe any particular situation where you felt completely out of your comfort zone?

Again, it is important to define the circumstances. What stands out the most to me is when I was a young naval officer, and I volunteered to be part of Nixon's "Peace with Honor" program as we wound down our involvement in Vietnam. As I mentioned earlier, I served as an adviser to the South Vietnamese Navy, helping to transition the equipment (in this case ships) we were leaving behind so they could fight the war by themselves. This meant going out on patrol as the only American or in some cases with an enlisted assistant for up to 30 days at a time or until our water ran out, teaching the Vietnamese how to use these assets. We were patrolling and showing the flag in the Ca Mau Delta, notorious Viet Cong territory where the villages were nominally neutral during the day and active VC compounds at night. I knew that I was not Rambo and would not be able to fight my way out of a tight situation (there were reward posters out - "dead or alive" - for advisers like myself) so I had to be creative. While I could have stayed on board my patrol vessel in each village, I chose to accompany my counterpart, the captain, as we showed the flag, trying to convince them that the South Vietnamese government was their friend. Visiting villages armed to the teeth did not exactly enhance my likability quotient, so I took the unusual step of buying a Mattel plastic machine gun that made funny noises and flashed bright colors when the trigger was pulled and carried that along with a big bag of candy each time I visited a village. I still wore my flak jacket and had my .45 pistol hidden inside it, but I wanted to appear as non-threatening as possible. It worked, and I was like the Pied Piper with most of the village kids following me and hanging on my arms to the amusement of the village elders since I was so tall and spoke some Vietnamese. This did not stop the attacks on the ship when we were on the rivers and for me, it took a few cases of receiving "incoming" fire to get used to it. Vintage WWII ships such as the old amphibious vessels I was serving on were so old that an AK 47 round would pass through at least two or three bulkheads (walls) when fired at close range. One of our missions was to patrol the rivers and draw fire from the VC so we could engage them. This was definitely an uncomfortable moment. As anyone who has been in combat can attest, it is a rite of passage that defies description.

If we ignore military service, I would have to say our visit to Iraq had me most on edge. I can handle potential threats when it is just me at risk, but the game changes when I have responsibility for a group. While there had been a lull in hostilities, protocol still required that we have armed escorts. In our case, it was a truck with a .50 cal machine gun mounted on the bed with six soldiers in the front of our vehicle, another similar vehicle in the rear plus two armed officers aboard our bus. It took a while for the rest of the group and me to adjust to this, but as we sped through the first dozen of what turned out to be 150 checkpoints during our visit (since we were considered "VIP's" and did not have to stop), I quickly acclimated. I had been most concerned about our exposure at checkpoints because of the possibility of remotely detonated IEDs. Later in our tour when we were visiting the Arch of Ctesiphon, the largest unreinforced brickwork arch in the world, my concerns reappeared when the government added an ambulance to our convoy. I swear that the shell casings on the ground at the arch were still warm...

What are your three favorite cities in the world, and why?

I presume this refers to cities that I have and will continue to return because of a particular attraction. I could qualify these by category, but to keep this simple I will be brief. Cathy and I always enjoy Bangkok. The people, the concentration of culture, food, and convenience of being an excellent jumping off point for further exploration of Asia makes it special. We also have an old friend and associate, Jeff Rexeisen, who we enjoy spending time with. If I were to pick a favorite destination to detox from the crazy world we live in, I would say St. Maarten. While not a city (it is an island), we normally stay outside of Philipsburg, so I think this qualifies (the French side is also pretty nice). We love the beaches, the restaurants, and the mix that it offers. Another contender is Dubai, not because I like the climate (it is among the world's worst) but because it is such a Disneyland of the absurd. Constantly striving for the superlative such as the world's tallest building or constructing ski slopes in an arid desert make us want to go back and see what the latest lunacy is. Fortunately, it is also an easy and inexpensive hub for many of our travels. London, Paris and Rome are also convenient and have their own special charms.

What is the ideal amount of time you prefer to travel on each trip before you are ready to go home and take a break?

Since we are both still working (or at least pretend to), our travels are normally limited to two or three weeks unless we are escorting one of our groups on a longer journey and have made sure that there are no overlapping groups that we need to monitor. While we would like to travel at least four weeks, but probably not more than eight, we still feel a need to reconnect with home. We have talked about moving to someplace that does not require our personal attention so that we can pack our bags and stay as long as we want. We envy those who can go for at least three to six months but have not yet psyched ourselves up to that.

In your opinion, where are the most beautiful places on Earth?

I am fascinated by the stark beauty and contrasts of the polar regions, particularly on a clear day with blue sky and an artistic assembly of clouds and animals. Majestic mountain scenery such as the Himalaya landscape always inspires me. There is something about the interface of a beautiful beach and blue sky that captivates me. A couple of places that come to mind are Cocos-Keeling Island and the Seychelles, particularly La Digue and Praslin islands. The beauty is always enhanced if you can share it with someone you love.

If you had an unlimited budget and space and time were no object, what would your perfect travel day look like (for example: start your morning in Bora Bora; afternoon on a safari in Kenya; night in Australia, etc.)?

Seeing the curvature of the earth from space has been one of my fondest desires. I have always envied my classmates from Annapolis, who went on to be astronauts including the current head of NASA, Charlie Bolden. I would settle for a suborbital flight, ideally passing over both poles with a delicious meal served in-flight by French and Thai chefs. My second choice would be to witness sunrise at the South Pole, fly to a remote island in the Pacific such as Cocos-Keeling for a cool dip and a great seafood meal and then continue north, parachuting down to the North Pole.

Which three countries would you recommend for adventurous travelers to visit, and why?

Each person has his own level of adventure. My idea of adventurous travel is not dodging bullets in some war-torn country for the sheer thrill of the moment or trying to reach some remote rock (although some of my friends might accuse me of that...). I would pick countries large enough and with a broad range of attractions so I could tailor the degree of adventure to my spirit of the moment and those I might be traveling with. Countries like China, India, and Russia, have such enormous potential and offer virtually any experience you want from mountains to deserts, jungles, impressive archaeological sites, history and culinary delights. The character of countries changes every year. I can always find adventure in smaller countries like Papua New Guinea, places in Central Africa or South America, but reflecting on my travels over the past 50 years I know that my big three would never disappoint.

If you had just one travel story to share with someone, what would it be?

When your life has been dedicated to travel, it is hard to separate out just one story. Although we are known for our group tours, I personally prefer traveling with Cathy alone by rental car so we can control the places we visit, the time we spend and not feel guilty about making too many photo stops. It also gives rise to the unexpected when you have a loosely structured itinerary. With this in mind, one of the more interesting trips we took was spending a couple of weeks driving through Germany, Austria, Italy and the Balkan Peninsula in July of 1989. Cathy was still working as General Manager of another travel company and she was able to make some strategic hotel reservations since we knew it was high season and Europeans love to travel. We spent many a delightful day visiting magnificent medieval cities, churches and fortresses. Sitting in a central plaza, sharing a bottle of wine and eating great local food was always a highlight. Yugoslavia was a different story. They were in the process of breaking apart, and there were tensions in many parts of the peninsula. It was still recovering from the yoke of Tito and the new repressions of Milosevic. We were not able to pre-book any hotels there since they were not tied to the Western hotel reservation system. We were very anxious to visit the Dalmatian Coast and parts of Slovenia, so we decided to take our chances. We arrived late in Ljubljana, the capital of Slovenia. Stopping at most of the main hotels and finding no vacancy, we began to get worried. Finally, we found a small hotel that had one room left. Sensing our desperation, I think the proprietor jacked up the rate, already very high because of peak season. Cathy innocently asked if there was a travel agent rate. With considerable feigned indignity and in the great Communist tradition, he responded: "We all pay the same rate here!" I almost asked him if they had a military rate since I was still on active duty but thought better of it... Our experience here forewarned us of what to expect on the coast, so we got an early start. Armed with our trusty guidebook, we spent most of the day checking out every hotel and resort within a reasonable distance of the beach. Each was completely full, and they had no recommendation as to what might be available. We expanded our search and luckily found the Ulika Naturist Center in Porec. The guidebook was very clear that it was a nudist resort, not "clothing optional." We gulped, looked at each other and resignedly said OK. While we had been to clothing optional beaches before, this was a first. As it turned out, the resort had one trailer left, but we had to become members of the nudist club and promise to abide by all their rules. It was family oriented and very above board, but I cannot begin to describe the emotions running through our minds when we ate at the restaurants completely naked or were pushing a shopping cart down the aisles of the supermarket among other shoppers all in the buff...

Do you ever feel you have missed out on certain aspects of life while away from home as you travel so much?

Yes. Friends I have made during my time in the Navy and while we have been traveling understand the "pick up and go" spirit every serious traveler has to a degree. We are able to reconnect quickly and catch up on lost time. Other people, and particularly relatives, have difficulty accepting that our suitcase in many respects is our home. We often spend more time living out of it than our closets in our house. Relationships suffer and friends fade away since you are not able to maintain a normal social life. Investments also suffer when you are not able to manage them on a daily basis, and one of the driving forces in any career path you might consider is how much vacation time you might have and how flexible is the work schedule. Having said this, our life is so much richer in different ways that I have no regrets. I will not go so far as to say travel is an addiction, but it does have a serious hold on me.

What advice would you give to others who would like to travel to every country?

To paraphrase an old saying popularized in Chicago politics, "travel early and travel often." Good health is a major factor, and I have seen far too many friends and acquaintances that otherwise had the means and desire to travel more, wait too long. The kids, business, dog, slow economy, etc. will always be a convenient excuse. You don't need to set a goal of visiting every country early on in your travels but careful planning and combining the right amount of time for your personal situation is imperative. You can treat your early travels as a "taster" to find out where your true interests lie. Travel should not be viewed as a competition since there will always be someone with more money, more time or more ingenuity to rise to the top. Make the most of what you have.

For someone who has been almost everywhere, what still gets you excited about packing your bags again?

The thought of the unknown. I was born with an overactive curiosity about everything, so exploration comes naturally. It does not have to be someplace I have yet to visit for I have already visited every country, most of them multiple times. A major event or change, a different mode of travel, seeing a familiar place through the eyes of others or simply trying to recapture a magical moment from the past is enough reason.

Looking ahead, what travel plans and goals are you still pursuing, and what is on your "Bucket List"?

For me anyway, I don't think there is a single "trip of a lifetime" unless it is when I ultimately meet my maker. Life itself is the trip, and I hope when my time is finished to have woven as many meaningful threads into its fabric as possible (I like the way this sounds... I think it should be on my tombstone!). On a more prosaic note, one bucket list item would be to explore more of the ancient Silk Road. Another would be to witness the migration of the wildebeests in Africa, but both of these are relatively easy. I don't know if it is possible, given my limited finances, but being able to visit both the North and South Poles are a lifelong dream. Cathy and I are interested in finding more about our roots (hers in China and mine in Europe) and seeing as many important World Heritage Sites (not just UNESCO) as possible. The bottom line is travel, travel, travel as often as we can!

Thomas Buechler, Switzerland

(Thomas Buechler in Lower Omo Valley, Ethiopia)

Where did you grow up, and what was your early life like?

I grew up in the beautiful village of Weggis, in the central part of Switzerland; went to the gymnasium in Lucerne, and later on to the University of Geneva studying international law. In my youth, I made very few trips abroad. One was a train trip with an interrail ticket that gave us the freedom to move anywhere in Europe for one month, so that was the beginning of my never-ending appetite for new countries and places. We went up to Rovaniemi in Finland, the polar circle, and had a kind of baptism ceremony there with a certificate. Funny, but I found it quite touristy.

What was the first international trip you took, and what do you remember most about it?

If you say international, I want to talk about the first really big trip, which was in 1980 from my native village in Switzerland all the way with the Trans-Siberian Railway to China. It was under the Socialist time, and tourists in the Soviet Union were welcome but had no priority. When the country had to assist the Polish government with tanks, and actually had to move tanks westward from the Mongolian border across Siberia, our little train had to stop all the time in the middle of nowhere. When night fell, we had a birch tree in front of the compartment, and when the sun came up in the morning, we found ourselves still in front of the same birch tree and did not move the whole night, but plenty of cargo trains were passing, loaded with T72 tanks. When we arrived in Irkutsk, we were already two days late, and for that reason, we did not have a wagon restaurant across Mongolia. When we finally arrived at our tour destination, Beijing, we almost missed the tour group we were supposed to join and the Miss Mao, the young, energetic lady guide proposed either a visit to the Great Wall or pay tribute to the Great Chairman Mao Tse Tung, and we had to choose. Guess what we decided? Of course, the Mao Mausoleum! Our argument then was that the Mao criteria was a political question, it could close down in one day, but the Great Wall would live on forever!

When did you go from traveling casually to making this a full-time goal, and what motivated you to travel to every country?

With my best friend and classmate, we made a bet when we both had reached about 20 countries, and it was about reaching 60 countries; that was the target, and I was very happy then.

It was the right time to purchase a huge world map and mark the points. At that time, I thought it would be a cool idea to visit all UN countries in the world. I had no idea, however, how difficult and time-consuming it would be. It took me hundreds of visits to hundreds of embassies in almost every capital of the world to organize visas, and I now have 12 old passports with about 450 pages full to the last square inch with visas and stamps. In Tashkent, Uzbekistan I broke the record: in just three days I was able to obtain visas for Azerbaijan, Georgia, Tajikistan, Kazakhstan, and the most difficult of them: a five-day transit visa for Turkmenistan.

It took me almost 40 years to travel to each one of the 193 UN countries. Some of the most interesting nations I have gone back many times. There are also some countries where I have just been very briefly: Algeria in 1979 was just a one-night affair by bus to a small village along the Algerian border (I stayed in a hotel that just opened the very same night, and was invited to the dinner banquet, how lucky!). Right now, after 37 years, I am preparing my second visit to Algeria that will cover most of the UNESCO World Heritage Sites in that country.

Also, I have a list and statistics about all my visits. At the top of the list are two Southeast Asia countries, the Philippines (visited 130x) and Thailand (73x). In Europe it's France (102x), Germany (131x), Italy (78x), Austria (56x) and the UK (103x, but this is somehow misleading as I was adding my 75 visits to Hong Kong under British rule to that count!). In Africa, I have done less repeated visits, and my best-visited countries are strategically located, like Kenya (7x) and South Africa (6x) where I really fell in love with its stunningly beautiful landscape, especially around Cape Town and the Garden Route. In South America both Argentina and Brazil (6x) are on the top of the list.

What have you done in your life to gain the freedom and finances to pursue as much travel as you have?

I worked in between my jobs, as a journalist for Swiss newspapers in Malta in the early 1980's, as resident manager of a beach resort and as a tour leader in the central part of the Philippines. Later on, I started an export company for fashion jewelry and attended trade shows in Hong Kong, Japan, Milan, Singapore, Dubai and other places. With the help of professional designers, I created my own collections and specialized in beach jewelry.

Has there ever been a time where you considered abandoning your travel goals?

No, it was quite the opposite. The more I have traveled, the more I became obsessed with it.

What do you consider to be your two favorite travel experiences, and why?

Both of them are in Africa. My visit to the "Pays Dogon" in Mali and a trip to Ethiopia to the various tribes in the Southern Omo Valley, like the Hamer, Konso, and Mursi (with the clay lip plate ladies) were the best adventure trips ever. In both places, I was able to take excellent photos. In Mali, we trekked along the Bandiagara Escarpment to the Dogon villages, met the medicine man, visited the burial grounds, attended a circumcision ceremony, and had a great time. We slept on the rooftop of a local terracotta house under the stars. I was with my Filipina girlfriend at that point, and the night was incredibly cold as we did not bring a warm sleeping bag. After a long night, I spotted with the first sun rays two white men on a neighboring roof; they turned out to be my countrymen from Switzerland, and we became friends, and are still, as of today. To enjoy and have fun, I don't necessarily need the comfort and luxury of western civilization, but I appreciate a certain standard of hygiene and a cold beer during happy hour! This is not always possible, of course!

What are the main things you seek to experience when you travel (culture, cities, nature, animals, adventure activities, etc.)?

It's a mix of everything. You can not separate the culture from its people. In the early days of traveling and as a student, I was more into historical museums, but nowadays I go for UNESCO World Heritage Sites, as I find them a good introduction to a new society. Even in countries that I already know and have been many times, it forces you to go deep into places and visit national parks and ruins that are really off-the-beaten track, to use *Lonely Planet*'s language. I remember the trip to visit Kilwa Kisiwani, off the southern coast of Tanzania. It took us days to reach the island by public bus. The most interesting UNESCO sites are not along the highway, and this goes especially for the third world.

Looking back from when you started traveling to where you are now, in what ways, if any, has travel changed you?

I guess coming from quite a conservative society in Switzerland, where women, for instance, were only given full voting rights in 1971, when I was 13; my travel experiences have changed me a lot, gradually becoming more open-minded and tolerant of other cultures and religions.

Do you speak any foreign languages, and if so, which have been the most useful for you besides English?

My mother language is German, and for seven years I learned French and Latin in school. It's a good thing I took up English, but I missed Spanish, and that would have been very helpful in most of South America and Spain, of course.

What was the longest extended trip you have ever taken, when was it and where all did you go?

My longest trip was a 6-month journey by train through Austria, Poland, Belarus, the former Soviet Union, Mongolia, and China. Then on to the Philippines, where we stayed five times longer than originally planned, and finally moved on to Sabah, Sarawak, Singapore, Malaysia, Thailand, Myanmar, and Bangladesh, before flying back home on a direct Dhaka to Amsterdam flight with Bangladesh Biman Airlines. I remember paying around $300 for that ticket, some weeks before that trip.

What two countries have exceeded your expectations and which ones left you feeling underwhelmed, and why?

I often go back to the same places, if the country has something to offer – I have been more than 70 times to Thailand, for instance; nice people, lots of culture, delicious food, perfect beaches and colorful nightlife. Cambodia too is one of my favorite countries. And of course, the Philippines, which may have the friendliest, funniest and most beautiful people in Asia. But I would also love to go back to the Seychelles archipelago to see some of its more remote islands.

I was surprised with the progress that the small African nation of Rwanda has made over the last few years; from the nightmares of the brutal civil war and the genocide, the country woke up to become one of the cleanest places in Africa. There is a program of community work, called Umaganda, where nearly 80 percent of the local population goes out to clean the streets of Kigali and the surroundings of their homes. Another government decree does not allow plastic bags any longer, so when visitors arrive with those bags, they will be confiscated at the airport or land borders. Supermarkets are all working with paper bags. It's the opposite of so much plastic bags I have seen all over Africa, along the busy roads, on fields, or on garbage mountains piled up, and burning. The worst scenario was in Mauritania. Before reaching Nouakchott from the south, tons of blue plastic bags where littering the fields. Another place of extreme pollution is the so-called "Smoky Mountain" in the suburb of Tondo in Manila, where tons of garbage is permanently on fire, and poor Filipinos, even kids, try to collect useful things.

I did not much enjoy countries like Chad or the Central African Republic where you have to make a huge effort to see a waterfall, for example, and where one wrong move, like taking a photo of a church in Bangui, almost put me in prison. They still have this law that visitors need a photo permit, even for a religious building.

When you travel, do you prefer to go with others or solo, and why?

I travel solo in difficult countries in Africa, but happily with Vanessa, my Filipina wife, when she feels at ease. Also, it is sometimes a real headache to organize the visas, especially for a Filipino passport, and I could probably write an article or even a book just about this experience, on different embassies around the world.

What has been your most uncomfortable mode of transportation?

I have only had uncomfortable modes of transportation! I have made so many trips across Africa with local buses, or the yellow shares taxis – practically in each of the 54 countries of the Black Continent. Hundreds of thousands of kilometers. But the worst experience was Mozambique to the border with Malawi, on the back of a local truck squeezed between locals with their products – chickens, goats, plus the stinky fish; some kids were vomiting. It was awful.

What is the strangest thing you've seen/experienced while traveling?

Both have to do with mistreatment of animals. I saw on a small island in the Visayas, the central part of the Philippines, some Japanese slaughtered a turtle, and it was really a cruel scene; and in Taiwan, I was in Snake Alley where they skin the snakes alive and drink the blood as long as it is still warm. Local men swear that it's better than Viagra!

What are the best and worst meals you have ever eaten while traveling, and where was it?

I have eaten in many famous restaurants, including the Burj Al Arab in Dubai, but I would not single out the best meal. But perhaps when I had those grilled lobsters in a little cove on Boracay island for my 50th birthday, that was for sure one of the highlights.

On the opposite, I've eaten dog meat in the Philippines, crocodile in Papua New Guinea on the Sepik River, snakes in China, and in Tunisia there was a dead fly hiding under my steak. One time on Alona Beach in Bohol, Philippines, I almost swallowed a metal hook that was hiding inside a fresh tuna fish.

Out of the thousands of places you've stayed around the world, what have been your best and worst accommodations?

The best was no doubt the Burj Al Arab; it was in an expensive suite with a butler and all the gadgets. Hermès perfume was for free and included in the room rate. The laundry bag that I purchased with the gold logo of Burj Al Arab did not last long; it was stolen at a B&B in Nadi, Fiji, a few weeks later. It was just too fancy for a backpacker like me!

My worst accommodation must have been in Africa, somewhere in Tanzania where we tried to make it from the Rwandan border to the coast. The bus broke down, and we ended up in a $3 room with plenty of mosquito's, but no comfort at all, not even running water. We were just killing those mossies the whole night – more than a hundred was the final count!

What is your favorite "off the beaten path" destination, and why?

What was "off the beaten path" in the 1980's, is not anymore on the list. For a long time, it used to be Boracay island in the Philippines; when a nipa hut was one dollar per night, and the beer was cheap. The famous Sugar Palm Beach is 4km long, and there was hardly a foreigner walking around, early 1980's. Last year, the tourism authorities counted more than 1 million arrivals on the island, mostly Asian tourists. The beach still has the same length, but the original beauty is gone. I have been to Boracay every year at least once since 1980, and the island has changed dramatically, and hundreds of hotels and commercial buildings were put up, but no master plan for development. Plus global warming and beach erosion have taken away huge portions of the beach. I still go back to Boracay, as I have long time friends there, but it's a different vibe now. There are alternative islands now, let's say in Palawan or even Indonesia and Thailand that are still relatively undeveloped.

What were your most challenging countries to visit, and why?

To organize the visas, it was Saudi Arabia, and my second to last country, Equatorial Guinea where most nationalities, except Americans, need a visa that is hard to get and requiring police clearance and an invitation from a local person. Lately, it seems that they dropped this requirement, and a hotel booking would be enough, so I finally got my visa in October 2015 in Berlin.

Of which travel accomplishments are you most proud?

I arrived in the town of Harper in Liberia, after crossing the Cavalla River in a dugout canoe. But it had been raining for weeks, and Harper was cut off from the rest of the country and the ship to Monrovia sank a few weeks before. The UN only used the airport, so no commercial flights going anywhere, and the road went through the jungle, with lots of trucks broke down and there was no supply coming in. My only option was to hire a motorbike with a reliable driver. It was the most incredible trip in my whole life and took the entire day. Harper via Fish Town to Zwedru. The highlight was the cold Club beer in Zwedru at sunset.

If you could travel back in time, to which era and place would you go, and why?

My lifestyle allows me to travel permanently back in time! And the Philippines is my favorite place, not only because I have many friends there, but simply because "It's more fun in the Philippines!"

People are extremely friendly and open minded to foreigners, and communication is easy, as long as you speak English. If not, they use "body language" which also works. You can easily travel independently and go on an island hopping tour. You will never run out of destinations as the whole archipelago has about 7,107 islands! Even me, after 35 years visiting and living in this great country, I still find new exciting places to discover: Sipalay in Negros Occidental, Apo Island close to Dumaguete City, which is such a great place for underwater sports, and the entire northern part of Palawan with hundreds of remote beaches and cays. My advice is to go now, because once there is an international airport with flights to neighboring countries, the "paradise feeling" might be lost forever, like what happened in Boracay!

Do you remember encountering particular people that left a lasting impression with you?

Sure, I had handshakes with ex-Australian Prime Minister Bob Hawke, who was at the same time on the volcanic island of Tanna in Vanuatu, and in the same beach bungalows, so I opened his wine bottle with my Swiss Army Knife. I also met the Crown Prince of Tonga during a private dinner in Nuku'alofa, he was studying in Switzerland and became king when his father died.

At the airport in Punta Arenas, I was allowed to speak to ex-Chilean President Ricardo Lagos, and I still have the photos of this meeting. My "holiest" moment, however, was when King Bhumibol Adulyadej of Thailand, and his entire family, suddenly stood in front of me in Bangkok's Wat Phra Kaew temple, and we had an eye to eye contact. I was the only "farang" (foreigner) allowed to stay on the temple grounds, during his majesty's visit. The reason for that was probably me being accompanied by a Filipina lady of whom the security personnel thought was a Thai girl!

But what makes also lasting impressions is to talk to extreme travelers and listen to their never-ending travel stories. People like Peter Forwood, who went on their motorbike to every single country in the world, or Don Parrish with whom I traveled on the MV Ortelius with during the Bouvet trip in April 2015. On top of that, I am in contact with most of the leading travelers during my job as verificator of the TBT (The Best Travelled) website where I double-check their travel claims and points.

Can you describe any particular situation where you felt completely out of your comfort zone?

Yes, that was in Havana, Cuba, in the early 1980's when there was little tourism, and some bandits dared to lure me to the area of a lighthouse after midnight, and then robbed me with a huge kitchen knife and all was taken from me.

First the watch, well it was a copy from Bangkok but expensive looking, and that was, of course, the mistake. I felt very uncomfortable, but then the police arrived quite fast, surprisingly, because it happened in the middle of nowhere, close to sugar fields. They brought me to a local hospital for treatment, and then to the police station where I had to identify the guys. They were caught quickly and put in prison, and I was in the hands of the Cuban Secret Police for a while.

What are your three favorite cities in the world, and why?

Bangkok: it has all the ingredients for an exciting lifestyle.

Cape Town: it has the perfect climate, the perfect vineyards, and lots of excursions to do.

Paris: it has whatever you would expect from a world-class city, plus some extras (where else in the world do you have a three-floor restaurant that just serves cheese and wine, but from all major regions of France?).

What is the ideal amount of time you prefer to travel on each trip before you are ready to go home and take a break?

I have no limit on a trip; it really depends on the itinerary. I can travel a couple of months or just one week; but on an average now, my trips typically last for about a month. I don't like to be stressed, so I plan enough time in each city, especially if there are interesting places to visit.

In your opinion, where are the most beautiful places on Earth?

That's really difficult; it's where the highlights are, it's where we can find an abundance of natural parks and animals, where we also have a concentration of World Heritage Sites. As such, I would say it ranges from the rough beauty of a place like the Pays Dogon in Mali, or the Fernando de Noronha archipelago in northern Brazil, to the Rice Terraces of Banaue in the Philippines, and so on. But you also have all the cultural heritage of India, China, Italy, Spain, France, etc. One single place I would like to mention is the Khmer temples of Angkor Wat in Cambodia.

If you had an unlimited budget and space and time were no object, what would your perfect travel day look like (for example: start your morning in Bora Bora; afternoon on a safari in Kenya; night in Australia, etc.)?

I would start the morning with some croissants at Champs-Elysee in Paris, then visit the Vatican Museum and have lunch at Cape Town's Waterfront. In the afternoon, I would do a safari in South Luangwa National Park in Zambia, relax for a late siesta in a hammock on the island of Zanzibar, before enjoying the nightlife in Bangkok.

Which three countries would you recommend for adventurous travelers to visit, and why?

Ethiopia: relatively easy for independent travelers to see the cultural highlights or tribes in the south.

Philippines: many islands, many beaches, communication is easy with English-speaking people.

Morocco: good food, many places to visit within easy reach of each other.

If you had just one travel story to share with someone, what would it be?

It is the story of the souvenir that I usually buy when visiting a country for the very first time. I was in Afghanistan in 2003, wandering around in Kabul's infamous Chicken Street and looking for the perfect souvenir to buy. They had lots of carpets, lots of semi-precious stones, and some handmade pistols, inlaid with wooden pieces and mother of pearl shells. I decided to buy one for $28 USD. A rare beauty, but I presume it was a copy of an original, working with black powder. It landed in my backpack, and we went on to Mazar-i-Sharif and Kunduz in the north, then crossed into Tajikistan and Uzbekistan, and the gun was never discovered. We visited the great Uzbekistan cities of the Silk Road like Bukhara and Samarkand, and at the end arrived in Khiva. It was a three-week journey through this very interesting region. When we went to board the domestic flight from Urgench to Tashkent, the capital, they discovered my souvenir from Kabul, and we were detained right away. They confiscated our passports. I was with a Filipina girlfriend at that time, and we were put on house arrest. They investigated the story and sent the pistol to Tashkent for verification. If the piece still worked as a real weapon, it would fall under the new anti-terrorism law of the country, with a maximum penalty of six years in prison. Fortunately, after a week waiting and attending a court hearing, we were released, and just paid a little fine. I promised myself I would never touch any more guns, not even a toy gun, during my trips!

Do you ever feel you have missed out on certain aspects of life while away from home as you travel so much?

For sure I had much less contact with my children than if I would not have traveled so much. I have brought them to Florida, the Bahamas, and some places in Africa and Southeast Asia. They now live in Switzerland, and my daughter Michelle travels whenever she can – she has already registered with The Best Travelled (TBT).

What advice would you give to others who would like to travel to every country?

Plan ahead, save money and go! If you like a place and fall in love, go back!

For someone who has been almost everywhere, what still gets you excited about packing your bags again?

The preparation for a new trip is almost as exciting as the trip itself. Except a few countries like North Korea, China in the 1980's, Libya just recently, and the Bouvet trip, I have not traveled with organized tours but did it all myself. Even difficult countries like Nigeria, Angola, Equatorial Guinea, Sudan or some parts of Russia, I did the whole preparation from scratch. And I love to do it. Many aspects nowadays can be double-checked on the Internet, and that is the big difference with trips I did in the 1980's.

Looking ahead, what travel plans and goals are you still pursuing, and what is on your "Bucket List"?

I want to finish the UN countries in 2016 with a trip to Namibia. I have purposely kept Namibia as my last country. It has a lot to offer in terms of wildlife, parks, some tribes, and the natural landscapes and dunes along the coast. But I want to do this with some good friends, not only to travel but to celebrate this great achievement of my life!

After this, it's the UNESCO World Heritage list, where I have so far visited about 630 places in 127 different countries. Few other people have done better, and I am top 5 there! Then it's also the territories and regions of the TBT website, as they divide the world into 1281 units, and I have just been to 840, at a rank 19. I also don't know much of the USA, and I plan to change this with an extensive visit by car, now that the gasoline prices have come down! It took me 30 years to visit all the independent countries in Africa that mostly give you just one point, especially on MTP. I hope it will take me less time to visit all 50 U.S. states!

Claus Qvist Jessen, Denmark

(Claus Qvist Jessen fishing in Indonesia)

Where did you grow up, and what was your early life like?

Born in 1960, I'm a kind of "alien kid", as I was adopted at the tender age of zero, so that the family I grew up with were not my biological parents. The latter two I found much later, and it seems that a lot of my doings throughout the years can be related to genetics rather than my adopted family.

Anyway, I grew up in a stable but absolutely non-traveling family, with a Danish lawyer father and a Norwegian psychology mother. Living close to Copenhagen, the Norwegian background of my mother ensured that all our summers, Christmases, Easter holidays and other vacations were spent in Norway. Nothing wrong about that, as Norway is a fantastic country, however, 15 years in a row in Norway is hardly border-line adventurism. On the plus side, my love for hiking and sports fishing grew during that period, which turned out to be not bad at all.

By education, and much unlike the rest of my less technically inclined family, I ended up as a chemical engineer, specialized in metals, corrosion and, in particular, stainless steel. The chemical engineering degree extended itself into a PhD in electro-chemistry and electroplating, although the degree became somewhat interrupted. The travel itch had sneaked its way into my blood, and, to the horror of my professor, I interrupted my studies for a six-month period and drifted off to Nepal and India. It turned out that I was the first-ever student at the Institute who interrupted his PhD in favor of "going walkabout". India and Nepal seemed the right thing to do at the time. However, I did go back to complete my degree – definitely less popular with the professors than before.

After the PhD, a longish spell in South America followed, fueling my ever-present love for the Inca culture and the southern nature. However, one has to live and after coming home, I ended up as a consultant engineer. Great job, by the way, but the travel itch just didn't want to leave. I really tried, but in vain, so at first I managed to persuade my boss to grant me leave three times one month annually, and when that proved not to be enough to stimulate the travel addict I had become, I left the engineering job completely in 1997 and went walkabout for several years – at first to West Africa and later back to Asia. Life was great, and it still is.

Around that time, myself aged 38, I discovered that my biological father was an engineer, a chemical engineer and even a PhD and a consultant engineer who had been spending a major part of his engineering life working abroad – mostly in the Middle East. It became even more spooky when I discovered that my biological mom was a chemical engineer as well. The musical side seems to originate from that side of my biological family, so things started to make sense.

And traveling? Well, my biological mother had worked numerous years abroad on various Third World projects. However, it all became even more strange when I discovered that a distant cousin of her turned out to be one of the true "classic" Danish adventurers, Jorgen Bitsch. He is one of the true pioneers of adventurous exploration in the mid-20th Century, and coupled with my engineering background and my hopeless travel itch; this really convinced me that genetics play a much bigger role in society than the psychologists like to admit. Engineering and traveling are simply buried deep in my genes, and I'm bloody proud of that. I just didn't know when I started off the first time.

What was the first international trip you took, and what do you remember most about it?

International? If we regard the rest of Scandinavia as "domestic", I was at the tender age of 19 when I actually made my first real "international trip". Well, technically it was not even international, however, by the distance it certainly was. The destination was southern Greenland and, despite being a low-budget fishing trip; it still is one of the most beautiful places I've ever been. It was the first time I ever saw icebergs, glaciers and the true arctic life. Greenland proved to be a full-scale attack on my senses, and by being close to a floating iceberg, you really discover how small you are compared to the might of nature. Nature in Greenland is truly awesome.

I'd really love to get back once. Unfortunately, Greenland happens to be one of the most expensive travel destinations on the planet, and as long as I can spend three months in India for less money than I have to spend one week in Greenland, it's unlikely that I'll be doing so for years to come.

When did you go from traveling casually to making this a full-time goal, and what motivated you to travel to every country?

Traveling to every country on the planet has never been a "full-time goal" to me. I guess that when I started off almost 30 years ago, I had the secret ambition of "going everywhere." However, after having seen quite a bit of the world, I guess that I discovered that having all the country stamps in the passport doesn't mean that you've been everywhere. It just means that you have seen very little from each country. People who race to get all the stamps rarely seem to linger more than a day or two in each place. A bit sad, I think.

As in many other aspects of life, traveling much more about getting to the top than actually being on the top, and, as a restless soul, I have never focused on "conquering" every single country in the world – especially if conquering means spending one hour in the airport or a border region. I prefer to use lots of time, and so far I have, on average, succeeded in spending about three weeks in every single country outside Europe I've ever been to, ranging from several months in India to a few days in the tiny micro-states.

If I ever succeed in getting all the stamps, that's just luck. To me, traveling is more a way of living, a great way of neglecting your calendar and the rent, and instead, live right now. Not tomorrow or the next week, but right now, learning about the people you are among. Long-time traveling is the ultimate way of living the present, as opposed to spending your life preparing for something which may never happen anyway.

Motivation? A great curiosity and a desire to see the world as it is, as opposed to the world you get to see through the filtered TV. And, of course, to get the chance to catch a funny fish belonging to a strange species I didn't even know existed. Spending some time in a West African market, or on the roof of a local Nepalese bus, or standing on the roadside somewhere in Patagonia, or fishing alongside the local fisherman in El Salvador teaches you more about the world and yourself than endless episodes of *Friends*.

What have you done in your life to gain the freedom and finances to pursue as much travel as you have?

I have never done anything specifically pointed towards "freedom". Well, maybe I have, as my education as a chemical engineer and metallurgist has recognized me as one of the leading experts on stainless steel and corrosion in all of Scandinavia, perhaps even Northern Europe. This makes it much easier to persuade the employer that I just need to go. Preferably now! Fortunately, my tolerant and very patient boss has accepted my "strange way of living," allowing me to spend much more time as a travel freak than most engineers ever get to do.

Basically, I get a lot of spare time, although the inevitable consequence is a lower pay. To make end meet, we (my wife and I) live fairly cheaply at home, use a terribly old car and avoid excessive expenses.

The "cheap life" applies for my time abroad as well. The more time and the less money you use when traveling, the more likely you are to interact with the locals. With loads of cash, you end up in a dull air-con minibus instead, together with the other tourists whom you may as well meet at home. So far, this attitude has allowed me, on average, to spend four months annually abroad. That balance seems to fit me, but others may disagree.

On two occasions, I have tried to skip my engineering career completely and go traveling forever. At least, that was my intention. However, I have to admit that I kind of miss my stainless steel! Sounds crazy, right? However, there's a reason I have devoted a large percentage of my adult life to electro-chemistry. I really like it, although the moment I stop liking my corrosion I will start to consider quitting. Fortunately, this is not the case yet.

Has there ever been a time where you considered abandoning your travel goals?

As above, I never really had any definite "travel goals", like being in every single country in the world, or having been in every state in the US. Not even my fishing contains specific long-term goals. Only a desire to catch this or that right now. With no specific travel goals, it's hard to "abandon the goals", and instead, I do whatever I can to fool around and enjoy life the best I can. You may call that a goal as well.

However, I have tried to abandon traveling. Several times, actually, because it really doesn't correlate with the standard way of living. Regardless if it's the job, the family, the friends, or even the local rock band you're playing in, leaving the country for months or even a full year takes a lot of patience from everyone else. In the end, this patience often runs out, so, for the sake of everybody, it would be so much easier if I just stayed at home. So I tried – but in vain. The itch is just too strong (yes, genetic!), a bit like being an addicted smoker in a world of non-smokers, and now I have just accepted that I'm weird and that I need to spend some months abroad every single year. It's hard to fight addiction, and I really don't want to. It's so much easier to succumb and enjoy.

My major problem has always been combining the two "careers". If you got the skills, being a full-time engineer is not that much of a problem. And, if you want to go traveling forever, that's no problem either, provided that you can arrange the finances, such as working for the UN or being a Saudi prince. The difficulty is doing both, combining an engineering job at home and traveling abroad.

For some reason, the Danish society, my different bands and most girlfriends (!) are not willing to accept any middle of the road solution and, consequently, try to squeeze out an ultimatum in order to force me to quit traveling. Bad idea, at least if you don't want to hear a negative answer. Never try to push a dedicated traveler. He is just as determined as a full-scale drug addict, and you are going to lose. Even if you win, you'll end up with an unhappy husband, and most likely he'll leave anyway in a couple of years.

Fortunately, I have succeeded in finding the impossible compromise by marrying a woman who loves traveling as well. Maybe less crazy and less adventurous than me, but it works, and so does the job. Not a bad combination.

What do you consider to be your two favorite travel experiences, and why?

I don't think that you can define one favorite travel experience - or two for that matter. I've had loads of them and more to come, hopefully. If instead I try to focus on the most important travel experience, things become slightly less difficult, and I can narrow the choice down to two different trips: My first time in South America, and my slightly illegal solo crossing of the Tibetan Plateau.

The reason for the significance of my 1990 South America trip was that it happened to be my first-ever solo adventure in the Third World. After traveling together for three months, my girlfriend had to go home and take care of her exams, while I decided to stay. Suddenly, I was all alone in the middle of nowhere, didn't know anyone and didn't know where to go - apart from having a return ticket home from Cuba five months later.

Ecuador was quite easy at the time, but the real challenge came when I stood in front of the Colombian Ipiales border. At that time, Colombia was torn apart by crime and drug wars, and crossing into the presumably unstable Mordor really took some courage. A deep breath, and off I went, got my stamps and, of course, Colombia turned out to be extremely friendly, and so was the string of Central American countries further north. Yes, I had to learn the language and to stay alert. However, the solo months really matured me as a traveler, and I came home a wiser and stronger man than I'd ever been before.

These five months taught me to be independent. To be alone when necessary, to look for the unseen opportunities, to behave and to be timid, to trust myself and avoid the dodgy characters, and to embrace the world with a positive attitude. These five months truly changed me, and there was no going back. My life had decided what to do.

The second experience occurred some years later and involved a slightly illegal crossing of the Tibetan plateau from west to east. I had set my eyes on the sacred mountain of the Tibetan Buddhists, the holy Mount Kailash in the remote and desolate West Tibet, however, getting there was far from easy. It involved a legal bus trip from Khunjerab through Kashgar and on to Yeching to the southeast, and after that everything was more or less illegal.

A Chinese coal truck carried me to the highlands up to 5000+ meters, where it crashed into a muddy river. Apart from a freezing night in Aksai Chin at 5500 meters, I survived and managed to get on a Chinese military truck the next day, disguised as an officer to prevent the truck from being stopped at the police posts. The town of Ali was reached, I was arrested, but for some reason talked my way out of being sent back. Perhaps the officer was too lazy. Anyway, I made it another 200 miles southeast to Darchen from where I spent a few days walking the holy "Kora" around the mountain - in a snow storm. For that, the heavenly powers have forgiven all my sins - I hope ☺. A day trip from Darchen even brought me up face-to-face with the sacred mountain itself. With the perfect backdrop of a crisp, blue sky, this is probably the most awesome and magic place I have ever been on the planet.

The trip to Lhasa proved less complicated (although with one more Chinese arrest), whereas the trip from Lhasa towards the Nepalese border contained a few challenges, mostly created by the stupid fact that I, very spontaneous and absolutely illegal, found out that I was going to climb Everest in the famous footsteps of the Mallory-Irvine expedition back in 1924!! Solo, with no previous experience, no equipment and not enough provisions did not prevent me from trying – or, at least, try to see how far up I could go before things became too steep. Not very far, as at Camp 1 1/2 in 5,800 meters, I ran into a serious blizzard, lasting all night and truly convincing me that this was just stupid. But at least, I tried.

What are the main things you seek to experience when you travel (culture, cities, nature, animals, adventure activities, etc.)?

My traveling has definitely changed with time. Some 30 years ago, my focus was largely on nature and animals, and, to some extent, adventure activities – especially fishing! My itineraries were always planned (if planned at all) according to "something" I wanted to see, or some fish I wanted to catch. Throughout the years, this has changed in the direction of the local culture. I can spend hours in a local market at Lake Victoria, just for the sake of being there, watching what happens and talking to the curious locals who seem to wonder what the strange white guy is doing here.

Throughout my traveling life, I have always tried to avoid big cities. Well, in Europe they are hard to avoid, and there is, in fact, no reason to avoid them at all. After all, the European cities carry the history of several centuries, and cities like Paris and London, or the old Eastern European ones in Prague or Budapest, are definitely worth several weeks.

In the developing world, things are much different, and few cities really appeal to me. This applies to most of Africa and South America, where the big cities should definitely be avoided. Still, to this day, I can see few reasons to go to places like Caracas, Abidjan, Lagos, Johannesburg or Port Moresby. These crime-infested and over-crowded dumps don't contain much of the village life I like to see, and the chances of you surviving the staggering crime rate are not impressive. I hate to force myself to be alert 24/7.

Unfortunately, embassies have a nasty habit of being situated in the capitals, so it's hard to avoid the big cities altogether. But I try and tend to go to the smaller towns and villages instead. The local markets appeal much more to me then the supermarkets of the big cities, and people tend to be more friendly as well. And, very importantly, it's really hard to find a good fishing spot in Addis Ababa or in Bogota! At least without getting arrested for disturbing the public order.

Looking back from when you started traveling to where you are now, in what ways, if any, has travel changed you?

Definitely yes, although it's hard to tell which changes actually come from traveling and which come from getting older (and preferably wiser!). I guess I have learned to appreciate things as they are instead of wanting to change everything into my own way of thinking. I have learned not to feel uncomfortable anywhere. If the locals can cope with the conditions, well, so can I.

Already my first trip to South America taught me one essential lesson: The importance of the language. Well, somewhere at least, as in India, regardless how long time you stay somewhere, people will keep on staring at you like a green alien from Mars. In Latin America, once you master a few simple phrases of Spanish, you are readily accepted and regarded as a life-long friend. The same actually applies with some Arabs, though less so than in Latin America. I really got to love the passionate Latinos.

Curiously, I find that my relationship with the terms "time" and "patience" is governed by where I am. Sitting somewhere in the Amazon or on a roadside in Bolivia or West Tibet, it's impossible to rush things. You just wait for the next lift, and you can't rush it. It just takes a lot of time, and you might as well accept things as they are as opposed to getting a heart attack by wanting to change the unchangeable.

When back in Denmark, people start getting annoyed if the bus is two minutes late. I think that the Danish comfort has taught people not to be grateful for what we've got. Traveling really puts things in a perspective, and I get kind of angry with the people who regard all their benefits as a matter of course. It isn't, so please be a little grateful.

Do you speak any foreign languages, and if so, which have been the most useful for you besides English?

Coming from a tiny country like Denmark (5 million people), it's incredibly optimistic to trust that the rest of the world obeys your own linguistic whims. They just don't, and consequently, Danes are happily forced to learn a few languages just to get by. And still we maintain our own "secret tongue," allowing us to talk about everyone without them noticing ☺.

Today, English is still useful everywhere and is definitely my second language. I would never recommend anyone to go abroad without at least a basic understanding of English - if nothing else than to be able to communicate with other backpackers, and, of course, read the *Lonely Planet* bibles.

In Latin America, Spanish is the one language to know. I have never really attended any Spanish classes or done any courses, but years of traveling has made me more or less fluent in small-talk Spanish. Especially in Central America, this makes a huge difference, as the average American tourist is 95 % mono-lingual. By commanding a basic Spanish, you distinguish yourself from the ignorant mainstream tourist, and it's so much easier to get accepted by the locals – and to get a better price! It's no coincidence that one of the first sentences I ever learned in Spanish was "Lo siendo, no soy Americano." It's still very useful.

In West Africa, it's hard to get by without a basic French, although the French they speak has little to do with the French I learned in school, or the language of Paris. Still it's quite useful to master a bunch of sentences. In contrast, my German has proved pretty useless abroad, as, thanks to the defeats of Wilhelm the 2nd and Hitler, German never became a linguistic world power. Thus, my German is pretty useless abroad, but quite useful at home as Germany happens to be our most important trade partner.

In most of the ex-Soviet, it's hard to get away from the crowds without at least a basic knowledge of Russian, and although I've never managed to become fluent, I get by. Just being able to spell your way through the Cyrillic alphabet is a great help if you get stuck in the Moscow Metro. The same applies for Bahasa Indonesia and Arabic. I really try, but I tend to have forgotten the most of it.

But abroad you always get credit for trying, very much like in Denmark. We tend to love immigrants who try to master the Danish language – and hate the ones who never bother despite spending 20 years on unemployment benefit. Same thing outside Europe.

What was the longest extended trip you have ever taken, when was it and where all did you go?

From 1997 to 2004, I didn't work as an engineer and spent most of my time abroad somewhere. If we narrow it down to continuously being on the move, away from Denmark, I managed two trips of each one year, one time eight months, twice six months, and a large number of "smaller trips" lasting anything from one to three months. And then all the really short ones, mostly in Europe.

What two countries have exceeded your expectations and which ones left you feeling underwhelmed, and why?

Actually, most countries, or more correctly, most people exceed my expectations. Expectations seem to be something you build up at home, from what you read, from what others tell you and so on, and these almost always deal with the "foreseeable attractions", such as the Taj Mahal or the Chichen Itza. However, once I get there, I usually spend much more time with the locals, chatting, drinking, discussing and so, and despite having been to thousands of "places", I never stop becoming happy when this happens. I guess that's the reason for me to keep on traveling.

For the same reason, very few countries have made me feel "underwhelmed". A few places, maybe, have been exaggerated beyond common sense (like our own "Little Mermaid" statue), but that's very few. It rarely happens that the people disappoint me, and if so, it's likely to be the officials, such a few overly rigid Ex-Soviet officers, or the corrupt Guinea policemen who, when we crossed from Guinea into Sierra Leone, did an excellent job to ensure that I'd never miss the place. French-speaking West Africa just seems to be incredibly corrupt. Quite openly, each and every policeman seems to collect "fines" for his own private consumption and the region is just no good for travelers who don't like to face corruption. There is a politically incorrect reason West Africa is the poorest region in the world and always will be.

When you travel, do you prefer to go with others or solo, and why?

Admittedly, I'm a kind of anarchist. Not in a political sense, but very my so when it comes to traveling. I'd hate to be in a group and do "everything as planned", and they'd probably hate me as well – the stupid guy who always want to turn left when the agenda says "turn right".

According to my wife, I'd make everybody else angry, so, for the sake of peace and quietness, it's better that I travel alone, or with my wife. The latter may qualify as a very small group, but it works great, as, whenever I feel like going fishing or doing something really crazy, she just sits home with a good book and waits for me to stop behaving like an idiot.

Traveling alone or as a couple really comes quite natural, as most of the places I'd like to go simply don't exist on the itinerary of group travel companies. Somewhere, though, like North Korea, you have to, but we were lucky to join a very small one (six in total, all politically incorrect), making it very bearable.

What has been your most uncomfortable mode of transportation?

Ouch! Lots and lots. I love hitchhiking, so I have spent numerous days and nights sitting or lying on top of a fully loaded truck carrying planks, pigs or the kitchen sink. Not very comfortable, but great adventures.

However, only counting "organized transport", I guess my most uncomfortable ride was the Mauritanian desert train, connecting Nouadhibou at the coast with the iron mines far inland in the Sahara. There was one dilapidated passenger cart for everybody, and the "seats" consisted of wooden planks with no cushions but lots of protruding nails ready to tear your pants. I was absolutely the only foreigner, however, my company was excellent. Really nice people – as always.

What is the strangest thing you've seen/experienced while traveling?

Hard to tell. I don't really believe in either gods or magic, so it's hard for me to classify anything as "strange". Perhaps that I managed to cross the Tibetan Plateau, watching a Benin voodoo ceremony without being turned into a toad, or surviving countless trips on a staggering number of dilapidated fishing boat in pursuit of my beloved fish.

But "strange"? Not really.

What are the best and worst meals you have ever eaten while traveling, and where was it?

Best meals? I really don't know, but I seriously love the Indian cuisine. The same applies for the Chinese, while it took a while for me to get used to Tibetan tsampa and butter tea.

The worst one? My basic philosophy is that if the locals can eat it, so can I, however, on a few occasions I have been offered things which crossed my unknown borders. One of these happened to be the fat, white maggots I was offered by the Shuar Indians in the eastern Ecuadorian lowlands. The maggots being three of four inch long and were swallowed live certainly didn't stimulate my appetite, and I politely skipped "lunch".

Out of the thousands of places you've stayed around the world, what have been your best and worst accommodations?

I'm not fuzzy, so I'm happy with a fairly comfortable not-to-dirty bed and a bit of quiet without too much noise from the party next door. However, if I should pick one, I guess it's going to be Bandos Island in the Maldives. The rooms were fantastic, the company the same (my wife!), and the surroundings nothing but excellent – including the best snor-snorkeling I have ever experienced.

Regarding the "worst night", I have quite a few to choose from, but most of them actually turned out to be quite funny – afterwards. Among these were a night in a creepy, shabby and shit-smelling "hotel" in Labe, Guinea, where I most likely made a personal record in donating blood to the bed bugs.

On the more funny side, I once spent an open-air night at a butchers market in Niah, Sarawak. I failed to find somewhere "real" to stay, so I just crashed out for free at the local market, found a spot for my luggage and spread out my mattress. The funny thing started when I, the next morning 5 a.m., wake up when a local butcher tried to cross me while carrying a pigs head. Waking up and staring up into the grin of a dead pig's blood-dripping head right above me was close to scary – and, once again, very funny. I've had quite a few of those type of nights.

What is your favorite "off the beaten path" destination, and why?

Perhaps West Africa. Far away from everything, no real tourist attractions and the combined "army" of Islamic fundamentalists and corrupt policemen are doing a great job frightening away the remaining tourists. Afghanistan's got the same "virtues", and, very nicely, the corruption level is somewhat lower than in West Africa. The eastern Tajikistan mountains of Gorno-Badakhshan is equally fantastic, and so is West Tibet. Both are a kind of highland desert but very far away from anywhere, which sharply reduces the number of mainstream tourists to zero.

Another great "off the beaten path" destination in New Guinea, second-largest island of the world. Regardless if you go to the eastern half (Papua New Guinea) or the western one (Indonesian Papua), the chances are that you bump into a few very traditional men in penis gourds and feathered headgear. It takes a bit of work to get away from the tourist path, however, that's what it's all about, right?

What were your most challenging countries to visit, and why?

Traveling off the beaten track always poses lots of "challenges", however, that's a part of the fun - once you overcome the obstacles.

One of the seriously annoying, and repetitive, obstacles are visa problems. Getting the required visa is really annoying, and few places on earth have succeeded to create a "visa wall" as Ex-Soviet Central Asia. Most of the countries have loosened their stone age policies, however, to Europeans, places like Uzbekistan and Turkmenistan maintain their old-school Communist way of handling tourists: You need an "invitation" and lots of pre-booked accommodation to get a tourist visa. This is all very easy if you travel in a group, but hell on earth if you try to do it independently. Still, it can be done, but not without hard work. Absolutely unnecessary, but it keeps thousands of public bureaucrats occupied.

Similarly, West Africa contains a lot of "visa problems", mostly revenge from Europe not wanting to accept millions of African immigrants. I've never been to Central Africa (like Angola, Gabon, and Equatorial Guinea), but I expect things to be even worse here. You really need a big wallet to go there.

Of which travel accomplishments are you most proud?

Describing my travels, I've never really used the word "proud". My 30 years on the road have neither brought me to the top of the Everest nor the Nobel Prize, so proud is hardly the right word. However, I guess that being able to combine my engineering job with extensive traveling is not a bad feat, and I'm certainly happy that I have managed to do it.

Do you remember encountering particular people that left a lasting impression with you?

Quite a few, however, if I have to limit the number to less than a few thousand, I guess that Ernesto Tseremp Juanka (Ecuador) is one. He was a full-blooded Shuar Indian and spent much of his life fighting for the Indians to retain their native forest, strongly opposing the national oil industry and their destruction of the Amazon, just to earn a few dollars more.

Ernesto played a major role in two different contemporary novels written by the Danish author Ib Michael, and when I stumbled across him back in 1990 (in a bar in Sucúa!), it was much like meeting Robin Hood or Ivanhoe. A fictive character coming true as a human of flesh and blood. And, to make things even better, I was invited to join him on a micro plane next day, flying deep into the Amazon visiting a tribe which had never before seen a white guy – and certainly not a white guy with a fishing rod. This was just great!

Another inspiring person from the same trip was a young female Kiwi traveler by the name of Judith, who just seemed incredibly confident being 5 feet tall and having hitchhiked all the way from Alaska to the Andes. I guess that was one of the reasons I had little hesitation doing the same – or at least a major part of it. Perhaps the world was a lot safer than I imagined?

Finally, although he hardly can be described as "foreign", the late co-founder of the Danish Travellers' Club, Mr. Poul Folkersen, definitely deserves a lot of credit as an eternal source of inspiration. Part gypsy, Poul was the kind of guy who literally burnt his candle at every possible end, trying in vain to combine a restless life as an adventurer and travel writer with the need for a steady income and the safety of a family.

In addition, being a very heavy smoker and a life-long alcoholic (and a master level bridge player!), Poul seemed to be burning all his bodily bridges every single day, ending up being kept alive by a piece of oxygen equipment - and still dreaming of "going somewhere". In the Travellers' Club of Denmark, the most prestigious prize, given to a traveler who really has broken the barriers, carries the name of Poul Folkersen, one of the last true crazy guys. But what a guy.

Unsurprisingly, Poul died in 2000. However, more than any, he fueled my addiction to go walkabout, and I really owe him a lot. If anyone, he is the closest I've ever had to a "mentor" although I never really caught up with his habits of heavy drinking and smoking. His playing bridge has been substituted with me playing chess on a Danish master level, and instead of his heavy smoking and drinking, I go fishing instead.

On the personal level, I'm a little proud that I happened to be the first-ever receiver of the famed "Folkersen Prize", basically for doing what I'm doing the best: traveling to anywhere without a safety net.

If you could travel back in time, to which era and place would you go, and why?

The whole island of New Guinea (east and west) seriously intrigues me. I've been to the mystic highlands twice, Indonesia in 2015 and Papua 2002, and in both cases I loved the traditional way of life displayed by the tribal peoples. However, how wonderful it would have been to go there back in the 1930s before the intruding white missionaries started teaching the locals that their style of life was sinful and that Western clothing was much better.

Similarly, it must have been great to travel the Pacific before the great Captain James Cook, seeing the traditional lifestyle of the Polynesian peoples of Samoa and Tonga. And, of course, enjoying the magnificent Easter Island, the fantastic Rapa Nui, around 1000 years ago, before the tribal wars tore down all the moai.

A few years before that, it would have been great to experience the mighty Inca Empire of Peru/Ecuador, before the arrival of Pizzaro in 1531. It must have been one of the most fascinating and most colorful empires in history. Similarly, the Pharao empire of Ramses II in Thebes, nowadays Luxor, would have been great. Just to be a fly on the wall – preferably a fly with a digital SLR camera.

Another great, though more contemporary experience, would have been to travel Afghanistan in the 1960s and 70s, before the Russian invasion and before the rise of the Islamic extremists which have rendered this beautiful country almost out of bounds. Even later, it would have been great to experience the Eastern Block from the inside, before the fall of the Berlin Wall in 1989. I never got any further than standing on a Western ladder, back in 1985, staring at the gray and militarized East Germany. Considering my age (born in 1960), this is likely to the be the greatest regret of my travel life. After all, this I could have done during my lifetime.

Can you describe any particular situation where you felt completely out of your comfort zone?

Almost always, I'm tempted to say. Actually, I do whatever I can to try to get out of my "comfort zone". If you intend to stay inside your zone all the time, it's too much like being at home, and I travel to get out! To see the "dodgy" parts of the world, you really need to get out of the zone.

However, sometimes it just gets a bit out of hand, however, unlike most people's belief, it's not the crooks who are the dangerous ones, but more the police. Or, well, the crooked police. Or just stupid police of which Africa is sadly full. I have been arrested a few times, and in most cases, it's been much further from my comfort zone than I'd like it to be. In Eritrea and Ghana, I have been arrested and detained for just having a camera, and in South Sudan, I ended up in a street fight with two "secret police" who simply couldn't cope with the fact that there was a white guy fooling around. They even have a Ministry of Tourism, but they can't be doing a very good job.

What are your three favorite cities in the world, and why?

Frankly, I don't know. There are so many beautiful towns and cities in the world, and places like Paris, Venice and New York are certainly high on the list of favorite cities. So are Kathmandu, Bukhara, Samarkand, Cusco, Esfahán, Yogyakarta, London and my own hometown Copenhagen, just to name a few.

Still, if I have to pick only three, one of them must be Herat, Afghanistan. Herat is not a flashy or flamboyant city in any way. The number of "real" attractions is limited to the very beautiful Govar Shad Mosque and some ancient relics, the nightlife is close to non-existing, and the food is very simple. Nothing special, really. However, Herat really crept underneath my skin because of its people. Not the attractions, but the people themselves. The streets are full of wildly looking bearded men, but Herat happens to be one of the friendliest and most hospitable places I've ever been to, and despite being there at a time when the Taliban was still partly in charge, it was just great. I many ways, Herat is a wild place, but my kind of wild. I really love Herat.

Sana'a, Yemen provides a bit of the same wild and ancient feeling, however, with the added bonus of lots of antique relics crammed into the old UNESCO-certified center. Sana'a is one of the oldest cities in the world, and everywhere you see the ancient mud-built high-rise houses equipped with white gypsum framing around the windows to keep the evil spirits away. The old town of Sana'a is like stepping back into history, away from the beeping cars and the traffic jam and into the different world of Aladdin and the Queen of Sheba.

Varanasi in Indian may be more chaotic (if possible!) and less historically beautiful than other Indian cities, but almost 30 years ago, Varanasi happened to be my first encounter with this strange and mesmerizing country. Nothing beats getting up 5 am in the morning, walking down to the banks of the mighty and muddy Ganges, and sit down facing the sunrise and just watch the whole city get to life. Varanasi is one of the most fantastic religious places on earth, although my latest visit was a bit disappointing. Organized tourism has taken over, and the virginity of the city has been somehow forgotten. I still, though, have a dream of grabbing my guitar and watch the sunrise while playing the "Cavatina" (from Deer Hunter). Perhaps not John Williams class, but I'll try.

What is the ideal amount of time you prefer to travel on each trip before you are ready to go home and take a break?

In the good old days, a couple of decades ago, my ideal would be "indefinitely". Just leaving home with a couple of plane tickets and no "real" agenda was the right thing to do at that time. These days, well in my 50s, my ideal length is a bit shorter, more like two or three months, probably caused by myself getting older. Or perhaps a stronger wish to combine my domestic engineering career with the less lucrative one as a traveler.

In your opinion, where are the most beautiful places on Earth?

This is big! And is actually an impossible question. It's a bit like describing your favorite piece of music. I can't. It depends a lot on the day, the situation, my mood, the surroundings, etc. so any hit list is bound to be very temporary. Tomorrow it may be different.

Still, regardless how I make my list, a few places are always bound to be close to the top. One of these is the mountains of Nepal. Its beauty is hard to explain to anyone who has never been to the Himalayas. However, the miles and miles of towering white mountains combined with the green rice paddies below and the gentle population is hard not to love. Similarly, Ladakh of India and Northern Pakistan, the latter with the added "bonus" of having a somewhat wild population, not too far from Yemen or Afghanistan.

Tibet is a kind of highland desert, in which the mountain chains are much further from each other than in Himalaya and Karakorum. In addition, the holiest Buddhist mountain, the very special Mount Kailash, is found far west in the remote West Tibet where very few white people have ever been. The Swedish pioneer, Sven Hedin, by the way, was one – and so was I.

For animal wildlife, the Galapagos Islands of Ecuador are hard to beat. Others may go for various African experiences; however, I vote for the Darwin Islands. For diving and snorkeling, Niue (400 miles east of Tonga) and the Maldives are definitely worth mentioning, and so are the icebergs of Greenland and the salty lake of Salar de Uyuni, south Bolivia.

The world is truly beautiful!

If you had an unlimited budget and space and time were no object, what would your perfect travel day look like (for example: start your morning in Bora Bora; afternoon on a safari in Kenya; night in Australia, etc.)?

I love angling and usually travel with a bunch of fishing rods. Consequently, my perfect day should include a few hours of tarpon fishing in the Barra del Colorado region of Costa Rica. Around lunch, I'd love to make a stroll among the giant flocks of king penguins on South Georgia, perhaps enjoying a couple of male sea elephants fighting hard for their territory. In the afternoon, time has come to enjoy a photo safari among the marine iguanas of the Galapagos Islands, perhaps dotted with a few giant turtles, where after I'll finish the day with a sunset G&T from one of the fantastic bars at the Maldives – or perhaps a cup of tea and bubbling shisha together with a bunch of bearded gentlemen in Herat, Afghanistan.

Which three countries would you recommend for adventurous travelers to visit, and why?

It all depends on what you define by being "adventurous". And, regardless how the term is defined, it's bloody hard to limit the choice to three countries.

If "adventurous" means a guy who insists on going right to the limit, and maybe a bit further, my No. 1 would be Afghanistan. This place is just wild, and at the same time incredibly friendly and hospitable. The Afghanis are fierce and very proud, however, if you come as a friend, there is no end to their friendliness. Personally, I have avoided the critical southern regions, but in the north, this very much applies. Northern Pakistan, Tajikistan, parts of Iran and the rest of the region is pretty much the same freaky blend. Just great, with loads of incredible people. The whole region is a bunch of gems. Very backward due to the stronghold of conservative Islam, but what gems.

Another "wild" favorite is Western Tibet. Most people on a limited time and a high budget only see Lhasa and perhaps Shigatse and the route down to Nepal, and that's a mistake. Tibet offers incredible possibilities of doing a walkabout, and in particular, West Tibet, the holy Mount Kailash, and the whole highland desert far away from anything opts for some serious backpacking. You'll hardly see another foreigner – just remember to hide from the stupid Chinese police who don't like you being there. I got arrested twice but managed to get off the hook.

For a third choice, I might vote for Patagonia. Depending on the side of the continent (Chile vs. Argentina), the landscape is very varied, and it's no minus that the trout fishing on both sides is very good - along with the chances of enjoying fantastic national parks, peaks and glaciers, along with a few hot-spots for whale watching, along with Magellan penguin, seals and sea elephants. A special spot is the very British Falkland Islands. Highly recommended for serious wild guys with a flair for camping and penguins.

If you had just one travel story to share with someone, what would it be?

Travel stories? Lots, like most others who have been spending some time abroad. However, a few stories really deserve to be re-told, such as my experience as an angler in the independent Somali "republic" of Somaliland.

Just judging from the geography, Somaliland just has to be a great place for sports fishing. Thousand miles of pristine coastline, and, unlike most of Asia and the Pacific, no tradition at all for ling-line tuna boats. This simply has to be the "Fish Mecca", so, of course, I had to go there (2005), despite the fact that Somaliland was far from quiet, and that piracy in the Aden Bay was steeply on the rise.

The first few days in the capital proved to be rather quiet. Hargeisa is a rather sleepy and dusty place with not much to do. As anywhere, the market is the most lively place in town, apart from the noon rush hour during which the whole town seems to be running around to buy their daily supply of qat. After that, everyone sits down and chews. And chews. And chews. And nothing really happens until next morning at 9 am. Somalia is not a place where stress seems to rule. More likely, people die from too much chewing.

However, I was there to go fishing, and a local taxi took me north to the coast, along with the two guards who were assigned to me. I didn't want them. However, the Hargeisa chief of police insisted, and I ended up spending a couple of day-loads of qat for the two lazy guys "protecting me" from nothing. Or at least, it seemed like nothing.

Once I got to Berbera. The real hassles started. Out of nowhere, another "guard" popped up, insisting that he was to "protect me". I tried to protest, but in vain, and in the days to come I was followed everywhere by the silly, drooling soldier chewing qat non-stop. Definitely a public servant.

After a happy afternoon fishing barracudas from the town jetty, I got into contact with some local fishermen in a café, and they were happy to take me fishing early next morning. Or so I thought, because later at the café, I suddenly got a phone call(!) from the police chief who strictly insisted that I was not allowed to go fishing without a permit!

"What!!" Fishing in Somaliland does not require a permit, however, not to cause problems for my new friends in the café, I abstained from the morning fishing and instead walked down to the marine office where a friendly guy confirmed: no permit required. Unfortunately, my "bodyguard" sensed that this was trouble, and I promptly got arrested and got myself a walk (at gun point!) to the Berbera police station.

After a lot of waiting (and policemen chewing qat), I ended up in the barren office of the police chief, a small, aggressively looking guy with a big balloon of qat on the one side of the mouth. After staring for a second at the crazy tourist, he started shouting: "You need a permit to go fishing in a boat! This permit you get back in Hargeisa". End of discussion, and I was sent back to the town center with the strict order of not going fishing.

This was, of course, a pure lie, made up just to avoid being confronted with something new, such as a white guy with a fishing rod, so the next day I was arrested again for trying to go fishing. After the second arrest, I got badly tired of the stupid police chief and, at my own will, walked straight up to the governor in order to get the verdict from the highest local authority. Surprisingly, I was granted access into the palace, and while "parking" my unwanted bodyguard outside, I entered the houses of the holy.

The governor proved to be a very nice guy. A well-dressed, elderly gentleman with golden glasses and a close-to-perfect English in a delicate wrapping of politeness and education. Definitely the right guy to talk to, so he got the whole story about the fishermen, the ignorant and stubborn police idiot and the endless number of arrests.

The polite governor listened patiently to my endless ordeal and finally called for the police chief to come to his office at once. Payback time, and at first, things went hunky dory. The police chief even clicked his heels a couple of time in an obedient salute to his superior, while I was standing beside trying not to interfere with justice – and not to smile too much. However, the chief was allowed some talk time too, and all too quickly he managed to persuade the governor that the bloody tourist definitely needed a non-existing permit.

Suddenly, the governor switched sides and started to explain the situation to me. "What if something happened to you? I could lose my job?". What a shame. Personally, should something really happen, I could lose a lot more, however, at a maximum of two miles from the coast, the risk was likely to be very small. I really tried, but in vain. The governor had decided to side with the uniformed idiot, and I was ordered to get a "permit" from Hargeisa. That didn't prevent additional problems. An hour later, I was arrested once again and forced to sit and sweat in the hot police station, until the police chief called me in. He wasn't happy, and the "meeting" ended up in him banning me from fishing from the jetty. Actually, I was not allowed to fish anywhere in Somaliland without a government permit. I just gave up. Went back to Hargeisa the following day and caught an early morning jeep to Djibouti. The virgin Somali coastline is still unknown territory for me.

Do you ever feel you have missed out on certain aspects of life while away from home as you travel so much?

Traveling like I do automatically implies a certain difficulty in being a family man. Actually, I am not a family man, and I never will be. However, I still managed to have two boys, and on more than one occasion I would have liked to be able to be in two places at the same time.

Traveling a few months at a time surely costs you a lot of social life at home, and it applies to most aspects of my domestic life. When you suddenly leave the country for six or twelve months - or more - friends have a tendency of dropping off. At least in the old days before the invention of Facebook, you were bound to lose contact with all your friends back home, and that is at a cost.

The same applies to various "activities". I used to play in a band (or, more correctly, a number of different bands), and being a bass player is close to impossible if you want to go walkabout for several months at a time. I was never close to being professional, but even as a good amateur, most bands hate when their trusty bass player is not available. Quite understandable, I have to admit. Serious traveling is very hard to combine with a "normal" life at home, simply because you are not there.

Fortunately, 20 years ago, the Travellers' Club of Denmark was formed, and this has proved to be a great refuge for lots of "homeless" travelers. Here, we have a great forum, sharing lots of funny stories among people who understand that traveling is like an infection. You just have to, and this has created great friendships inside the club, even though some of us leave the country for several months. There is kind of understanding for being weird.

What advice would you give to others who would like to travel to every country?

Don't do it! Really. Focus on the adventure of being somewhere instead of just thinking of the next stamps in the passport. Thinking in terms of been-there-done-that is no good way of traveling. I prefer to respect the people who spend lots of time abroad, rather than those who "conquer" six or seven countries within two weeks. Traveling this way is like going to the opera and then leave 10 minutes inside the overture.

For someone who has been almost everywhere, what still gets you excited about packing your bags again?

The Internet has certainly made it much easier to prepare for the unexpected. Compared to 30 years ago, an easy Google quickly provides us with lots of information and photos from all corners of the world, however, if you (like me) love the unknown, it's not that difficult to get a few surprises on the way. Well, it's kind of hard to be surprised by the Pyramids of Giza or the Eiffel Tower, but once you get a little further away from the beaten track, it's still quite easy to get surprised.

I love these surprises, and, who knows, I may catch a few funny fish I have never caught before. Traveling should always include a certain degree of uncertainty. Life is very much a game of improvising.

Looking ahead, what travel plans and goals are you still pursuing, and what is on your "Bucket List"?

Actually, my traveling has become a bit like a balloon: What I've seen is inside the balloon; what I want to see is the surface of the balloon, so the more I see, the larger the balloon, and the more I want to see. In addition, the Travellers' Club (Denmark) is a seriously dangerous forum! You gets loads of information and even more inspiration from an entirely different angle than that on the TV or from journalists, and that's highly inspiring. Consequently, my never-ending bucket list is a dynamic organism, always expanding and always in motion.

For years, my top of the list has been South Georgia and Antarctica. Due to the price, I've never been there, but I will. Unfortunately, I prefer to go somewhere far away from the rest of the tourists, and that certainly doesn't make things cheaper - especially as I'd love to spend lots of days on South Georgia, preferably among the southern elephant seals during the period when the five-ton males are fighting to collect the biggest harem on their particular part of the beach. Perhaps I should try to get a job in Grytviken...

Mountains? Well, 30 years ago, K2 or Everest or just the Mallory-Irvine Route to Camp 3 would have been on my list, however, age creeping in, I have kind of give up such stupid ideas. Actually, I once tried to tackle the Camp 3, but was beaten by the bad weather. Not to be repeated.

And then I'd really like to catch a big marlin using light tackle in a small boat...

Jack Wheeler, U.S.A.

(Jack Wheeler with KPNLF guerrillas in Cambodia, 1984)

Where did you grow up, and what was your early life like?

I grew up in Glendale, California near L.A. It was the idyllic childhood of the 1950s 'American Golden Age', especially in Southern California. My dad worked for a local television station; my mom was a homemaker, we were all blissfully unaware of the world outside Glendale.

The only time I left Glendale as a young boy was in 1954 at age 9. My parents took my sister Judy and I on a giant road trip throughout the West – the Grand Canyon, Bryce, Zion, Yellowstone, Custer's Battlefield, Crater Lake, Yosemite. I was stunned by what I saw; the impact of the American West's natural beauty and grandeur has never has left me.

At 11, I got into tennis and the Boy Scouts. Torn between the two, I got off to a slow start with Scouting, taking over six months to get from Tenderfoot to Second Class. I spent the summer of 1955 trying to make First Class and get my Camping Merit Badge. While at camp, I had a daydream that I could make First Class by September, Star by December, and be a Life Scout (the highest next to Eagle) by March, making each in the 3-month minimum for advancement. When I made the mistake of telling the other kids, they laughed at me, and it made me mad. By March of 1956, I was a Life Scout and no one was laughing.

Now 12, my whole life was dedicated to Scouting, to reach the required 21 Merit Badges and fulfill the other requirements for Eagle. The minimum from Life to Eagle was six months, and I was determined to make it, which I did in August, whereupon I was notified by Scout Headquarters (then in New Brunswick, New Jersey) that I was the Youngest Eagle Scout in the history of the Boy Scouts. I was invited to New Brunswick to receive my Eagle medal by Chief Scout Executive Arthur Schuck, and then to the White House where, with my parents, I met President Dwight Eisenhower.

It was a life-altering experience to have the President of the United States put his hands on my shoulders, look me in the eye, and tell me, a 12-year-old boy, "I am proud to have met you, Jack."

What was the first international trip you took, and what do you remember most about it?

In 1958 before the Matterhorn, my family and I went to Moscow where I saw Stalin entombed with Lenin in Red Square. (Khrushchev had Stalin removed in 1961.) It was impossibly creepy.

I was only 14, yet I knew that these two men had murdered millions, that they were among the evilest men who had ever lived, that they were moral equivalents of Hitler. The reverential silence, the worship of evil, displayed by these

Russians all around me as we slowly shuffled past their corpses was terrifying and mysterious.

When we came out again onto Red Square, I felt overwhelmed by a question: Why would people worship evil?

Why would they worship monsters as heroes, monsters who took away their freedom, who slaughtered and starved them, put them in concentration camps, caused them to live a life of fear?

It puzzles me to this day. Especially since the Russian kids I met in one of their schools were very friendly to us. Interaction with them profoundly affected me. When I made notes with a cheap Papermate pen, the kids couldn't believe their eyes. I asked our Intourist guide Valya why they were so curious. She studied the pen, which to me was the most ordinary thing I could imagine, and said, "We do not have such things in Soviet Union."

I stared at her for a moment while her words registered. I had a few extra pens in my pocket and gave them to the kids. They were almost giddy with excitement, and I thought: "What kind of a country is it that can maintain an Iron Curtain and threaten the West with atom bombs, yet doesn't know how to make a ballpoint pen?"

The answer came to my mind as a revelation: "It's a country that can be had." 25 years later, that revelation would enable me to create what the press called The Reagan Doctrine.

When did you go from traveling casually to making this a full-time goal, and what motivated you to travel to every country?

Those are two entirely separate questions. For the first, the answer is when I was 14 and read *Richard Halliburton's Complete Book of Marvels*, suddenly opening the world to me as a place of endless wonder and adventure. It was his account of climbing the world's most famous mountain, the Matterhorn in Switzerland, that transfixed me.

The timing was lucky because my dad had just gotten his television station, KTTV, to pay for our going to Europe and film it for a TV special. Going to Europe was exotic in 1958, but the real selling point was Russia – taking an American family there was a big deal back then.

I tell the story of why my father said yes when I asked if I could climb the Matterhorn at 14 in *What Life Is All About*. When I reached the top with my guide, Alfons Franzen, Dad was flying around the summit in a small plane, and we waved to each other. One of the most profound moments of my life to this day, it was the experience we shared at his death in 1980.

It was a moment that set me on my life's direction. People collect things. They collect stamps, or coins, or porcelain. At 14, I decided what I wanted was to collect extraordinary experiences. You could lose your stamps or coins, but you can never lose what you have done with your life. A collection of unbelievably memorable adventures can never be taken away.

So I set off alone, to swim the Hellespont like Leander in Greek mythology (*LIFE* magazine, Dec. 20, 1960), get adopted into a tribe of Amazon headhunters (the Shuara Jivaros in Ecuador), and hunt a man-eating tiger in South Vietnam while still in high school. By the time I was 17, I was the subject of Ralph Edwards' This Is Your Life television show. By the time I was 21, I was named one of America's Ten Outstanding Young Men (TOYM) by the US Jaycees.

I haven't stopped since, but it never occurred to me to get to every country in the world until about 10-11 years ago – it's always about experiences not country-counting for me. One evening while my wife and I were having dinner talking about some remote part of the planet, she asked, "Just curious – how many countries have you been to?" I told her I didn't have a clue.

So I looked up the State Department list of Independent States and counted – it was 140. When I told her, she asked, "How many countries are there?" "Depends on how you count," I replied. "Obviously the UN Member States, of which there are 191 (Montenegro added in 2006, South Sudan in 2011). Add the Vatican as a UN Observer State (Palestine added 2012). Add two countries that are clearly sovereign nations but the UN won't let them join: Taiwan and Somaliland (plus Kosovo since 2008). Forget colonies like Greenland and French Polynesia, and phony countries that are really colonies like Russia's Abkhazia or Morocco's Western Sahara. So my count is 194." (Now in 2016, 198: 193 UN, 2 UN Observers, three sovereign non-UN: Taiwan, Kosovo, Somaliland.)

She thought for a moment, then with a smile and her eyebrows raised, asked, "Why don't you try for them all?" At first, it was a strange thought. I never went to a country just to go there but to do something cool and memorable. I told her I'd think about that.

Afterward, I started doing something I hadn't before. Whenever I led an expedition someplace, like to the CAR (Central African Republic), I began making it a point to explore a neighboring country like Chad or Cameroon. I'd go to find something interesting to experience and to see what made this place tick as a country.

My "Every Country" project was completed last year (2014) on a scientific pilgrimage to São Tomé and Príncipe (Príncipe is where Einstein became Einstein - see my *Science in Africa*).

What have you done in your life to gain the freedom and finances to pursue as much travel as you have?

Real high adventure didn't cost much when I was young – no fancy hotels in jungles. I saved up by giving tennis and judo lessons. In my college years, I alternated semesters at UCLA and running a business in South Vietnam. There were no adventure travel companies in those days – to do something adventurous you had to figure it out yourself. Eventually, I wrote a book, *The Adventurer's Guide*, where I told how I did something and how the reader could do it too.

There were chapters on "Climbing the Matterhorn", "Living with Headhunters", "Swimming the Hellespont", "Hunting a Man-Eating Tiger", and "Exploring Outer Mongolia". It got me on a host of television shows like *Johnny Carson* and *Merv Griffin*. Merv made me his co-host for any adventure-themed show, when he'd have guests like Thor Heyerdahl or Jacques Cousteau.

It was this enormous publicity that enabled me to start my adventure-expedition company, Wheeler Expeditions. I began with the first commercial expedition to the North Pole in 1978. It had never been done before. I've been to the North Pole now 21 times.

This went on for 25 years. Then in 2003, I launched a subscriber-based geopolitical website, To The Point. This gave me a purpose for going to countries I'd never been to before – I'd write about them, explaining their history, how they came to be, and in many cases, how they might cease to be.

I had a reputation for doing this, as I predicted the demise of the Soviet Union years before it happened. Many countries are artificial constructs. They never emerged organically out of history, but were either created by colonial powers such as Britain, Germany, or France – or they are a part of colonial empires of conquest within their own borders like the Soviet Union until we broke it apart.

So I bring a unique outlook on geopolitics that people are willing to pay for – and that justifies a lot of unique travel.

Has there ever been a time where you considered abandoning your travel goals?

Twice. When I was 19, I started a business in South Vietnam exporting cinnamon to spice companies around the world. I kept it going until I managed to graduate from UCLA (in anthropology) and get back there – but it soon collapsed when the Viet Cong killed my Vietnamese partner and blew up our cinnamon groves. I ended up in Hawaii broke and found solace in reading Ayn Rand's *Atlas Shrugged*.

(Don Parrish, who has a chapter in *Chasing 193*, is smiling now. I thought I was the only person on earth inspired by both Halliburton and Rand until Don was too. No wonder we've become good friends.)

Rand, and subsequently Aristotle turned me on to philosophy so much that I decided to get a doctorate in it. Thus, I spent three paradisaical years in Hawaii with a gorgeous Hawaiian maiden who also was a Randian, being in the graduate school of philosophy at the University of Hawaii in Honolulu, and having so much fun with fellow Randians driving the campus lefties crazy. The rest of the world was a long ways away.

After I had got my MA, I got a job offer to teach and get my Ph.D. at the University of Southern California in LA. I would take summers off to get into trouble somewhere in the world – all over Africa, the Middle East, the Pacific and elsewhere. One real high point was reaching a group of Aushiri Aucas in the Amazon – the ones who kill all the missionaries. It was a "first contact," and memorably intense.

I wrote my doctoral dissertation on Aristotelian ethics and *The Adventurer's Guide* at the same time. It was a wild intellectual ride. When I got my Ph.D. I knew I didn't want to teach anymore. I wanted to be a professional adventurer.

On the book tour, attending a lecture I gave at the University of Las Vegas was the most extraordinary woman I'd ever met. Her name was Jacqueline. She was from the Alps of France, and she was the star showgirl of the Folies Bergère. I moved to Vegas and launched my expedition company with her.

Jacqueline and I lived with a cannibal tribe in New Guinea (the Wali-ali-fo, my second "first contact"), went to the North Pole, took elephants over the Alps via the actual pass (the Col du Clapier) used by Hannibal in 218 BC. The business was really taking off, we were planning our wedding, when we discovered that Jacqueline had breast cancer. She died in my arms three months later, on March 12, 1980.

I retreated from life not knowing if I wanted to live or not. I got a small apartment in Malibu to walk the beach and mourn. The one thing that kept me alive was sky-diving. On a North Pole expedition in April 1981, I set a Guinness World Record for the "Northernmost Parachute Jump," the first free-fall skydive onto the sea-ice at 90 North, which as Guinness states (in the 1984 edition), "is a record that cannot be bettered after setting."

I had gotten to know Clint Eastwood via Merv Griffin; we ended up alone on an iceberg in Greenland during the filming of *Firefox*. I launched the original "Seven Summits" expedition (to climb the highest mountain in each of all seven continents) with Frank Wells (then VP of Warner Brothers). But by 1982, the grief became too much to bear, and I gave up my expedition company.

Then a friend ended up in the Reagan White House, and my idea of how the Soviet Union could be had was revived. It dawned on me that a number of anti-Soviet insurgencies were emerging in various Soviet colonies – but neither my friend nor anyone else in the White House believed it. I had something to live for again. I took off for six months talking my way into guerrilla-held territory in Nicaragua with the

Contras, Angola with UNITA, Mozambique with RENAMO, the TPLF in Ethiopia, and the Mujahaddin in Afghanistan.

When I came back, I showed my pictures of these freedom fighters to the White House. It was November 1983, and the people there credit that meeting as the birth of what the press was later to call The Reagan Doctrine, the strategy to rid the world of the Soviet Union. (We didn't call it that, however. We just called what we were doing "FTC" – you can figure out what we wanted to do with "The Commies.")

But I was still a mess personally – until I met a woman who saved me. Her name – her real name on her birth certificate – is Rebel Holiday. Rebel healed my crippled soul. I had found my life partner. We were married in St. Tropez with Congressman Charlie Wilson (of the Tom Hanks' movie *Charlie Wilson's War*) as my best man. There are pictures of our wedding in Charlie Wilson and Ronald Reagan's War.

I restarted my expedition business while continuing forays into guerrilla territory and reporting back to the White House. I was myself again, thanks to Rebel.

What do you consider to be your two favorite travel experiences, and why?

It's really hard to pick two. Blowing up the Soviet High Command at Bala Hissar in Ghazni, Afghanistan has got to be up there. The Guinness North Pole solo skydive, the Hannibal Expedition, any one of the three first contacts I've had with a tribe from the outside world.

(I've mentioned the first two, the Aucas in 1972 and the Wali-ali-fo in 1977. The third was with an uncontacted band of San Bushmen in the Kalahari of Botswana-Namibia. It affected us all very deeply. One of us, John Perrott, formed a charity to help the Bushmen people, SavetheSan.org).

It's a long, lifetime list, and I've enjoyed them all. The one that means the most to me is my being the unofficial liaison between the Reagan White House and all the various Anti-

Communist insurgencies that emerged in the 1980s mentioned above, plus the Hmong guerrillas in Laos, the KPNLF in Cambodia, and the Karen-ni in Burma.

I spent much of the 80s with these insurgencies as they fought to liberate their countries from Soviet imperialism. I also spent time with the all the democracy movements emerging in Eastern Europe and within the Soviet Union itself. It's why I'm credited in a number of histories of the Cold War as the originator of the Reagan Doctrine that was successful in breaking the Soviet Union apart like Humpty-Dumpty.

Now that's a series of experiences, and you want a story about a particular incident, so here's one. It took place in the exotic locale of Capitol Hill in Washington in October 1996. A Congressman I know, Dana Rohrabacher (R-CA), insisted I attend a meeting with some Russians in town – the Deputy Mayor of St. Petersburg and his entourage.

This was a time of Boris Yeltsin and good feelings with Russia, so after the meeting – it was the end of the day – Dana asks the Russians if they'd like to have a beer. They think that's a great idea, so we retire to the Irish Times pub on the other side of the Hill. After a pint or two of Guinness, Dana and the Deputy Mayor decide to have an arm wrestling match to see who really won the Cold War.

Too much Guinness – but this story is true, there were/are several witnesses (such as Ed Royce, current chairman of House Foreign Relations). The Deputy Mayor puts Dana down in a New York second. Holding his arm and looking very bewildered, Dana sees me and says, "Wheeler, defend the honor of your country!"

The Russians, of course, want to see another Amerikanski get his ass kicked and start calling, "Hey, tovarich!" – So I think, why not? The Deputy Mayor had blond hair, blue eyes, and a smirk. Okay. We set it up, and I let him give me his shot – I didn't want to crush him like he did Dana, I just eased him down. Instantly, up went his left arm. Really? Okay... and down he went again. He wasn't really very strong.

But as I stood up to leave, thinking that was over, up stepped the Deputy Mayor's KGB bodyguard. He was huge and wanted to dislocate my shoulder. Somehow, I don't know how to this day; I managed to beat him, both arms.

So weird story, which was forgotten until January 2000, when Dana and I were having lunch discussing what was going on in the world, and he asked about Russia. Suddenly, a man's picture in the newspaper I had seen that morning clicked. I asked him if he remembered the Russians we arm wrestled four years ago in the Irish Times. He finally did and asked so what? "You don't remember who the Deputy Mayor of St. Petersburg was?" I asked.

"No," he answered. "Who cares? He was some Deputy Mayor." "Well, Dana, I just recognized his picture in the (Washington) Post today. He's been elected President of Russia. His name is Vladimir Putin."

Again, true story with Congressional witnesses.

What are the main things you seek to experience when you travel (culture, cities, nature, animals, adventure activities, etc.)?

The new. Someplace I've never been to before, to discover what's interesting about it. Or what if anything is important about it geopolitically, not only to write about it for To The Point but also for the geopolitical briefings I give to people in Congress or international companies I consult for.

Looking back from when you started traveling to where you are now, in what ways, if any, has travel changed you?

One change, in particular, comes to mind. It was late 1987, and I just got back from an extravaganza - Afghanistan with the Mujaheddin fighting the Soviets, an overland expedition from Beijing to Tibet to Kathmandu, Mozambique with the RENAMO anti-Soviet guerrillas, et al. I was sitting on a couch at home telling our four year-old Brandon about where I'd been, when he said barely above a whisper, "I missed you, Dad."

My life was different after those four words. I realized I could never again go off into the world without taking Brandon - and later his younger brother Jackson - unless it was to a war zone.

Do you speak any foreign languages, and if so, which have been the most useful for you besides English?

Not a one. It's amazing how much communication is non-verbal. I spent a month in Afghanistan with a Mujahedin commander named Qari Baba - he looked like a cross between Genghis Khan and Buddha. He didn't speak a word of English, and I didn't speak Pushto. We had a fabulous time together and became fast friends.

What was the longest extended trip you have ever taken, when was it and where all did you go?

That six months I first spent with a number of anti-Soviet guerrilla movements mentioned above.

What two countries have exceeded your expectations and which ones left you feeling underwhelmed, and why?

There are more of the former than the latter. Only two? Rwanda, certainly. I wrote about it in "Gorillas, Savages, and

Redemption" (To The Point, March 2011). I think Rwanda's leader, Paul Kagame, deserves the Nobel Peace Prize.

Another would be Malta. In "The Siege of Malta" (December 2009), I describe how it's where civilization emerged from the Stone Age, where the Knights of Malta saved the Christian West in 1565, and where that assault has begun anew. An extraordinary place.

Underwhelmed? Sadly, South Sudan. In "The Newest African Farce" (March 2011), I explain why the latest UN member state is unlikely to succeed. That's unfortunate, but the reality is, virtually the entire map of Africa needs to be redrawn.

Another would be Nauru. It's the most pathetic excuse for a country I know of. It's "The Land of Fubar" (October 2013).

When you travel, do you prefer to go with others or solo, and why?

It depends on who the others are! Of course, I'd rather travel with my wife or my sons. And with a number of friends with whom I've been exploring the world for decades. I don't tolerate whiners and complainers, though – everyone who travels with me knows I'll send them back home immediately if they do that, so it happens rarely.

But taking people to remote places is a heavy responsibility. So it's a real luxury for me just to get lost in the world all by my lonesome, where I don't have to take care of anyone except myself.

What has been your most uncomfortable mode of transportation?

A captured Russian truck with blown shocks driving thousands of kilometers across the roadless African bush with the UNITA anti-Soviet guerrillas in the 80s.

What is the strangest thing you've seen/experienced while traveling?

"NorkLand." Anyone who has ever been to North Korea understands why. It's beyond surreal. The Norks have drunk the Kool-Aid, it's Orwell's 1984 made real, where they really do love Big Brother. Most fully demented country on the planet. I've been all over it – even to their sacred mountain of Paekdu – three times. Never, ever again.

What are the best and worst meals you have ever eaten while traveling, and where was it?

The best steak in the world is the nerve of an elephant's tusk. The first step in the recipe is to shoot an elephant. Extract the nerves from the tusks – it's like a New York stripper that comes to a point. Slice it into steaks; pan fry it with butter over the campfire. Not even a porterhouse at Peter Luger's in Brooklyn comes close.

The most bizarre meal I've ever had was in Cholon, Saigon's Chinatown, in 1961. We were seated circling the usual round table enjoying normal dishes when waiters removed everything including the white tablecloth. In the middle of the table was a small hole about two inches in diameter. A spoon with a very long handle and a very small bowl was placed beside each of us.

A waiter brought out a live monkey, crawled underneath the table and strapped it down, so the top of his head poked through the hole. He then leaned over the table with a large sharp knife and sliced/pried off the upper part of the monkey's skull exposing its brain. The monkey must have been drugged or something as it didn't make a sound.

The waiter then poured boiling oil into the brains, everyone picked up their spoon and dug in.

Out of the thousands of places you've stayed around the world, what have been your best and worst accommodations?

A Grand Suite at the Sacher Hotel in Vienna overlooking the Opera House is exquisite. A Dung-ri-la next to a Chinese garrison on the Tibetan Plateau isn't.

What is your favorite "off the beaten path" destination, and why?

Tristan da Cunha. It's the people that make it so incredibly special. See "Freedom Paradise Found" (April 2013).

What were your most challenging countries to visit, and why?

Any country with an active war zone that you walk right into is challenging. In Afghanistan and the others rebelling against the Soviets, I had a purpose in doing so. After that purpose was fulfilled, I've never had a desire to walk into another.

Of which travel accomplishments are you most proud?

FTC... (what we called The Reagan Doctrine, remember?)

If you could travel back in time, to which era and place would you go, and why?

1776, to Revolutionary America to meet the founders and creators of the most successful country in human history - and to ask their advice on how we can recreate the freedom they gave us, which has now been lost to such a tragic degree.

Can you describe any particular situation where you felt completely out of your comfort zone?

I'm sure there have been, but none come to mind.

What are your three favorite cities in the world, and why?

Perth, Singapore, and Munich. Perth for the Sail & Anchor Pub in Fremantle, Singapore for the snooker table at the Raffles, and Munich for the Hofbräuhaus. Mostly, though, big cities are places to get out of and into the world.

What is the ideal amount of time you prefer to travel on each trip before you are ready to go home and take a break?

It depends on how long I can stand being away from Rebel if she's not with me. Even after over 30 years, more than a month away from her is a very long time. Also, Rebel's cooking is better than most any restaurant.

In your opinion, where are the most beautiful places on Earth?

The world is neither beautiful nor ugly, it just is. The beauty is inside us, in the incredible human capacity to experience the world as magical. A sunset in the ocean, the sun filtering through pine trees and lighting up a gurgling stream with sparkles, your wife's smile, the sound of your children's laughter, we are surrounded by beautiful things and places.

That said, there are places of overwhelming awe. The most magnificent mountain scenery on earth is at Concordia in the Karakoram of northern Pakistan, the junction of the Godwen-Austen and Duke of Abruzzi glaciers forming the Baltoro glacier. You are surrounded by 7,000 and 8,000-meter peaks, including K2, the world's second highest mountain. To get there, you pass by the Trango Towers, the world's highest rock spires.

The most beautiful scuba-diving I think is in Palau. The most beautiful island for me is La Digue in the Seychelles (although Norfolk Island comes close). The most beautiful city is Cape Town, and the most beautiful sunset is the

North Face of Mount Everest when the setting sun turns the whole Tibetan mountainside rose-red pink while the jet stream blows a plume of cloud off its peak.

If you had an unlimited budget and space and time were no object, what would your perfect travel day look like (for example: start your morning in Bora Bora; afternoon on a safari in Kenya; night in Australia, etc.)?

It's hard for me to imagine something that's pure fantasy, only something that's possible in reality.

Which three countries would you recommend for adventurous travelers to visit, and why?

Well, I'd first have to ask what kind of adventure rattles their cage and tailor three with that focus. How extreme, what skill level, what are they capable of? It's what you can do in a country that counts, not just going to a place on the map circumscribed by artificial lines called "borders."

Also, there are astounding places within countries but not the countries themselves. The island of Socotra is an absolute mind-blow, but the country it belongs to, Yemen, is currently (and very sadly) belly up. The same for the Tassili-n'Ajjer Plateau in southeast Algeria, or the Ténéré and the Lost City of Djado in Niger. The same for many other countries.

So, OK, three out of 193, that's the game. First, America. I thought I'd seen a lot of our country by the time my youngest son, Jackson, was 8 and we launched his Nifty Fifty project - for him to see and experience something cool and memorable in each of all 50 states (and for me to take him!).

Do this - of course, with your kids if at all possible - and it will blow you away how much there is of natural grandeur, geology, history, the opportunity for exploration and adventure, plus most of all, how wonderfully friendly Americans are just about everywhere you go.

Second, New Zealand. South Island is an absolute wonderland of every adventurous sport and activity you can imagine.

Third, China. The opportunities for exploration are almost bottomless. Unfortunately, the Chicoms have destroyed Tibet, which is now just a theme park for Chinese tourists. And climbing Everest now is just a traffic jam. But there are other giant mountains galore like Minya Konka, Amne Machin, and Muztagh Ata - almost 25,000 feet and you can ski/snowboard down it.

From the Guoliang Precipice Long Corridor to the Hani Rice Terraces to Wa headhunters on the untamed border with Burma (although they'd rather grow poppies, dance in their incredible Wood Drum Ceremony, and drink their baijiu moonshine - the best in China - than hunt enemy heads now) to... well, you'll never get to the end of it.

If you had just one travel story to share with someone, what would it be?

The Indian Ambassador to the US once had a private luncheon at his residence in Washington for the Dalai Lama to which I was invited. Sitting next to him, I said, "Your Holiness, I must tell you a story..." Here is that story.

In 1987, I drove across the Changtang Plateau of Tibet north to south. When we reached Kham, I began looking for Khampas.

(As the Dalai Lama well knew, the Khampas are the nomad warriors of Tibet. The CIA sponsored a rebellion by the Khampas against the Chicom seizure of Tibet in the late 50s-early 60s, led by legendary agent Tony Poe - who during the 80s would become my dear friend. The Chinese are terrified of the Khampas to this day.)

I spotted four riders trotting along a high ridge. I told our Chinese driver to stop the jeep, got out, told those with me to stay here; I'll be back. When the Chinese driver saw the

Khampas, he freaked: "No, no! Stop! They will kill you! Stop!" he yelled in panic. I told him to calm down, just stay here. I began walking up to the ridge where the riders had by now halted.

As I approached them, they had turned their horses towards me in a row. They looked straight out of a movie, long black hair interwoven with the Khampa red silk topknot, long mustaches, wearing knives, swords, pistols, muskets, and cartridge-filled bandoliers across their chests, the horses blowing steam out of their nostrils. They looked like they could kill me without hesitation.

"I walked right up to them, put my hand in my vest pocket, took out a picture of you, Your Holiness, and handed it to one of the men. I took out another, another, and another, so each had a picture of you. Instantly they jumped off their horses. They were transformed. Before they were stern and wary, now they were all smiles, touching the picture of you to their foreheads. They didn't know who I was or where I was from. All they knew was that I was their friend.

"I had given each of them the most valuable thing it was possible for them to possess - a picture of you, which, as you know, the Chinese issue a death sentence for any Tibetan having one. They crowded around me, put their hands on my shoulders and pushed down - they wanted me to sit and have a cup of yak butter tea. I looked far below to the jeep and waved to my friends to come. They did - the Chinese driver stayed of course - and we proceeded to enjoy the most memorable cup of tea we'd ever had with these wild Khampa warriors. When we finished, one of them unwrapped his red topknot from his head and presented it to me in gratitude."

The Dalai Lama was impressed at this. "Oh, very high honor from Khampas," he said. "The honor was mine, Your Holiness," I replied, "in my being able to give them your picture."

(Jack with Dalai Lama)

Do you ever feel you have missed out on certain aspects of life while away from home as you travel so much?

I've been blessed in my life with luck enough to have a balance between home with my wife and family, and to have an adventurous life as well. I have yet to figure out why I'm so lucky to have such a supporting wife.

In your first edition of Chasing 193, the fellow who impressed me most with achieving such balance in his life is Robert Bonifas. It's that balance in life you want to strive for, not a single-minded obsession.

What advice would you give to others who would like to travel to every country?

The first and most important is: Don't go to a country just to check it off the list. Having been to a country just to say you've been there, just as a tick in the box, means nothing. Nothing. It's what you did there that counts, what you experienced, what you learned.

My advice is to go to those places that fascinate you, that call to you, that you want to make a part of your life. You have one life – that's it. One chance to make it special. Fill it up with memories. Not with ticks on a checklist. When your grandkids ask you about a country, you never want to say, "Well, uh, I was there for just a little while and looked around..." You want to be able to light up and say, "Oh, wow, while I was there I did the coolest thing, here's the story..."

I'd like to suggest that before you commit to this every country goal, you really drill deep and ask yourself why? What do you actually, truly, meaningfully-to-you intend to accomplish? And of equal importance, what would you give up? Would you, say, divorce your wife, abandon your family?

There are a lot of things in life far more important than traveling to another country. I've been ridiculously lucky to have a wife and life-partner who lets me go off into the blue yonder while she works on the business she loves. (Yes, she does go with me somewhere adventurous whenever she can.) I've also been so very lucky to take my boys with me on expeditions when they were growing up - or else I'd have stayed home.

Do your best to create your own luck, to forge your own life, but be very sure of your priorities.

For someone who has been almost everywhere, what still gets you excited about packing your bags again?

There's no everywhere, not even close. There's an old saying, "The more I know, the less I know" - i.e., the more you know regarding any subject, the more you realize how much more there is to learn. It's the same with travel - the more of the world you see, the less you see.

That is, the more of the world you see, the bigger it expands in your mind. There's a tiny speck in the Pacific called Niue. Go there and explore it - it's now a lot bigger for you than a tiny speck on the map. You'll never get to the end of all the history, the beauty, the wonder, the magic of what there is to experience on our Earth. There will always be people to befriend and learn from.

The bottom line is: if you have an adventurous attitude toward life, you'll always be excited about packing your bags and being off to experience more magic in the world.

Looking ahead, what travel plans and goals are you still pursuing, and what is on your "Bucket List"?

I don't have a bucket list. What would you do if you complete it? Kick the bucket? No, you need a list so long you'll never get to the end of it. There will always be another adventure to add to your life.

Henrik Jeppesen, Denmark

(Henrik Jeppesen, right, in Tripoli, shaking hands with Khalifa al-Ghaw, the Prime Minister of Libya's new General National Congress)

Where did you grow up, and what was your early life like?

I grew up in the Thy-district of northwestern Jutland in Denmark, where Denmark later got its first national park. My early life was mostly about sports, where I was a good cyclist and among the best in my age group in Denmark in the year 2000. When I decide to do something, I do it a hundred percent. Travel is those hundred percent at the moment, but back then it was all about cycling. I knew just about everything about it and was a cycling expert on national TV during the Tour de France, at the age of 12. As I will explain later in this book, it is very important not to push yourself too hard. I did with cycling and slowly lost interest. In 2002, I decided to stop and have not had an interest in cycling since. I instead got a keen interest in football (soccer for American readers). I was not a talented footballer, but I began watching games and became passionate about it. I still like football today, but my interest is limited to two local teams I follow over the internet. In my teenage years, it's fair to say I was a bit different in many ways. I had a big interest in geography, politics and movies and was never interested in the Danish drinking culture. My first interest in travel probably came from the many different films I saw from around the world. I especially liked South Korean, Italian and Brazilian cinema and found it fascinating how different they were from your typical Hollywood production. Hollywood could never make a *Cinema Paradiso* (Italy) or *Memories of Murder* (South Korea), which are two of my favorite films. I was never depressed or unhappy with my life, but there wasn't much to do in Thy unless you like the Danish drinking culture. I couldn't wait to get older and travel the world. In the meantime, I went on a few trips with a truck driver to a few countries in Europe. It was very exciting and surely gave me the travel bug. My first goal in my early teenage years was to visit 50 countries, as I was afraid to go far and only wanted to visit "safe countries". I never in my wildest imagination thought I would be part of a book about travelers going to every country in the world.

What was the first international trip you took, and what do you remember most about it?

I went to Germany when I was a few years old and remember nothing from that journey. The first trip I remember is when I was 12 years old, and I went with my family to the South of France. Being a cyclist at the time, I managed to climb the Mont Ventoux the day before the Tour de France peloton. In 2006, I decided to travel for six months solo and went alone to places like Egypt and Southeast Asia, at age 17. In Egypt, I remember making many mistakes and, of course, being ripped off. I, however, enjoyed the Pyramids, Luxor Temple, and experiencing an entirely different culture from what I was used to. I grew up in a very safe place and wasn't used to big cities. Maybe that is why I was robbed in Liverpool on one of my first solo trips.

When did you go from traveling casually to making this a full-time goal, and what motivated you to travel to every country?

It must have been around the time I reached 100 countries. I do travel goals step by step. First, I wanted to visit 50 countries, then 100, then all, then all territories. Visiting all countries is an entirely different story than just visiting 100 of them. If you visit all of the Europe, the Americas, and Southeast Asia, you are almost there. In the beginning, I never thought about going to countries like Afghanistan, Sierra Leone, Rwanda or Cameroon, but they all turned out to be great experiences. What put me off was my comfort zone. I was afraid of traveling to so-called dangerous countries, but the more I traveled, the more comfortable I became. It is all about doing enough research and work with companies others have successfully used. Regarding visiting all countries, I am happy I don't have to visit many different parts of each country for it to count. Many parts of Syria, Afghanistan, the Central African Republic (CAR), Somalia, Yemen, etc., are very dangerous, but you can visit at least one area that is safe. My motivation to visit all countries in the world is to see a bit of everything, but having traveled extensively in many countries, I must conclude I will never get to see a bit of everything. Your impression of a country very much depends on the city or area you get to visit. Going to Copenhagen isn't the same as going to my area of Thy. Going to Miami isn't the same as New York. Going to Beijing isn't the same as Xi'an, and so on. Even if you visit every region of the world, lots of differences can be found in most regions. I plan to visit every little spot of my country, but that would take a lifetime or more to do in many countries. By visiting every country, you get an impression of the parts of the countries you visit, but to see everything is not possible in a lifetime.

What have you done in your life to gain the freedom and finances to pursue as much travel as you have?

This is where I am different from any other person that has been to all countries, at least as far as I know. As others have written, to visit all the countries you must have time and money. I never had much money and especially not when I completed business school in the summer of 2010.

In late 2009, I received an e-mail from my bank manager saying we needed to talk, as my bank account was around minus $2,000. I explained I had too much expense but would bring it back to positive as soon as possible. The government of Denmark pays you to go to school, and after selling things I no longer needed, I had a bit of money in the spring of 2010, around $1,500 which was what I had to start up a blog.

I began traveling full-time after completing business school that summer. I purchased the domain, Hotelpassion.info and began contacting hotels telling them that I was young, flexible with my dates, had a blog, and was hoping to publish a book in the future. I immediately had results as most hotels offered a hugely discounted rate, that was cheaper than booking a 2-star hotel. Although I could have stayed cheaper in hostels, I saw the huge discount as a way to get my blog started and hopefully soon get complimentary stays. JW Marriott in Bangkok was the first hotel to offer me complimentary accommodation for a blog post. I was amazed as this opened up the possibility of traveling full-time for years to come, should this idea work with hotels around the world. I made an arrangement with a bank to have a loan with a very low-interest rate to see how many countries and luxury hotels I could manage to stay at before I would run out of money.

In 2012, 100-something countries in, I ran completely out of money. I went home and looked for a job but I didn't find one. Instead, I thought to myself, what if it would be possible to get some airlines to support my project to visit all countries? I immediately got results by showing my blog of more than 500 hotel reviews, and by being young with lots of countries visited. I decided to keep traveling on a few dollars a day and skip meals when no cheap food would be available. A combination of home stays, luxury hotels, and sleeping in public places made it possible for me to travel with no money for accommodations. Whenever an airline agreed to give me a ticket, I would cover that country and the nearby area with a low-cost carrier, public transport, or hitchhiking. I remember Pegasus Airlines sponsored me to go to Tbilisi, Georgia where I hitchhiked to their border with Azerbaijan and went with shared transport to Armenia. Shared and public transport is very cheap in most non-western countries and going overland can save you a lot of money. I would usually eat a lot at breakfast and buy cheap food at the supermarket for dinner. One of the advantages of staying in luxury hotels are the welcome amenities(that often are fruits), making it a suitable lunch replacement. As I will explain later, being focused on everything you spend, and being creative, is the way to visit every country if you don't have the money everyone thinks you need to chase the 193.

Today, I am still somewhat broke, but I manage to earn a little bit from my blog and from updating a company website once a week. It has given me the possibility to book tickets on low-cost airlines in advance and helped a lot with the stress levels of doing this project. I know I will become debt-free the day I have the time to focus on earning money instead of a constant focus on getting to the next country. While it can be stressful and sad at times to be poor on the road, I like "playing the game" of doing all countries on the cheap. One of the questions I get asked quite a lot is if all potential sponsors are supportive of my idea, the answer is 'no.' My trick and what works is to e-mail as many people as possible in each destination and usually things work out. Companies in the USA and the UK are the hardest to deal with, probably because they receive the largest amounts of requests while most companies in less-traveled countries say 'yes.'

Has there ever been a time where you considered abandoning your travel goals?

No, but there have been days where I felt like never traveling again. Usually, I wake up the following morning and send tons of e-mails to plan new trips. We can all have a bad day, but I would say I have had only a few in my travels if we take away the days I have suffered from food poisoning. I got use to loneliness on my early travels, and it's rarely been a problem in my years traveling full-time. I am used to being alone and miss my family at times, but a call always helps. The year 2011 stands out as a particularly bad year. My uncle and dog died on the same trip I was making, and this is where I felt the loneliest in my travels. My mother's call to my hotel room at Taj Cape Town stands out as a very sad night in my travels. Will anything ever make me consider abandoning my goal of visiting all territories? Yes! If I don't find a way to reach the British Indian Ocean Territory (BIOT) or the Norwegian claim of Antarctica I will have to be happy about "only" visiting all the countries defined by United Nations. It's beyond my control with some of the territories. I went to Samoa to catch a boat to Tokelau on a long-planned trip, but it was canceled the day before going. For now, it's about taking one destination at a time, and I hope to visit all territories eventually.

What do you consider to be your two favorite travel experiences, and why?

Among many, I would have to mention the many private island resorts in the Maldives and the entire country of

South Africa. It is close and difficult to pick two. The Maldives is a country where you can combine extraordinary natural beauty with some of the best hotel experiences money can buy. Many of the private islands resorts are outstanding. I have stayed at 38 resorts in the country and hoping to reach 100 in the summer of 2017. Safari lodges are another thing I love. You have the time of your life and a combination of world class safari with unique accommodation in a very remote location. It's wonderful, and Singita especially stands out with world-class accommodation, food and service. Besides world class safari, South Africa has world-class beaches, fantastic countryside, food and don't forget value for money. Travelers love Southeast Asia for its cost of living, but in my opinion, the value for money is far greater in South Africa as the food quality is much higher. Great pizza is less than $2, and restaurants equivalent of Michelin restaurants are not much more than a fast food meal in Denmark would cost you. In Denmark, I can't afford to eat at nice restaurants but can do it every day in South Africa. I have probably been in a taxi in Denmark five times in my entire life, but in South Africa the transportation app, Uber is cheap, and you have a private driver in minutes. The climate is nice year around. Only their winter can be cold at night, but that is the European summer and the best period to visit my family and friends in Denmark. Besides the above, Cape Town is my favorite city in the world, and I like the highly underrated Johannesburg where I recently lived for two months. South Africa has its problems like any other country, but it's where I feel the happiest and can wake up excited every day to the endless possibilities of things to do – opposite of living in Thy, Denmark.

What are the main things you seek to experience when you travel (culture, cities, nature, animals, adventure activities, etc.)?

I can appreciate any experience; however, I must admit I put countryside and nature over cities. Ideally, I would like to live close to an international city with easy access to have the endless possibilities. The French marketing organization Relais & Châteaux is a collection of properties that must meet many requirements, most of which I tend to look for in my travels. Small property, local experience, fantastic food, stunning location and with its unique character. I also like some of the overland journeys in Africa, as long as the road conditions are good, and dust and pollution can be avoided. This is one of the reasons I rank Rwanda very highly. Stunning nature, cultural experiences on good roads with hardly any dust or pollution. To sum up, after visiting all countries, I look for something unique, something new and something different in my travels while still being comfortable.

Looking back from when you started traveling to where you are now, in what ways, if any, has travel changed you?

I have completely changed in many respects, and I don't know where to start. I look back at a 17-year-old kid that did not know what to do with his life and how I look at things today. I was not a very open minded person ten years ago, but that has completely changed. I look at the world a lot differently today. Ten years ago, I never imagined I would prefer to live elsewhere than my beloved, Denmark. I had no idea I would love the places I end up loving.

Do you speak any foreign languages, and if so, which have been the most useful for you besides English?

Besides my mother tongue of Danish, I speak English fluently and can understand Norwegian and Swedish. Instead of learning new languages, I am doing my best to get my English as good as my Danish. I write travel articles in English, and it is very important to keep improving. I used to speak German back in my school days, but since I only need it once or twice a year, I have lost it. Italian is a beautiful language I love listening to, but I find it pointless to learn it as I never really need it. Spanish and French are useful for Latin America and West Africa, but I have always managed to find someone that speaks English, even in the poorest French-speaking countries in Africa.

What was the longest extended trip you have ever taken, when was it and where all did you go?

I did almost five months without visiting Denmark in 2015. I visited Germany, China, North Korea, Tibet, Mongolia, Hong Kong, Singapore, Thailand, Bhutan, Dubai and around two months at my base in South Africa, staying at different properties. Usually I would go back to see my family and friends for at least a couple of days every two-three months, but with a base in South Africa, a couple of times a year is fine.

What two countries have exceeded your expectations and which ones left you feeling underwhelmed, and why?

Overwhelmed:

Rwanda. This small nation, known for the 1994 genocide, is one of the best countries in the world to travel and different from most countries in this part of the world. It is very safe with relatively good infrastructure. President Kagame has done an excellent job of getting the country back on track, and you don't find the corruption you do in many other African countries. People are friendly, and you don't need to worry about being threatened to pay a bribe like I have many times through Africa. Rwanda is the 'Land of a Thousand Hills', and my trip from Kigali to Gisenyi and back stands out as the best bus journey I have ever been on. Fantastic and with shockingly good comfort. A clean $5 bus on good roads with hardly any dust or pollution. I also traveled overland to Bujumbura, Burundi and it's another beautiful journey I will never forget. Some parts of Africa are truly magical. I can only thank the people that inspired me to visit every country, as I would never have visited Rwanda if it wasn't for that goal.

South Africa is my favorite country for many reasons. When I was young I planned only to visit "safe countries", but I had heard so much about South Africa that I made a decision to go. At the time, I thought that if the best hotel in the world (awarded multiple times), Cape Grace, decided to accept my request, I will visit. They did, and I was overwhelmed with the city, its people, the food and just about everything about Cape Town. When I am not in South Africa, I constantly think about it.

Underwhelmed:

I thought Sal Island, Cape Verde would be a nice, beautiful beach destination, but it was instead a boring place for middle-class Europeans with nothing to see. Big tourists resort with their low-quality all-inclusive concepts, and that's it. I am not planning to visit it again.

Bora Bora was another disappointment. It is one of the most beautiful destinations in the world but insanely overpriced with really bad service. I very much disliked the fact that many resorts hire lots of Europeans to do service that takes it as a vacation instead of providing the world-class service you would expect for the price. I don't travel as far away from Europe as possible to stay in a resort where the majority of the staff is from France. Instead, I can recommend to fly into Raiatea instead and stay at Le Taha'a, a member of Relais & Châteaux, with fantastic food and great service from local staff.

When you travel, do you prefer to go with others or solo, and why?

I very rarely travel with someone. Mostly as my friends and family in Denmark has little or no interest in world travel. I now have like-minded friends in other countries, and I hope to travel less solo in the future. Traveling alone is great for a journey to every country as you constantly have things to plan and organize, but experiences are always better when shared!

What has been your most uncomfortable mode of transportation?

Buses in Africa. The nearly 30-hour bus journey from Lomé, Togo to Niamey, Niger is the worst I have ever done. I did it as the flights were very expensive and impossible for me to get sponsored. I thought the journey would go through Burkina Faso (where I had a double entry visa), but they instead went through Benin where I had no visa. I had already been told by the Benin Embassy in Rabat that I didn't need a visa, but I was told to go back to Lomé to obtain a visa. I began to panic as I had a flight to catch from Ouagadougou, Burkina Faso and had no time to wait in Lomé for the Benin visa. I told them about my situation and said I was willing to pay extra if necessary. The bus driver also wanted to help and spoke English. The bus driver asked me to pay a surprisingly low amount, and that was enough. I was given a transit visa and off we went. Before taking the Lomé to Niamey bus in the evening, I had slept one hour in the lobby of Palm Beach Hotel. I expected to sleep on the bus journey, but the road condition, with dust and sand flying in the air, made it impossible and the worst journey I have ever done.

What is the strangest thing you've seen/experienced while traveling?

The entire surreal experience of North Korea where it felt like everything was staged. North Korea is not one of my favorite countries, but it is without a doubt the most interesting country to visit and I would highly recommend it to anyone. Koryo Tours does an excellent job where everything is well-organized from beginning to end. The guides meet you at the airport, and the first stop is an empty, beautiful park where it feels like you are part of a movie set. Although you can't travel by yourself in North Korea, having the guides around wasn't a problem and actually enjoyable. The tour operator prepares you well for what you can and can't do, and you just follow that. North Korea is not a place to worry about comfort on the ground. The tour operator and the guides are up to the same standards as you will find in many other countries. The hotels, on the other hand, are not. It's also one of the few places left where people smoke everywhere. I was lucky to be staying in a quite empty hotel which was acceptable for sleeping. And that is all you use your hotel for in North Korea. It's an adventure from morning to the evening where you will see some of the strangest things in a country that is entirely different from any other in the world.

What are the best and worst meals you have ever eaten while traveling, and where was it?

I have eaten at many Michelin-starred restaurants, and it is not small overpriced courses like people that haven't been to any believes. It is simply the best food money can buy. The worst meals would be one of the four times I have been food poisoned. It might have been more if we count all the times I've had problems breathing after a meal. It started in Bali in 2013 where I went to the emergency room as I couldn't breathe. It took only a few days to recover. I am not sure what caused it, but most probably a Japanese soup at InterContinental, which I still wonder why I had to try. Then followed the worst experience of my life. Food poisoning in the Andaman Islands. The hotel made me fish soup and after around 20 minutes I was in the worst pain I have ever been. I got a little better and was able to fly back to the mainland, but as soon as I am on the plane I can't breathe. The cabin crew gave me oxygen, and I got three empty seats to lay down. It was the worst flight of my life, and I was in constant pain. I couldn't even sit up for landing. Back on the mainland, in Chennai, followed the loneliest week of my life in bed and big pain. The hospital did not provide me with the right medicine at times, and I was completely stressed out. Since then I have been very careful about what I eat and have no desire to try local food in third world countries anymore. In the following months after that fish soup in the Andaman Islands, I had constant problems after eating. I don't forget a bus on the American highway at night where I couldn't breathe and would have left the bus if I could. My advice is to spend a little time on finding the right things to eat for every meal when you travel in third world countries. You can't be too careful.

Out of the thousands of places you've stayed around the world, what have been your best and worst accommodations?

Best: Singita's collection of safari lodges are the best experiences money can buy. Aman Resorts and some of the Relais & Châteaux country hotels are also up there. Glenmere Mansion and Ballyfin are two independent properties not to be missed. Singita comes with a price tag, and only when you stay there, you will understand how a "hotel" can cost so much money.

Worst: Tuvalu's only hotel, Vaiaku Lagi Hotel. I spent hours cleaning it. It would have been better for me to sleep in a tent on a beach like I did in Kiribati on the same trip.

What is your favorite "off the beaten path" destination, and why?

Besides Rwanda, which I mentioned above, I like a lot of other less-traveled places. The small, volcanic Caribbean island of Saba is a special experience and unlike the rest of the Caribbean. No beach, a population of approximately 2,000 people and a unique ecosystem make it well worth visiting. Flights are cheap from Sint Maarten so if you are ever planning a visit to that Caribbean island, make sure to go to Saba for at least a day. While, I am not certain if I would ever live on an island, I love visiting most small islands. The people are usually very friendly; they usually have their unique culture and hitchhiking is both comfortable and enjoyable almost everywhere. Sitting on an empty beach on Tinian Island in the Pacific was a special moment as well as visiting Palau, one of the smallest independent countries in the world. I have named it the easiest country in the world to hitchhike on my website. When it comes to small islands, I also have to mention safety. It is very safe in most of these places, and if you are in doubt if you can hitchhike, a small island is a place to try it first. I have hitchhiked with more than 1,000 cars and nothing ever happened to me. Even Brazil has a very safe island called Fernando de Noronha. Another easy place to hitchhike and although it does have some tourism, I think we can put it in the category as one of my favorite off-the-beaten-path destinations.

What were your most challenging countries to visit, and why?

Equatorial Guinea. First, the embassy in Pretoria, South Africa told me they would like to help me, but they did not get approval from Malabo. Secondly, I decided to give Libreville, Gabon a try as other travelers have had success there recently. I waited for a total of nearly ten hours over four visits before I was guaranteed a visa if I came back four days later. I had met with the ambassador and negotiated the price down to $140 instead of the $300 they wanted. Other travelers have been asked to pay $600 at this embassy and similar amounts at some of their other embassies around the world. I came back Monday morning and was told sorry; it is not possible, and there was nothing they could do. I was shocked. I had spent an extra four days in Libreville for this important visa I never got. I later got it in Lagos, Nigeria after explaining my project. Besides Equatorial Guinea, Ghana was a difficult visa to get. I tried at many different embassies, but only managed to get a 48-hour transit visa in Abidjan, which didn't do Ghana justice. I loved the journey, though, which was surprisingly comfortable. Abidjan to Accra is a beautiful journey in a bus of a Western standard. The shorter Accra to Lomé journey is nice as well, but the border crossing was a bit scary as I had been told by many to be very careful with my belongings.

Of which travel accomplishments are you most proud?

I am proud of the past six years. From being broke with an uncertain future to a total of nearly 300 countries and territories visited. Getting all these sponsorships approved and people believing in my project makes me proud. Rovos Rail, The Blue Train, Four Seasons Explorer Cruise, Singita Lodges, many Michelin restaurants and Four Seasons resorts, among more than 1,000 other luxury hotels I have stayed at. I am also proud of being able to visit so-called dangerous countries on my own, and that I have hitchhiked with more than 1,000 cars around the world. When I look back how afraid I was of visiting London alone when I was 17, I have come a long way.

Do you remember encountering particular people that have left a lasting impression on you?

Too many to mention. Hundreds if not thousands of people have gone out of their way to help me. The people that have picked me up and insisted on taking me straight to my the place I'm staying for the night. Hitchhiking at midnight from the airport in St. Maarten to Radisson Blu Resort in St. Martin was quite a journey. A girl felt sorry for me and took me all the way, as she knew I would not get any rides. An Iranian English teacher also picked me up on the highway at Tehran International Airport and showed me a bit of Tehran before dropping me off at my hotel. The Icelandic businessman in Papua New Guinea that gave me a lot of money after a lecture in Port Moresby. The Air Burkina employee that felt sorry that no hotels would host me in Ouagadougou and offered me to stay with his family. Besides this, he showed me a lot of his city on his motorbike. Jamal, who is responsible for foreign press in Libya, not only guaranteed me a visa but also contacted Afriqiyah Airways to get me free flights, all within 20 minutes after adding him on What's App. When in Libya, he took me to a press conference with the Prime Minister of the government based in Tripoli. Around a minute after the press conference, I was asked to come on stage to meet the Prime Minister and have my photo taken with him.

If you could travel back in time, to which era and place would you go, and why?

I think we are living in a very exciting time, and my travels around the world would surely not have been possible if it wasn't for the internet. I like old movies and going back to the 30s and 40s would be interesting, as long as I can quickly return to 2016 again.

Can you describe any particular situation where you felt completely out of your comfort zone?

Visiting Port-au-Prince, Haiti and the Cité Soleil area that United Nations consider "The most dangerous place on earth." My tour operator in Port-au-Prince had never taken anyone there before, but we went in for a short visit in a bulletproof car. A few minutes after we left we had a car accident, and I still wonder what would have happened if we had the accident inside Cité Soleil. Visiting Syria in December 2015 and Libya in February 2016 was not too bad compared to Cité Soleil.

What are your three favorite cities in the world, and why?

Cape Town, Rio de Janeiro and Queenstown. Three of the most beautiful cities in the world, although Queenstown is perhaps too small to be called a city. The three cities all have fantastic food, friendly people and high quality of life. It's probably the three cities where I have felt the happiest and all feel different from your typical big international city. Cape Town and Rio de Janeiro have beaches and Queenstown has stunning natural scenery.

What is the ideal amount of time you prefer to travel on each trip before you are ready to go home and take a break?

If I had the possibility, I would like to travel for just a week or two so I can plan each trip perfectly. My problem has been not living in a city with an international airport, but instead in a remote part of Denmark. There are a lot of costs involved getting to and from airports, and with my budget, it does not make sense just to go away for a week or two. I have recently moved my based to South Africa, and it is perfect for flying to other African countries, but not ideal for world travel. It looks like my idea of going away for a week or two at a time will remain an idea. At least for the near future.

In your opinion, where are the most beautiful places on Earth?

There are many beautiful places on Earth, but beauty can be many different things. Let me mention some. The Maldives, the Seychelles and Bora Bora are all beautiful places to visit, but for the experience, I like the Maldives for its many private island resorts. Cape Town is the most beautiful city in the world, probably followed by Rio de Janeiro and Sydney. The nature of New Zealand and desert of Namibia is also not to be missed. The island of Socotra also deserves to be mentioned as a very special place that hardly sees any tourists.

If you had an unlimited budget and space and time were no object, what would your perfect travel day look like (for example: start your morning in Bora Bora; afternoon on a safari in Kenya; night in Australia, etc.)?

I would wake up in a water villa at Gili Lankanfushi in the Maldives, followed by their fantastic breakfast. Lunch at Samhoud Places in Amsterdam, followed by a quick safari at Singita Grumeti Reserves in Tanzania. Late afternoon would be a bus journey across Rwanda, before flying down to Cape Town in the evening to stay at the Mount Nelson hotel in my favorite city in the world.

Which three countries would you recommend for adventurous travelers to visit, and why?

Rwanda, which I have previously mentioned.

Palau: The easiest country to hitchhike and with very friendly people.

West Africa: It's a region, though, not a country. A trip through this part of the world is an eye opener, and you will hardly see any tourists in most of these places. I did most of it overland, and while it can very uncomfortable, it is in many ways fantastic and something every world traveler should try.

If you had just one travel story to share with someone, what would it be?

There are too many equally good stories. Something that changed me, the way I traveled and made me a more brave traveler, was my first big hitchhiking adventure. It was 126 kilometers between Otahuna Lodge and Grasmere Lodge, two of the best luxury lodges in New Zealand. I have hitch-hiked to many remote hotels around the world since this one and had many wild adventures, but this was the first. It was surprisingly easy, and I got there late afternoon, just in time for dinner. The following morning I had planned to get up very early and hitchhike back to catch an early $20 Jetstar flight to Queenstown. That plan changed quickly when the waitress told me the owners had decided to take me back to the airport to make sure I would make my flight. One of the nicest gestures in my travels, Without hitchhiking, it would have been difficult to complete my project at a young age as taxis are very costly. I have been in many situations where an expensive, overpriced taxi would be the only option if I had not had the "ability" to hitchhike.

Do you ever feel you have missed out on certain aspects of life while away from home as you travel so much?

As I am still in my 20's, it is perhaps a bit too early to conclude. When I read the first edition of Chasing 193, I saw many of the world's most traveled had missed out on many aspects of life. Many were single men in their 50's or 60's, and many had no children. Reading the book made me happy about my decision not to chase every single region of the world or the hundreds of remote uninhabited islands. I have missed out on a certain aspect of life traveling around the world for the past years, but nothing that is important to me except having a relationship.

What advice would you give to others who would like to travel to every country?

It would be an endless list of things that can make a journey to every country a lot easier. It's easy to say, 'Just do like me. Do a travel blog, set a goal to visit all countries in the world and e-mail a lot of companies'. As I was the first with such a plan, it will probably be lot more difficult for someone that would like to copy it. Most people say you should make money and take time, but that might take many years. Instead, it is possible for almost anyone to visit all countries in the world even without a blog, if he or she sticks to ten rules:

1. Be focused.

Decide if you really want to do this or not. Decide to do it a hundred percent. Keep in mind it takes a lot of time to plan trips on a very low budget. I made a decision early on to sacrifice and reminded myself often, 'You can't have it all'.

2. Have a zero budget for accommodation.

Use Couchsurfing.com and other sites to stay in the private homes of travelers around the world. If you don't manage to find a place to stay for the night, sleep in public places. Many airports are fine. If you do have a bit of money, keep a small budget for accommodation and use Airbnb as your plan B. On Airbnb tell the host you are on a low budget and on a journey to every country and bargain hard. Part of your plan B could also be the last-minute hotel booking apps such as HotelTonight and HotelQuickly. I don't like staying at hostels, but if you do that is of course also an option. If you are like me and need a private room, some hostels have private rooms, and again: Bargain hard and explain your project.

3. Low-Cost Airlines and no check-in bag.

Low-cost airlines are the way to go, and they are all over the world. Sign up for their newsletters with special offers and get tickets for close to nothing. Ryanair, Easyjet, Air Asia, Tiger Airways, Spirit Air (travel light), Wizz Air, Norwegian, Wow Air and Fastjet are especially valuable.

4. Low-Cost Buses.

While low-cost airlines have been around for years, low-cost buses are the new thing, and they are all over the world. Book in advance and you can bus tickets nearly free of charge in many countries. Megabus.com is a website where any budget travel should spend a lot of time. New York to Atlanta for a dollar is not a scam; it's a reality. You should also check out Greyhound Express, Naked Bus, Boltbus.com, Ouibus, Berlinlinenbus, National Express, Mein Fernbus, Rød Billet, Abildskou, Polskibus, Simple Express, Swebus, Omnibus, Student Agency Bus and hundredths of other low-cost bus companies around the world. Google is your friend.

5. Be creative with visas.

Visas are the number one thing we, world travelers, dislike about what we do. If I could buy a special passport with visa-free entry to all countries, I would have been to all countries two years ago, I'm sure. It's hard work and research pays off. All embassies are different. In Europe, you might need an invitation to an African country you want to visit, but you can get it in one of their African embassies in a day with no requirements. I can recommend the following: Sudan visa in Aswan; Ivory Coast visa in Nouakchott; Cameroon visa in Libreville; Central African Republic visa in Pretoria; South Sudan visa in Nairobi; Ghana and Burkina Faso visa in Abidjan, to just name a few. Rabat, Morocco is, however, the number one place to get visas for African countries. Rent an apartment for two weeks in Rabat and get as many visas as you can. Guinea, Guinea-Bissau, Mauritania, Niger and Liberia were all easy to obtain with no requirements besides passport photos and filling the forms. If I had the time, many other African countries were also possible, including Mali, Republic of Congo and Ivory Coast – all of which confirmed it would be easy and take a day or two. Finally, contact local tour operators and ask if they can help with a visa on arrival in countries where you need a visa. You will be surprised you can get a visa on arrival in many countries where you thought you needed to visit an embassy or apply in advance.

6. Never take taxis: Hitchhike.

As I explained elsewhere, hitchhiking has saved me a lot of money. It is difficult to take the first step. I would recommend doing it on a Pacific island for the first time, where everyone does it and where it is considered completely normal. I met an American in Kiribati that didn't like hitchhiking and took expensive taxis in the Pacific. We ended up traveling together around the Pacific. I insisted we should always hitchhike. Today, he is a hitchhiker himself and loves it as much as I do. There are many places where hitchhiking is difficult, but hardly ever impossible. I would recommend using Hitchwiki.org as a good guide for hitchhiking and, of course, my guide to hitchhiking the world that you can find on my website, HenrikTravel.com. If you for some reasons don't plan to visit the Pacific anytime soon, you might also try on the smaller Caribbean islands. However, for the warmest experience, I highly recommend Iran where I refused to pay for an overpriced taxi and instead put out my thumb at the international airport in Tehran and was taken straight to my hotel room by one of the warmest people I have met in my travels. The Iranians are the friendliest people in the world, and I think it will be a real tourist destination in the future. Oh, you can get a visa on arrival easily in Tehran with a letter from a tour operator. Easy process. What are you waiting for?

7. Avoid restaurants. Eat at Supermarkets.

If you are broke, get to the local supermarket anywhere in the world and eat the cheapest, but acceptable, food you can find.

8. Follow actively on Twitter.

Follow travel bloggers and deal specific accounts on Twitter to not miss out on free points, miles, promotions and incredible deals.

9. If American: Miles.

Americans have a significant advantage when it comes to frequent flyer miles with their endless list of great promotions. I am not an expert in this field as we don't have these possibilities in Denmark. Instead, I would recommend following the following blogs: The Points Guy, One Mile at a Time, Million Mile Secret, Frugal Travel Guy and Extra Pack of Peanuts.

10. Be positive and thankful.

Be grateful to each and every person that helps you on your journey. We can all have a bad day, but do your best to be positive and treat everyone you meet as they treat you. You will have stressful days, and you will have days where everything goes wrong. It's part of "the game". Don't rush through all countries. Spend most time in the countries you love, so your love of travel stays with you. You can easily get tired of traveling if you are constantly in places you don't enjoy. Remember a journey to all countries takes time. For most people that attempt doing it, it takes almost a whole lifetime.

For someone who has been almost everywhere, what still gets you excited about packing your bags again?

I like traveling light and even did a six-month experiment traveling without any bags at all. I don't like packing, so nothing gets me exciting about that. I, however, still get excited about visiting new destinations I haven't been to, going back to my favorite places, or having an extraordinary experience, at a world-class resort or Michelin-starred restaurant. By visiting all of the countries of the world, you can say you have been everywhere, but you have not necessary experienced everywhere. On some days, I love traveling so much I feel like exploring every single day until I die, as there is so much to see and do. I, however, realized that constantly being on the move, without breaks, is hard – especially in third world countries. I will continue to travel a lot, but I believe I will never get the same initial excitement that I did at the beginning, where everything was new. There will, however, always be exciting parts of every trip and that keeps me going. The most important thing for me is not to be stressed and push myself too hard to travel constantly, as I did in 2014. I was mentally shut down with stress for a few weeks before Emotional Freedom Techniques helped me. Since then, I have become much better at not pushing myself too hard. Work smart, not hard.

Looking ahead, what travel plans and goals are you still pursuing, and what is on your "Bucket List"?

Visiting all countries is special and unique, but besides this, I would also like to complete all 325 countries, territories and unique destinations defined by the Travelers' Century Club (TCC), but due to the logistics in getting to the most difficult ones, I have no set deadline for this. Rather than calling it a "Bucket List", it is more short-term goals. My other goals are to complete all American states and stay at 100 private island resorts in the Maldives. I truly love the experience of staying at these resorts, and the USA is just a wonderful country to travel around with a lot to offer. Even after completing the 50 states, I plan to visit often. Regarding travel, I have nothing else on my "Bucket List". For almost six years, I have hardly had anything but travel in my life, and I have sacrificed a lot to get this far in completing my travel goals. Life is more than just traveling, and although I want it always to be a big part of my life, it should not be all you have. At least, not for long.

Harald Buben, Austria

(Harald Buben – Barvikha Hotel & Spa Moscow)

Where did you grow up, and what was your early life like?

I was born in Graz, where the most famous living Austrian, Arnold Schwarzenegger, is from. Since then, I grew up and always lived in the Styrian town of Groebming. This is a typical Austrian alpine settlement, within the Enns River Valley, surrounded by high mountains, picturesque houses, and an ideal place for skiing, hiking and mountaineering. There is all-year-round skiing on the glacier of the 3,000 meters high Dachstein Mountain. We are less overrun by tourists than the neighboring Schladming. The area is part of the UNESCO World Heritage Site Hallstatt - Dachstein - Salzkammergut. My childhood was accordingly idyllic. As a kid, we all spent lots of time outside and grew fit and healthy in this beautiful nature here. Maybe there was an early longing to look outside of the valley, but we all love to come back to our "Heimat" as we say here. Starting at age 14, I spent each summer in the United States, working in the pizza restaurant of my Italian fatherly friend in Atlantic City. Tony taught me early on to work harder, be quicker and sleep less than others. When I came back to school from my holidays, I not only had my pockets full of money but I also spoke English like in an Italo-American mafia movie.

What was the first international trip you took, and what do you remember most about it?

My first more extreme trip was in two Suzuki LJ 80 soft top soft doors Cabrio 4x4s with a Swiss friend to the border of the Congo, and back. I was 18 and just had my driver license. At the time, there was no GPS. We were completely wild, didn't give a damn, and got severely lost in the Algerian Tassili Range. After several days of heat and fear, we finally hit the road to Tamanrasset. I never liked preparation and prefer to battle it out. I have total confidence that in the end, all will be good. Well, on that trip we had several close calls, including being robbed at gunpoint in Nigeria, and the stress deteriorated our friendship to the point where we separated on the way back. I drove alone through the eastern border of Algeria into Morocco, which has now been closed for a long time, and never saw my friend again. I know of course that he made it back alive.

When did you go from traveling casually to making this a full-time goal, and what motivated you to travel to every country?

Most of my travels have been for work. We have clients in more than 130 countries. One day, about ten years ago, I was sitting in the living room of such a client, a well-known Formula 1 driver, together with another guest from Germany. We immediately clicked and talked about travel continuously. I thought that I was quite a well-traveled person but soon realized that I was doing the same places over and over again. That person was Kolja, who is also featured in this book, who introduced me to the idea of systematic country collecting. A couple of weeks later we met again at a congress of the Most Traveled People in Munich with Charles Veley and Jorge Sanchez, among several other extreme travelers. I have been hooked ever since, and I try to slowly knock off the whole UN country list, in accordance with my business travel. I am now at about 170 countries. As a matter of fact, I have traveled to places just for the country point, and then won new clients for my business there. That is, of course, the best of all worlds.

What have you done in your life to gain the freedom and finances to pursue as much travel as you have?

After the pizza connection in the States and graduating from high school, I did my first round-the-world-trip together with my childhood buddy Christian. By coincidence we traveled through Coober Peddy, the world's opal capital in Australia and, believe it or not, out of the blue we started exporting opal stones to Austria which was a really good business for a while. Nevertheless, Christian and I finished our university studies alongside. I am a certified lawyer but never practiced. Those gemstones introduced us to jewelers in Europe and the luxury goods and watchmaking industry. We saw a demand and started producing sophisticated packaging for luxury watches. Then with the renaissance of expensive mechanic watches and the arrival of watch collectors we saw the demand for watchwinders. Later we put these watchwinders into objects like collector cupboards, large cigar humidors, or stand-up tourbillon clocks. Last not least, we now build whole safe rooms for clients with collections of precious watches, jewelry, antiques, guns or other collectibles. We have our own manufacture in the traditional jewelry city of Pforzheim in Germany, but our HQ still remains in Groebming. Our business requires a lot of R&D, so we need to re-invest a lot of profit, and, therefore, my travel needs to be compliant with our cost controlling.

Has there ever been a time where you considered abandoning your travel goals?

I have on two occasions deleted my MTP (Most Traveled People) account because I just didn't want to be bothered anymore by the idea of country collecting, but I always came back. I very much look forward to the moment when I have knocked off all the UN countries, and I am a free man again. I am saying this with a big grin of course. It's an addiction. Quite recently, in 2015, I had so much hardship on one single trip that I pondered abandoning my travels altogether. My ticket started with a flight to the US but continued with later stops in Panama, South America, Russia, Iran, Turkey, Sudan and Chad. I should have nicknamed it the "axis of evil". First, they didn't want to let me onboard in Vienna with such an obviously crazy routing, then I spent several hours being interrogated by border police in LA. When I showed them pictures of my company and the clients, in particular, "Arnold" that persuaded them that I could finally enter the country. Two days later, I rented a car at Asuncion airport in Paraguay at three a.m. and drove into town. Two bastards on motorbikes shot into my rear tire, tore open the doors of my limping car, and robbed my Berluti handbag, including cash, and worse the iPads and all that. It was my first attack in 28 years of travel, after that incident in Nigeria. The next trouble on the trip came when I was deported from Istanbul-Atatürk Airport. The Turks had not properly stamped me in on my prior entry from Northern Iraq, and this incident backfired. Now I'm all good again. When I stood in the heat of the Chad-Cameroon border the next day, trying to explain the guards that I only wanted to do a border walk, it almost became too much to bear. I know that I probably travel differently from other people. I do at least 250 flights per year, I can do up to 10 days and nights without proper sleep, and I have six passports, which rotate all the time, for visa applications.

What do you consider to be your two favorite travel experiences, and why?

The cross-Sahara trip at age 18 was unbeatable, even if it went sour at the end. It was all new to me, I love the desert, and driving endlessly by car. Nowadays, I could switch on the motor in Groebming and switch it off in Cape Town, without stopping in between. It's just so hard to find a suitable co-driver, haha. The other favorite trip was through all of Russia, mostly in winter. We first drove to the Nordkapp, entered Russia near Murmansk, continued via the Caucasus to the Caspian Sea, onwards on the Trans-Siberian Highway and the Road of Bones, finally to Magadan, Siberia. It was total madness and total freedom. Often we drove day and night. We both love smoking cigars in the car, and this time, it meant lowering the windows at temperatures of -50°C to -62°C outside. Crossing the Verkhoyansk Range, near the Pole of Cold, in the middle of the night, on slippery earth roads, a 500-meter drop to your right, in those killer temperatures, with no human settlement hundreds of kilometers around, that was the ultimate thrill. But I was always confident we would make it in the end.

What are the main things you seek to experience when you travel (culture, cities, nature, animals, adventure activities, etc.)?

I have zero interest in culture and sightseeing. For me traveling is about adventure and being in motion all the time. There is a lot I learn from my clients and friends about the local situation, so I never watch TV or read the newspapers. It makes a big difference if you have access to good information.

Looking back from when you started traveling to where you are now, in what ways, if any, has travel changed you?

I have probably always been the same. I also always treat people with the same respect. My father taught me to be optimistic and develop a good karma. Everything comes back to you, either in what you do good or bad. I have donated to many people in need, and maybe one thing the traveling showed me is that it is not correct to speak about a third world, hungry children in Africa, poverty in India, or so on. It is disrespectful to those people. When I identify a real problem somewhere I will be part of the solution, but I will never subscribe to an abstract charity need and transfer money to some abstract charity organization. I always help directly.

Do you speak any foreign languages, and if so, which have been the most useful for you besides English?

I speak English and a bit of Russian, and two or three funny words in many other languages.

What was the longest extended trip you have ever taken, when was it and where all did you go?

That may have been three years ago.

I started driving early in the morning to Vienna airport doing a new speed record with my Porsche Panamera: 317km/h on a regular German highway. It gave me the necessary push to do this upcoming trip knowing the adrenalin should last. And otherwise, I would have missed my plane. I flew to London for all day business to continue in the late afternoon to Larnaca, Cyprus to have an evening meeting, then rushing to the Turkish part of Cyprus to collect the point. At night, I took the convenient flight to Beirut arriving there at 0.30 a.m. where my good friend Dr. Rony, the owner of the LCU University, picked me up. Beirut is famous for its nightlife, and we sat together till sunrise. The whole day followed by meetings till the late night when I took off to Singapore to visit the Formula 1 Grand Prix the next day. In Singapore, we have our own flagship store, so it was business, Formula 1 paddock, and then all night karaoke with business partners. Again no bed. Then I met my closest friend Kolja to do the Micronesia Island Hopper together. From Singapore straight by taxi to Kuala Lumpur. We were very lucky we made it on the plane because the Cebu Pacific flight to Manila leaves from a different airport. This was the start of a crazy string of flights, again without seeing a hotel bed for a long time. Our Continental Micronesia plane had stops in Palau, Guam, Truk, Pohnpei, Kwajalein, Majuro, Honolulu to finally reach Los Angeles in the morning, although by now our internal clock was completely screwed up. We made sure to get immigration stamps in each port. In Guam and Honolulu, we even had time to go downtown for the length of a cigar. From Los Angeles, after another full day of business meetings, we took the night flight to Mexico City, landing during another picturesque sunrise. A quick shower in the airport hotel, then business meetings in Mexico City and an evening drive to Guadalajara where we found the first real bed in the Camino Real Hotel after 70 hours on the road, or rather, mostly in the air. Next morning, in a rental car we drove 1,000km through our missing northern Mexican country points (Mexico states) to Monterrey, from where I flew alone to Tijuana, to cross the border by taxi and in another rental car to LA. Here I immediately boarded Turkish Airlines for the night flight via Istanbul to Kazakhstan. Had a business meeting that day in Astana and Almaty, then at night to Bishkek, Kyrgyzstan by taxi. Evening business dinner at the Hyatt Regency at 11 p.m. and then a night taxi to Osh, which is a 10 hours drive. I have to say I slept in the taxi to be fresh for the onward trip to Khujand, which is one of the more exotic border crossings on this planet, changing cars three times. I was under pressure to reach my Khujand flight at night via Moscow back to Istanbul where I arrived the next day to meet my friend Georg. Istanbul was one-day business and two days partying and drinking. On this trip of 14 days, I had only two nights in a hotel. Average two hours sleep, and every night lots of Corona beers, besides working like crazy. The good thing is that I can work on aircraft, and I usually manage to answer all my email backlog on long haul flights.

What two countries have exceeded your expectations and which ones left you feeling underwhelmed, and why?

Since I never followed the mainstream media, my expectations were never distorted. I expect things to be more or less the same everywhere, and usually, they are. I see no advantage in seeking the differences. In most countries I found to have something in common with the people. I think that a typical tourist sees the differences, a real traveler sees over the differences, and a true global citizen should be at home everywhere.

When you travel, do you prefer to go with others or solo, and why?

My business travel is inevitably solo, and sometimes the country collecting too. But there is nothing more joyful than reviewing a rough day on the road with a Cohiba, an ice-cold Corona, and a close, warm friend.

What has been your most uncomfortable mode of transportation?

We had bought a wreck of a Nissan Patrol in Gambia and drove day and night through the Casamance, Bissau, Guinea, Sierra Leone to the inauguration party of President Ellen Johnson-Sirleaf. The car constantly had a new problem, lights off, clutch jumping, petrol filter jammed, but it always bounced back like a human being. The roads, in particular in Guinea, were flooded and sometimes unpassable. It was incredibly tough to make it to Monrovia in time, but we did.

What is the strangest thing you've seen/experienced while traveling?

After a business meeting in Ulaanbaatar, I took a taxi to the Russian border where I arrived 5 minutes before closure. I absolutely had to make it over the border, because my buddy already waited in Chita in Siberia. After much arguing, the Russians let me pass, but in order to punish me, they let me walk ca. 1 kilometer of no-mans land, instead of offering a car ride. When I reached the main road, I was very luck that a taxi was still there. It was -40°C, I wore a normal business suit and coat, and I had dragged my Tumi trolley behind me without gloves. It was unbelievably cold, even for an Austrian born in the mountains. When my taxi reached Ulan Ude, after several hours, I was still shivering. Then I took the wheel from my exhausted driver and tackled the remaining 700km night drive to Chita myself.

What are the best and worst meals you have ever eaten while traveling, and where was it?

My favorite is big steaks, and I know a good steakhouse in most places, from Buenos Aires to Tokyo. Funnily, I particularly like the food quality in Russia. That's because they don't use so much chemistry and antibiotics. GQ in Moscow is outstanding. Or the restaurant complex in Krasnoyarsk. Also the Spasso in Bangkok. And Bareiss in Baiersbronn, Black Forest. Of course, nobody cooks better than the Austrians, and the Steirereck in Vienna and Pogusch, Styria is a recommendation I like to give to all our visitors. Meatballs with lots of melted Parmesan and linguini on the side would be my last wish, but I doubt they will serve it when I'm confronted with my final situation.

Out of the thousands of places you've stayed around the world, what have been your best and worst accommodations?

Since I sleep no more than 2/3 hours in most cases, I get along with anything. But regarding ambiance, I particularly like the Barvikha in Moscow. The patio at the Four Seasons Mexico City. The Sheraton Grande Sukhumvit, where I have a special suite. The Faena in Buenos Aires. La Reserve in Geneva and the Chedi Andermatt, both in Switzerland. The Alasia in Limassol, Cyprus, and together with my wife, the Reethi Rah in the Maldives.

What is your favorite "off the beaten path" destination, and why?

Chechnya, because I have good friends and good business there, and I could experience the transformation from the danger zone to a Dubai-style boom town. All of the Caucasus has treated me well, be it Georgia, Armenia, or Azerbaijan and I was among the first foreigners to recently cross the newly opened border from Dagestan to Azerbaijan near Derbent, alone by taxi. I also liked the Turkana region and

Omo Valley in the Ilemi Triangle of Kenya, Ethiopia, and South Sudan.

What were your most challenging countries to visit, and why?

Entering Libya, in March 2011, during the Arab Spring was quite a challenge. We drove from Cairo to Benghazi and wore bulletproof vests.

Of which travel accomplishments are you most proud?

I learned to travel with minimum luggage. My bag fits under the seat in front of me, but I still look crisp and clean for business after ten days on the road. Traveling light adds so much comfort to any trip.

Do you remember encountering particular people that left a lasting impression with you?

Because of our products, I am fortunate to meet really extraordinary people. At least a dozen heads of state, many Forbes-list members, including the very top, and some famous actors and artists. And behind the lesser known names, there are likewise many extraordinary life stories. We don't advertise our client relationships, so I can only talk about two:

With Michael Schumacher, I had the pleasure of learning to skydive, free-falling from 3,000 meters, in Eloy, Arizona. That was an amazing trip with added thrills. I also had some adrenaline experiences with him in fast cars.

My fellow Austrian Arnold Schwarzenegger is such an inspirational and positive personality, a cigar aficionado like me, and a big watch collector, of course.

And then there were some other encounters, at random on the road:

I was in Saudi-Arabia's capital Riyadh, in the lobby of the Four Seasons Hotel, with our very young store manager Faiz, originally from Eritrea, when Gordon Brown came in with a small entourage. Faiz immediately walked towards him and greeted him like an old acquaintance, introduced us, conversed in a short, small talk. When I asked Faiz afterward how he came to know the former British prime minister, he smilingly admitted that he had never met him before, but while in the country he certainly wanted to give him a friendly welcome. That's chutzpah. And a good habitus. Undoubtedly, Gordon Brown thought that Faiz was a young local VIP whose face he had forgotten and probably wanted to play it safe and polite. We couldn't stop smiling for hours.

Another memorable encounter was in the middle of nowhere in the hinterland of Liberia, in a small village called Nela, where our car broke down, and we found the young operator of a repair shop and petrol station, the plastic canister version, not yet with modern pumps. Dudley was only in his early twenties but he already traded in building materials, and he desperately looked for financing for a dump truck and a water tank. In this war-torn country, everything was in short supply, but demand was growing and this hands-on junior entrepreneur, despite the odds, was really on the way to making it big. Whereas the corrupt political scene in the capital Monrovia and the constant offerings of shady diamonds or oil deals rather put me off, Dudley and I are still in touch by email.

If you could travel back in time, to which era and place would you go, and why?

It is sad that the era of supersonic flights ended with the Concorde, and given the amount of time I spend on airplanes, I wish that this technology would come back. Including in Russia, which is so big, and traveling in their

Tupolev 144 Concordski at Mach 2 would really make sense for me.

Can you describe any particular situation where you felt completely out of your comfort zone?

I immediately drop into a depression when the movement stops. Once, I was stuck in Lokichoggio, Kenya for a day, waiting for the UN shuttle flight to Juba, South Sudan. There was nothing to do. I hated it. And on a road trip through Mauritania, we were stopped by the military near Ayoun al Atrous because of a heightened terror warning in the region. Again blocked for several hours, outside my control. Not to be the master of my speed and destiny makes me uncomfortable.

What are your three favorite cities in the world, and why?

I really like Moscow, Beirut, Istanbul, and Mexico City. So much energy in those places.

What is the ideal amount of time you prefer to travel on each trip before you are ready to go home and take a break?

My wife wants me to be back home on weekends, if possible, so usually I do trips of a week or a maximum of two. I have no interest in extended traveling. My home is too beautiful.

In your opinion, where are the most beautiful places on Earth?

I have such a great home base, and my business is about beautiful things, that's why on my trips I rather look for hardship and don't seek beauty. That may be hard to understand for some, but it's how I am. If I have to give an answer, it's probably the sand desert of the Sahara and the snow desert of Siberia, that I find the most appealing.

If you had an unlimited budget and space and time were no object, what would your perfect travel day look like (for example: start your morning in Bora Bora; afternoon on a safari in Kenya; night in Australia, etc.)?

I would like to do the ultimate trip, as my fellow Austrian Felix Baumgartner, jumping from the stratosphere with a parachute.

Which three countries would you recommend for adventurous travelers to visit, and why?

Road trips through Siberia, Central Asia, and northern Africa provide the most freedom with the least amount of tourists.

If you had just one travel story to share with someone, what would it be?

I was exiting Uzbekistan to Afghanistan and the extremely thorough Uzbek customs found $1,000 US hard currency more on me than I had declared when entering the country. They insisted that I had to go back and "spend it." So I walked back to the next tree, pretended to pee, and dug a small hole in the sand with my foot and hid the money there. Customs did another thorough search but to their surprise couldn't find the money. The next day, on my way back in from Afghanistan, at the same border, of course, I declared the $1,000 on the customs form, to have correct papers this time. Another border guard asked, "show me the money." I pointed towards the tree and said it's there. This went on for three times, and the border guard thought I was cuckoo. Finally, he shook his head and let me in. I went for another pee, and the money was still there.

Do you ever feel you have missed out on certain aspects of life while away from home as you travel so much?

I could have spent more time with my son. Still I would do everything the same way again, including all the mistakes I made. I realized it doesn't make sense to change the way you are, or to think you should have done something different, as it is history anyway and why should I feel guilty for something I have done and which was OK for me the moment I did it.

What advice would you give to others who would like to travel to every country?

Don't even start it. It becomes an obsession. Travel the way you like, and not what others tell you. And get your finances together. It is not a cheap affair.

For someone who has been almost everywhere, what still gets you excited about packing your bags again?

It's like sex. The urge suddenly comes out of nowhere, and I'll jump on the next available plane.

Looking ahead, what travel plans and goals are you still pursuing, and what is on your "Bucket List"?

My list is still very long in comparison to my wife who wants to do stand-up-paddling next time in the Maldives. For me, it's Machu Picchu. Trekking in Tibet. The South Pole. The North Pole. A trip to space. Flying in an MIG in Russia. In a car around the world, no business and no time limit. Breaking the Panamericana World Record. From Moscow to L.A. by car, crossing the frozen Bering Straits.

Watson E. Mills, U.S.A.

(At Taj Mahal)

Where did you grow up, and what was your early life like?

My earliest memories are of Richmond, Virginia where I lived until I completed my undergraduate education. I was born into a middle class family. My father was a salesman and my mother taught piano and worked as a substitute grade-school teacher. When I was 15-years-old, I left home to attend a military academy and there I encountered young boys who had seen much of the world unknown to me. I took a keen interest in geography and enjoyed reading novels about faraway lands. When I finished university I continued my graduate education for another seven years, and even thought my interests in other countries continued, my educational expenses consumed what meager resources I had. So foreign travel had to be put on hold. When I joined the faculty of a small, liberal arts college in Virginia in 1968 I thought maybe foreign travel would finally be possible. I had been teaching there for a little over a year when the college president asked if I could help him out. He had begun organizing a tour group to travel around the world but his declining health would make it impossible for him to lead the tour. Would I do it? Of course I had not been outside the USA and didn't have a clue as to how to lead a tour. But I guess ignorance is indeed bliss, and so in July of 1970, I and a group of 24 students and local folks (from outside the college) departed (westbound) and traveled to Japan via Hawaii, Hong Kong, India, Thailand, Israel, Greece, Italy, France and U.K. The 30-day trip, 1st class hotels, all meals, and ground transport, transfers, tours and admission fees, including air, sold for $1,499! Somehow I pulled it off and I was completely hooked on seeing the world.

What was the first international trip you took, and what do you remember most about it?

It was the around-the-world tour I led in 1970. I remember getting off the plane in Tokyo and realizing where I was and seeing the neon lights along the main streets of downtown. Since I had seen neither Times Square nor Piccadilly Circus this was an amazing sight to be sure. But on reflection, it was so amazing to me only because it was first. On that same trip I would see the Taj Mahal and the Acropolis as well as Saint Peter's Square and the Eiffel Tower. Places I had read about all my life came into reality for me. WOW. I was hooked.

When did you go from traveling casually to making this a full-time goal, and what motivated you to travel to every country?

It was the previous trip mentioned that opened my eyes to what was out there (beside what I could read about in books); however, on an assistant professor's salary, foreign travel still seemed more of a dream. So I began to organize tour groups on my own. In 1971 I led a seven country European tour; in 1972 I took a group to Israel and Greece, and in 1978 I led a group to Spain. Of course, leading a group of students is an exhaustive and difficult way to get to travel; however, for me, it was the only real choice. And then in 1979, my fortunes changed when I got an appointment as a professor at Mercer University in Macon, Georgia. And even though I had traveled overseas a few times, without a group in tow, now my resources would permit more trips without having to lead a tour group. Also, at Mercer, there were funds available for professional, job-related travel, and I utilized these funds to the fullest. No more tour groups – just travel to the places I wanted to visit.

What prompted me to want to visit every country? I saw an article in a travel magazine about the Travelers' Century Club (TCC). I got all the information about the club and joined immediately, as I was already up to over 120 countries. This would have been sometime in the late 1990s. Then I subsequently joined in the Most Traveled People (MTP) group, and I was on my way.

What have you done in your life to gain the freedom and finances to pursue as much travel as you have?

Of course, university professorships are notoriously underpaid positions, so I had to approach funding my travel lust in other ways. I have had more than 20 trips abroad using frequent flyer awards. My daughter-in-law is a (retired now) flight attendant for Delta and has given me more buddy passes than I can count; the university where I worked until I retired has sent me outside the country more than 20 times. Also, I arrange my own travel and have utilized every money saving device then you can imagine – and some you probably can't! I remember reading slick, glossy catalogs like GEO Expeditions and finding trips I would like to take but could never afford. There was one that included an overland leg from Lhasa, Tibet to Kathmandu, Nepal with an optional stop at the Everest Base Camp. The price tag was astronomical – but I put together the identical trip for about 30% of the GEO cost. Of course, besides financial resources, one has to have the time away from work. This was, at least, one plus to a university professorship! Much available time off to wander the world.

Has there ever been a time where you considered abandoning your travel goals?

No, not really. There have been health issues along the way, of course, and financial strains of one sort or the other, but to-date I have made 130 international trips and fully expect to do more.

What do you consider to be your two favorite travel experiences, and why?

For me, this is a difficult question because there have been so many experiences that I truly cherish. But as requested I will mention only two.

(1) In 1999 my son met me in Nairobi and, after spending some days there, we boarded a light aircraft and flew to a safari lodge deep in the bush. There we saw the migration of the wildebeests – while crossing the Mara River in the Serengeti. One safari lodge on this trip overlooked Mount Kilimanjaro in Tanzania. One knowledgeable safari guide drove us to see two cheetahs asleep under a tree and a huge herd of more than 30 elephants. There were so many prides of lion that I lost count! We also visited Uganda to see the

source of the Nile River and then enjoyed a cottage along the shore of Lake Victoria. I often relive this trip through my photos and videos. I think seeing the wildlife and relaxing around the campfire at the wilderness lodges has been etched into my memory because I came to marvel at the immensity and diversity in the natural world that is all around me. Of course, seeing it all with my son made the experience all the more memorable.

(2) Earlier that same year I sank a huge amount of my resources into a long-anticipated trip with Quark Expeditions to Antarctica. This trip had been a dream of mine for a number of years. I flew to Santiago where the group met for orientation before a charter flight the next day to the Falklands. There I boarded the Russia icebreaker for the 10-day voyage. I was in a room with two other people – one lad from Australia, the other from Germany. I will never forget the rough waters of Drake Passage at the confluence of the two great oceans nor the playful whales that entertained us during the long days at sea. But finally, early one morning, I boarded the Zodiac and was transported to the continent of ice where I stepped off amid tens of thousands of penguins! It was cold to be sure but what I saw in those expeditions ashore and just cruising along the coast was truly amazing. And after leaving the ship at Ushuaia (itself an amazing sight nestled at the foot of the Andes), I flew to Asuncion where I took an overnight bus to see Iguazu Falls. I had been to Victoria Falls in Zambia and Niagara Falls as well, but I must say this was a truly incredible sight.

What are the main things you seek to experience when you travel (culture, cities, nature, animals, adventure activities, etc.)?

Of late my standard operating procedure is to Google "things to do" in a specific city/area. Then I make a list of those that interest me and do further research on each location/site, e.g., opening hours, cost, location, etc. Then I set the number of days in a specific location according to what I want to see while there. Sometimes I use Viator.com to book a tour or more likely I Google "travel agents in xxx" and book through them – after all these are the folks that Viator uses to fulfill their tours! Or sometimes I rent a car or, armed with Google Maps, I walk having selected a hotel near at least some of the places I want to see. Also, many foreign cities have excellent (and cheap) public transportation which is definitely the way to go IF you plan ahead and know what you are doing. I often use one of the free translation services available on the Internet to translate into whatever language something like "I am trying to find the xxxx" I print out the translation along with the English it represents and off I go. But to the questions asked of me: I want to see the sights and experience the culture. I enjoy meeting the people and observing them going about their daily activities. I am a little too advanced in years to do much adventure travel, though in 2015 I did pet a tiger in Thailand and in 2014 rode a camel in Morocco near Aït Benhaddou!

Looking back from when you started traveling to where you are now, in what ways, if any, has travel changed you?

Travel has enriched my life beyond measure. It has given me a deep and genuine appreciation for the USA. It has stretched my mind to understand and appreciate cultures that are different, even radically different, from my own. I firmly believe that sustained international travel easily rivals a college education in terms of human development. So I believe that my travels have enriched my life in ways that no other kind of experience could have done. But coming at it from a different angle, I must say that as I age, my approach to travel has changed, too. With two knee replacements, I am not as mobile as I once was. So now I have to rate proposed trips on a scale of physical difficulty – something GAP Adventures does routinely and which I very much appreciate. So when I took the GAP trip that included a visit to the southern part of the Sinai, I knew ahead of time that I would not be able to climb the 3750 steps from St. Katherine's Monastery to the top of Jebel Musa. So before I went I found online about Bedouin boys who rent camels for a ride 3/4 of the way up. I made the arrangements and at 2:30am one morning under a beautifully clear, star-filled sky, I headed out for an incredible sight – the sun rising over the Red Sea viewed from near the top of Mt Sinai. So I believe that as your health changes (read "declines") you can still travel if you choose wisely and plan ahead.

Do you speak any foreign languages, and if so, which have been the most useful for you besides English?

During my university years I took French, Spanish, German and Greek. But to say I "speak" them would be quite a stretch indeed. I do try to bone up on language skills a bit before each trip. The travel-orientated phrase section in the back of each *Lonely Planet* guide is helpful. Free cassette tapes or CDs are available from most public libraries. I have found that if an English-speaking traveler makes an effort, however poorly executed, to speak to a foreigner in their native tongue, the locals appreciate that effort so much and are frequently even more helpful in answering your questions – often in English.

What was the longest extended trip you have ever taken, when was it and where all did you go?

It was in 1997. I had some time off from the University, so I signed on to do some consulting work abroad for a New York publisher. I was based in Great Britain for six months though I traveled often in Europe (France, Switzerland, Austria, and Luxembourg) and even went to Beijing for a week. I spent three weeks in Ireland, including Belfast. Also a week in Scotland and extensive periods in Wales and

England. I flew to the Isle of Guernsey and later to Tunis where I spent several days. Still later I flew to Algeria. I did a week in Siberia as well. All of this and being paid, too!

What two countries have exceeded your expectations and which ones left you feeling underwhelmed, and why?

The two that exceeded my expectations are India and China. I have been to India three times. The sheer size of the place is overwhelming. The people are gracious and the sights, well, what can I say? On my first visit, I made the triangle trip from Delhi to Agra and on to the desert capital of Jaipur (where for the first time I rode an elephant up to the Amber Fort and Palace). This trip took place before the advent of digital equipment, and I squandered almost all of my film at the Taj and the Amber Fort. Also, in those days (1970) viewing of the Taj by moonlight was much less problematic than today. Also, the sounds and sights of Old Delhi made quite an impression on me. The confluence of a rich and glorious history and abject poverty can be a sobering experience for someone from the west. The regional differences in India are also something that can be appreciated only if one wonders outside the confines of New Delhi. By western standards a visit to India is inexpensive and yet most rewarding.

I have been to China eight times. On my first visit in 1997 I arrived on the Trans-Siberian Railway from Irkutsk, Siberia via Mongolia. So my first view of the Great Wall was along that route – a section of the Great Wall that was, by the way, in a terrible state of repair. But in Beijing, I found the people friendly and helpful, and oddly enough, English is widely spoken in places tourists frequent. I remember all the bicycles and the heavy smog. Also, the 'Golden Arches' of McDonald's next to the huge portrait of Chairman Mao! I was impressed by the public transportation system and by how very cheap (and clean) the taxis are. On a later trip there I arrived from the west via the Silk Road that took me across Torugart Pass into China (from Kyrgyzstan). Because of the necessary permits and bureaucratic red-tape, this was a difficult though nonetheless rewarding excursion (and believe it or not the representative from China meet me at the pass right on time). I discovered that the western part of China is also quite beautiful and seems to march to a slower tune than Beijing. One of my favorite memories of China is of the two trips I have taken on the Yangtze River through the Three Gorges. Also, I throughly enjoyed a two-day trip to Xi'an where I experienced the Terracotta Army in all their splendor. At Dalian, in northeastern China, I strolled in the largest square in the world, and while in Shanghai I rode the Maglev Train at a speed that can only be imagined by American train riders. China is inexpensive and has something of interest for everyone – a truly fascinating place. If I am able, I will travel there again.

The two countries that I have visited that left me thoroughly underwhelmed are Guinea and Nigeria. Of course, Western Africa is notorious for its virtually non-existent infrastructure. Conakry is reminiscent of Haiti – listless people lining the dirt streets with their faces reflecting their sense of despair. I remember beginning to feel that I had fallen off the face of the earth. My hotel was nice enough though the armed guards and high fences were somewhat off-putting. The hotel manager came to my room and explained to me the perils of venturing outside the confines of the hotel and how he could not be responsible for my safety. There was an Internet connection in the lobby, although I would not describe its speed as FAST! There was little to see in Conakry, so I only took one tour (with some other tourists). I was glad to see the airport. I left with renewed appreciation for the USA.

On my one and only trip to Nigeria, I arrived in Lagos by bush taxi from Accra, Ghana traveling through Lome (Togo) and Porto Novo (Benin). That was a two-day ride and I paid a small fortune in bribes at border crossings. The nine-passenger Peugeot station wagon was crammed full of paying passengers, and all the luggage was strapped on top. But it was an experience I will never forget. When I paid all the different folks at the border of Nigeria and said goodbye to my bush taxi and actually entered the country, I was beset by a hoard of taxi drivers wanting to take me to my final destination. They literally surrounded me, boxing me in. I later learned that they labor under the illusion that all westerners are wealthy! – An illusion, at least, as far as I am concerned. Finally, I saw a policeman and I went against prevailing opinion (never ask a foreign police for help) and sought refuge with the aid of the officer. He did help a bit holding the encircling thong at bay, and after a minute I was in a taxi (with bars on the windows) heading for the checkpoint to enter my hotel. After showing my passport and a search of the vehicle I arrived at the hotel's check-in. Again, I was repeatedly cautioned about leaving the hotel property. So again I took one tour (with others) on a minibus – although not much to see. I kept wondering where all the oil money was going – and I think I knew – in the politicians' pockets. I had read horror stories about passengers trying to board their flights out of Lagos, but once I paid a few bribes at the airport curbside, and again at check-in, I was on my way. And never to return!

When you travel, do you prefer to go with others or solo, and why?

Solo because it would be difficult if not impossible to find someone who wants to go where I want to go! There is one exception, however. I really enjoy traveling with my son. He has an wanderlust in his genes, too, I suppose. We have traveled together to Russia, Finland, Chile, Cape Town, Kenya, China, Alaska, Peru, Bolivia, U.K., France, Jordan and Israel.

What has been your most uncomfortable mode of transportation?

This would be a tie: (1) the aforementioned bush taxi from Accra, Ghana to Lagos, Nigeria and, (2), the 4 wheel drive mini-SUV from Mopti to Timbuktu in Mali, Africa. The trip took eight hard hours over non-existent roadways, e.g., tracks through the desert. And it involved a ferry boat across the Niger River. But I must say, that despite lacking the conveniences of home, this ride through the desert was something else. I will never forget it.

What is the strangest thing you've seen/experienced while traveling?

I have long been interested in WWII and so when I was traveling in Poland I rented a car in Krakow and drove to Auschwitz-Birkenau. These are actually two separate camps 3km apart. I toured Auschwitz first and though my knowledge of the Polish language is practically non-existent, I sensed something out of the ordinary was happening because the staff members were talking excitedly over one another and scrambling around, shouting into telephones, etc. But it was not until I took the bus to Birkenau that I figured out what was actually going on. Just outside the "Gate of Death" where the trains delivered the Jews and others to the gas chambers, stood a group of about 100 people, many carrying signs denying that the Holocaust ever happened. Some were skinheads, but many looked like ordinary folk. They were yelling at the visitors to the camp, though not in English. But that aside, I think most people getting off/on the bus got the idea of the viewpoint they were expressing. This is the strangest thing to me because, even though I knew about those who deny that the Holocaust even happened, I have yet to grasp why these folks would choose to demonstrate for their beliefs just outside the most notorious death camp from the Nazi era. There were probably more police there than demonstrators so I never felt I was in danger.

What are the best and worst meals you have ever eaten while traveling, and where was it?

The best meals I can remember were served on the river boat in China that took me along the Yangtze River through the Three Gorges. The meals were what I would call a "sitting buffet." The tables were round and rather large seating 10-12 people. In the center of the table was a round, rotating, "Lazy Susan" laden with small dishes of many different foods – some of which I had not a clue as to what it was! But really good to the taste. So I watched the others and soon got the hang of it and enjoyed a tiny sampling of many, many dishes at each meal.

The worst was a "meal" served at my hotel in Banjul, The Gambia. I do not know what the table d'hote was supposed to be that day, but I can tell you it was horrible. The inside of my mouth was on fire. I rushed to my room and, lacking mouthwash, rinsed out my mouth with after-shave lotion. Now that is an awful meal!

Out of the thousands of places you've stayed around the world, what have been your best and worst accommodations?

This one is easy. The best is the Explora Lodge in Atacama, Chile. I was there for four nights with my son in 2015. Talk about a room with a view. This was truly an incredible sight. The food was fantastic, and every amenity imaginable was readily available in our suite. Outside, glaciers were plentiful and snow-capped mountains abound. This place was one of which dreams are made.

At the other extreme is a guest house I where I stayed along the route from Lhasa, Tibet to Kathmandu, Nepal. I was in a room to myself. Good thing, too, since the "toilet" was a hole in the floor in the corner of the room (without any partition whatsoever). The stench was so great that I ended up sleeping in the parking lot on the hood of the SUV in which I was traveling (the doors were locked). Never again.

What is your favorite "off the beaten path" destination, and why?

I would have to say Timbuktu in Mali. To get there, I used a buddy pass to Paris and spent a couple of days there before flying to Mopti, Mali, on Point-Afrique Airlines. Now getting that ticket while in the USA was difficult in the extreme. But by definition Timbuktu is a remote place. I had planned on flying to Timbuktu from Mopti, but these air tickets can only be bought once in Mopti. I tried and failed. The language barrier could have been to blame, but the friendly manager of my hotel came to rescue, and he organized a mini-SUV with two others at a price well below the airfare. There was a sealed road, of sorts, for the first two hours. Then we were on a sand track which gave out after another two hours. Then we were making our own road as went through the desert finally arriving at the Niger River, which we crossed on a ferry boat. We had departed before day break so we arrived at Timbuktu at around 2pm. The afternoon sun was definitely on the warmish side! But around 6pm, the guide took me out into the desert and I witnessed a sunset over the Sahara. It was so quiet and peaceful. Not another soul for as far as I could see – only the faintest flicker of a single lamp from a distant Tuareg camp. I had made it to Timbuktu and lived to tell about it.

What were your most challenging countries to visit, and why?

North Korea would be at the top of my list because it is so difficult for American citizens to get a visa. I stumbled across Koryo Tours on the Internet and this company had successfully arranged for USA citizens to visit. So I bought a tour, which originated in Beijing. This was in 2006. I arranged to arrive in Beijing to catch the flight to Pyongyang near the end of an around the world trip. Some days before I was to arrive in Beijing, I received an email informing me that all tours to North Korea had been canceled due to severe flooding in that country. But that, if I had already left home, I should report to the Koryo Tours office upon arrival in Beijing, which I did. The tour company was more than generous in arranging other travel which I enjoyed very much. They offered me a trip to northeastern China to the major seaport city of Dalian.

I tried again for North Korea in 2008 and this time spent five days there. The flights were on North Korea's Koryo Airlines – the world's only one-star airline. They use old Russian turbo-prop planes (Tupolev Tu-204s) that were first flown in Russia in the 1950s. Due to safety and maintenance concerns, Air Koryo was added to the list of air carriers banned in the European Union in March 2006. The flights feature one channel of censored in-flight entertainment. The food... well, you best eat before you leave Beijing! On the flight over to Pyongyang, I happened to be seated beside the tour guide from Koryo Tours. I asked him about the small golf-cart like vehicle that was just visible beyond the wing tip moving alongside the aircraft during takeoff roll. Without a hint of sarcasm he said: "Oh, that guy picks up any pieces that fall off the plane so the next flight won't run over them." I was delighted and relieved when the plane touched down in Pyongyang.

The much sought-after visa is separate from your passport (though Koryo Tours graciously emailed me a copy of mine later). Arrival is straightforward enough though a bit time consuming. Cell phones must be deposited at the airport – why I am not sure since there are no cell towers in the country. Permission from the guide is a precursor to taking any picture anywhere. To get the visa I had to agree ahead of time in writing to visit the tomb of the Great Leader (while wearing a tie) and that I would bow before his body. I mean you have got to really want to go to North Korea. But I will say that the trip was definitely worth the effort required. My small sub-group of U.S. and U.K. citizens attended the Mass Games while in Pyongyang and this was an amazing sight to say the least. We also visited the USS *Pueblo*, which is still at anchor, and spent several hours at the DMZ. I was able to sit at the table on the exact spot where the U.S. "surrendered" to the triumphal North Koreans. Go figure.

Also, I would include here the breakaway Republic's that gained independence with the dissolution of the Soviet Union: Estonia, Latvia, Lithuania, Kazakhstan, Kyrgyzstan, Tajikistan, Turkmenistan, Uzbekistan, Belarus, Moldova, Ukraine, Armenia, Azerbaijan, Georgia and Russia. Of these 15, I have visited 13. There remain for me two of the most difficult to visit: Tajikistan and Turkmenistan. The major obstacle lies in the letter of invitation (LOI) that is required for visitors from, among other countries, the USA. Although this can be purchased online, in most cases one has to book travel from the agent that issues the letter. You can receive an emailed or faxed copy of the LOI, but the original is sent to Ministry of Tourism in the country to be visited, and they issue the visa usually within two weeks. Here is the killer: said visa is good for 30 days which means there can be little, if any, pre-planning and the airfare is likely to require you taking out a second mortgage! I am still attempting to visit the remaining two Stans', but it looks bleak for me.

Of which travel accomplishments are you most proud?

Some years ago I came across the *Smithsonian* magazine's List of "28 Places to See Before You Die." The travel accomplishment of which I am most proud is that as of 2013 I have been to all 28 of these places. To accomplish this, I had to do some major-league planning and also I had to allocate some significant funding towards this goal.

Do you remember encountering particular people that left a lasting impression with you?

I met a young lad who worked at the Mount Kilimanjaro View Lodge in Tanzania during my visit there in 2010. He also performed many other chores around the lodge – working in the kitchen, cleaning the rooms, etc. He possessed a very versatile skill set! Once he repaired the generator which had been down for more than a day. I have great difficulty in walking on uneven surfaces, and he frequently assisted me up and down the steep hillside on which the lodge is situated. He had passable English and asked many questions about life in America. He told me about his life experiences in Tanzania. On some mornings I would awake to find a proposed itinerary for the day slipped under my door. As with most of the employees at the lodge, he was extremely poor but nonetheless entertained great hopes for his future education and employment. I could not help but be touched by his eagerness and enthusiasm amid such a bleak station in life. He made me appreciate all the more the abundant opportunities I have enjoyed living in the USA.

If you could travel back in time, to which era and place would you go, and why?

I assume you mean for a visit and not to stay permanently. That being the case, I remember crossing the Gobi Desert in Mongolia when I took the Trans-Siberian Railway from Irkutsk to Beijing. I remember daydreaming about living long-ago in this bleak place that is vast, harsh and silent. Its profound emptiness and terrible isolation, its colossal sand dunes, and its ice-filled canyons gripped my imagination. About noon time, a group of horsemen clad in their traditional dress rode close to the slow-moving train. In the distance along the way, I saw countless yurts where these folks lived and worked. I wondered what it would have like to live as one these nomads. The scene was burned into my consciousness and I remember it vividly still today.

Can you describe any particular situation where you felt completely out of your comfort zone?

I was finishing up a swing through Kyrgyzstan, Azerbaijan, Kazakhstan and Uzbekistan when I arrived at the airport in Tashkent for an outbound flight. I checked in without difficulty and headed for passport control. I noticed what I thought was a heavier than usual presence of police with dogs and Kalashnikov's – although not an unusual sight in this part of the world. At least most of the dogs were muzzled! As I waited my turn and drew nearer to the barrier, I heard an exchange between the immigration officer and a tourist whom I took to be a westerner. The room fell silent. I could not hear the actual exchange just its tone (read "shouting") and I immediately suspected all was not well. My impression was confirmed as, after a few moments, the man was escorted away, physically, all the while protesting loudly. Now I was third in line from the barrier and, to my dismay, a similar altercation erupted when the next person crossed the red line, though he was not physically removed. After more heated verbal exchanges I was pretty certain I saw money change hands. The last person before me walked up. Again, there was a heated exchange, and this poor soul was ultimately dragged away, too. I quickly slipped a $50 bill inside my passport and strode as confidently as I could up to the window, smiling my biggest and broadest smile. The officer said nothing but worked with my passport outside of my sight line. He glanced up at me twice as if he were checking my face against the picture. Finally, after what seemed like an eternity, he stamped my passport and returned it to me without the $50. Later, on the aircraft, the guy next to me said there had been two incidents with drugs at the airport that morning, and everybody was in a bad mood! I learned, too, that he slipped only $20 into his passport!

What are your three favorite cities in the world, and why?

London. I have been there so many times that I know my way around. Of course, the language is no problem and the whole city seems to be geared to tourism. There is a wonderful, if aging, metro system with clear and helpful signage. The people are friendly and helpful. History abounds literally at every turn. There is so much to see and experience. The theater district offers it own special kind of entertainment. Once I saw a performance at the Globe on the River Thames – a theater built to the specifications and on the exact spot of the original. I really enjoy having a pie at a pub soaking up the atmosphere of an earlier time. There are many day trips available, so London is a great hub for outlying adventures. Train and airplane travel is plentiful. The only drawback for me is the simple fact that London is one of the most expensive cities in the world. For me, visits there require a lot of planning.

Cairo is another favorite city of mine, although all my visits there were pre-Arab Spring and I cannot assess how tourist-friendly the city is these days. But my five visits were quite nice indeed. Obviously, Cairo and its day-trip environs represent a treasure trove of sights to experience. Where else can you explore the single, remaining instance of the Seven Wonders of the Ancient World, ride a camel in the desert, enjoy a dinner cruise on the Nile River and marvel at the physical gyrations of a genuine belly dancer in a single day? Nowhere, I know of! Taxis are cheap and street food there is really good. English is widely spoken, too. I particularly enjoyed spending time in the Egyptian Museum. Train and bus service is quite good, though a bit slow compared with Europe.

Thirdly, I would have to say Berlin. To me, the unique mixture of history and the trendy new and modern nightlife makes this city one of the most appealing in all of Europe. While Berlin is quite expensive, the public transportation system is excellent. The city boasts a new airport. Train service is legendary. WWII sights abound as do some remnants of the divided Berlin during the days of the Wall. The tree-lined boulevards with wide sidewalks are reminiscent of Paris. There is an abundance of quality museums and restaurants. I visit here every chance I get.

What is the ideal amount of time you prefer to travel on each trip before you are ready to go home and take a break?

2-3 weeks.

In your opinion, where are the most beautiful places on Earth?

Patagonia; Canadian Rockies; Norwegian Fjords; Inside Passage to Alaska; Niagara, Victoria and Iguazu Falls.

If you had an unlimited budget and space and time were no object, what would your perfect travel day look like (for example: start your morning in Bora Bora; afternoon on a safari in Kenya; night in Australia, etc.)?

Watch the sunrise over the sand dunes in Namibia; early-morning safari in the Chobe Desert; a mid-morning swim in waters off the Gold Coast of Australia; a stroll along the Great Wall near Badaling; lunch at a café atop the Eiffel Tower; after-lunch nap in an over-the-water villa in Papeete, Tahiti; late afternoon scuba diving around the Great Barrier Reef; dinner and show at Maxims de Paris; fireworks at the Magic Kingdom in Disney World; the midnight buffet aboard the *Queen Mary 2*.

Which three countries would you recommend for adventurous travelers to visit, and why?

Tibet/Nepal. The overland trip from Lhasa to Kathmandu via the Mount Everest Base Camp is a journey that features not only the sheer beauty and wonder of the Himalayas but also presents significant physical challenges to the adventure traveler. Some even arrange to overnight at the base camp and explore the base of the world's tallest mountain.

Russia/Mongolia/China. I think the trip from Moscow to Beijing via Mongolia on the Trans-Siberian is tailor-made for the adventure traveler. It, too, presents some challenges but the rewards are great. The train itself is legendary. The scenery is magnificent. The red-tape is enormous, however, but I would count this five-day trip as one of a lifetime.

If you had just one travel story to share with someone, what would it be?

Several years ago I fulfilled my dream of traveling from Beijing to Lhasa, Tibet, on the "top of the world train." This route is an engineering marvel of the first order. Of course, the epic journey to "the roof of the world" includes scenery that will leave you breathless. The 4000km journey through eight provinces begins at 8 pm at the Beijing West Railway Station and takes 48 hours. On the day of my departure, despite my many trips to Beijing, I failed to allow enough time for the taxi from my hotel to the station. The traffic was impossible and my stomach was in knots when the taxi finally pulled in at the station only minutes before departure time. Even at this hour on a weekday night the West station is overflowing with travelers. But as if by a miracle, I found the track number and then my carriage number. Luckily there were others still boarding as well. A stern-faced guard examined my ticket, passport and the travel permit (required to enter Tibet). Once inside the car, I walked down the carpeted corridor to my cabin and located my pre-assigned bunk. Almost immediately the train began to move! I had paid extra for the soft-sleeper class which has four bunks, two on each side. The cabin is tiny but comfortable. There is a wall-mounted television with headphones, although movies on the English language channel are very limited. Best of all there is a huge window for enjoying the incredible sights along the way. Fresh oxygen is pumped throughout the cars.

The idea for this railway dates to 1919. But it was deemed impossible to build. Chairman Mao, in 1955, did further investigation but, again, no action was taken. But in 1984, several years after Mao's death, the first section of 800km was built. The 21st century would dawn before the most difficult stretch of the route would begin to built. This 1,142km, high-altitude track from Golmud to Lhasa has been referred to as "an unprecedented project in the history of mankind."

This section cost over $4 billion USD and required 100,000 engineers and construction workers. The four-year project called for tracks to be built higher than 4000 meters along more than 85% of the route. The highest point is actually over 5,000 meters. In addition to being the highest railway line in the world, this route holds several other world records, including the highest train station and highest railway tunnel.

There is scarcely any land as far as the eye can see that hasn't been farmed, built on or mined. Every muddy river has several bridges reaching over it and dams along its course. The hillsides look like layer cakes made of rice terraces. But in the morning I noticed that the farms had disappeared, and now I see a strange-looking emptiness that stretches out as far as the you can see. On the right side of the train, I see the snow-topped Kunlun Range. I have never in my life seen such beautiful scenery. It was a trip of a lifetime.

Do you ever feel you have missed out on certain aspects of life while away from home as you travel so much?

My only child was grown and out of law school before I became serious about traveling, so, no, I don't think I missed out.

What advice would you give to others who would like to travel to every country?

Plan, plan, plan. Set your goals and stick to them. Use the many travel sites and blogs on the Internet to find ways to squeeze the most out of each journey, both in terms of time invested and dollars spent.

For someone who has been almost everywhere, what still gets you excited about packing your bags again?

Seeing new places, learning about other countries and cultures, trying new things, and appreciating the opportunities given to me.

Looking ahead, what travel plans and goals are you still pursuing, and what is on your "Bucket List"?

My son and I are discussing trips to the Chobe Desert and Victoria Falls as well as a trip to Bangkok and Siem Reap. I have made these trips before but look forward to sharing them again with my son, Mike.

My personal bucket list includes Libya, Iraq and Afghanistan. Although I do not relish having to have my passport translated into Arabic, I look forward to finally visiting Tripoli's Freedom Square, which was once a symbol of Gaddafi's regime. The "Green" square, the largest in Tripoli, became famous during the 2011 revolution when thousands gathered here to usher in a new era after Tripoli finally fell. Also, I would really enjoy visiting the Assai al-Hamra (the Red Castle) as well as the Arch of Marcus Aurelius and Al-Majidya Mosque. Also, Libya's coastline is dotted with spectacular ancient ruins that can be visited in short excursions from Tripoli. For example, Leptis Magna, a short drive from Tripoli, is well known for its cobbled streets, the Arch erected in honor of Emperor Septimus Severus, the marble Hadrianic Baths, the basilica and the large amphitheater. Further afield (three hours) is Cyrene with its ancient fertility temples, beautiful Temple of Zeus and Roman stadium.

Of course, Afghanistan and Iraq present their own problems (and risks) for tourists. The State Department discourages US citizens with stern warnings; however, I hope that the day will come when I can see something of these places as well.

William Baekeland, Ireland

(Arriving on Palmyra Atoll, April 2016)

Where did you grow up, and what was your early life like?

It is very fortunate that London, England is where I spent a large amount of time growing up. It is a beautiful world city that is inspiring to a growing mind. Much of my early life was spent around Europe, visiting the grand opera houses and historic museums and art galleries, teaching me a lot about the history of the world, and opening my mind up to all sorts of other curiosities that existed in more exotic parts of the world. Opera and classical music in beautiful venues also served as a gateway to the past as well as a path for the future, which led me to further studies in music. It's been a great privilege to have been able to play some of the largest pipe organs in the world.

Early on in my life I also traveled to the United States a few times, crossing the Atlantic by ocean liner – a pleasant enough experience but without too much for a child to do, with many sea days. The sight of sailing into New York harbor more than compensated for many days of nothing to do for a child. I also took several flights onboard the Concorde airplanes, it remains a unique and historic travel experience, albeit one I perhaps cannot fully appreciate as I was too young before it went out of service. A far more interesting journey was from England to Australia by ocean liner, visiting so many exotic places along the way: Gibraltar, Rome, Alexandria, Bombay, Singapore to name a few. It really gave me a love for traveling by sea and for seeing strange new lands.

Always having grown up with large numbers of books, and a complete *National Geographic* magazine collection gave me the chance to read about all aspects of world history, affairs, geography, and culture. Being given the chance to view the ancient world that I had read about was, perhaps, a turning point in my life. Going across Europe by train to Aleppo on the routes of the Orient and Taurus Expresses was like slowly going back in time and the mystique of a city like Istanbul at that young age, left a deep impression.

Education was taken in several countries all in, giving a broad spectrum about how different people learned things. There are big differences in attitudes in the UK, Switzerland, America and the Nordic countries, and you really understand why this is when you grow up around people in their formative years in their schooling systems.

Overall my early life was very pleasant, I was fortunate to already see many enchanting places around the world and learn so much about the things I now hold deep interest in. I am most glad that I was able to pursue to the fullest the things I developed passions for. Growing up, I soon learned what success in a country really is, and what made my own world very different to that of many other peoples – countries that allow people to be free to develop themselves to the maximum are the most successful ones. The many countries that do not are unsuccessful. When I was a teenager I was surprised in admiration when I learned it took Ayn Rand to write her 'John Galt's speech'. I learned that the only thing we have which is a tool for our survival is our mind. This was an important lesson, learned early on.

What was the first international trip you took, and what do you remember most about it?

Aged just a few weeks old, I really have no recollection of my very first international trip. I do know, however, that it was across the English Channel to Deauville in France for a few weeks, then by train to Paris and the boat back to England.

Several years later when I was around six, this trip was more or less repeated, and although I had been to several places in between these two trips, I can remember bits and pieces of my second visit to Deauville. The hotel had an impressionable fairytale like feel to it and for a young child, was quite enchanting, and I've been back many times since that first trip. The wide sand beaches were far more appealing, and I entertained myself for hours and hours on end trying to create architectural masterpieces (as best as I could manage with a few buckets, sand, and seawater). I am very interested in structural variations around the world, and I suppose it was on childhood holidays to the beach where this interest started to form. Arriving in Paris after the seaside was like returning to the center of the world. A week was spent visiting all of the typical sites, the Eiffel Tower, the Louvre and Notre Dame, as well as many galleries and museums around the city.

When did you go from traveling casually to making this a full-time goal, and what motivated you to travel to every country?

Getting to every country in the world is far from a full-time goal. It is a big part of my wider travel goals, as it is necessary to visit all the countries to see the sites I wish to see and to get a wide spectrum of the planet. This is primarily to compliment my theoretical education of the world. This is the main goal and what motivates me to travel to every country.

I am not traveling 100% of the time and I many other interests and pursuits which I get on with. Often I say that travel is 10% of my interest but just happens to take up 90% of my time. Now I am more focused with my travels and do shorter trips, more frequently. With good planning and good logistics, it is possible to achieve a lot in a short amount of time. I don't get much satisfaction out of spending more time than I need in places which which do not warrant extended amounts of time. For some places, this way of thinking doesn't quite line up with commercial airline schedules.

This having being said, I would not travel much at all if I was unable to experience the outstanding natural beauty that the world has to offer. The true joy of travel is being able to witness these places and all of the unusual and exotic plants and animals which we share the world with.

What have you done in your life to gain the freedom and finances to pursue as much travel as you have?

The biggest obstacle that one faces traveling the world extensively is willpower – one must be very determined to make it a priority. Without it being a priority, one may very well fall easily to the prey of the mindset of fear and lethargy.

Time is also a big factor to consider with travel. I feel I have wasted a lot of time with travel, in that I have not made the most of my time while traveling. It is something that must be planned properly if you are to make the best use of the time available. Time, of course, is not in endless supply.

Has there ever been a time where you considered abandoning your travel goals?

It is a constant consideration. If extensive travel goals are too fixed and rigid, it can easily become a chore to undertake. Travel is a wonderful way to learn about the world and have an enjoyable time doing so. There is also the balance of other things in life. I do not consider it to be healthy to have the mindset of perpetual travel. To me, while it is fulfilling in many ways to travel, it would be emptying to experience this as a constant.

I have a general idea of the places I wish to see – to more or less be perfectly geographically and scenically varied across the entire world. This combined with some experiences, specific sites of personal interest, makes for a healthy, realistic travel goal, which does not need to lead to conflict and the feeling of a need for abandonment.

Sometimes during trips, I have abandoned my original plans for the trip in question, for various reasons. A number of times I have realized that I just planned things badly and either underestimated or overestimated time and levels of interest for things. I get better at this with time and experience of course. Speaking with other travelers who may know a region or place better is a big help for this. On other occasions, I've suffered from 'better deals coming along'. Once I completely dropped my travel schedule to fly back to Europe from Noumea, New Caledonia at very short notice. At the last minute, I learned of a performance of my favorite English opera, Venus and Adonis by John Blow. It's very rarely done, and this time, it was in a small town in Austria of all places. This is an extreme example, but once in a while it happens.

I have no desire to travel indefinitely, once I have seen the places I would like to see, I am happy to remain put at home and just visit some easy and close by places – there are so many other fields of interest in this world to pursue, which are not so time costly.

Many of the places I have so far visited, and several places I still wish to visit involve a degree of hardship and suffering, some involving a large degree of this. Once I have been to such a place, I leave knowing that it is very unlikely I will ever go back.

What do you consider to be your two favorite travel experiences, and why?

It is a constant consideration. If extensive travel goals are too fixed and rigid, it can easily become a chore to undertake. Travel is a wonderful way to learn about the world and have an enjoyable time doing so. There is also the balance of other things in life. I do not consider it to be healthy to have the mindset of perpetual travel. To me, while it is fulfilling in many ways to travel, it would be emptying to experience this as a constant.

My favorite travel experience is one I have experienced many times and will experience many more times to come. Standing on the deck of a ship approaching an unknown (to me) island, or wilderness location, and the great sense of anticipation that comes with it is one of the best feelings to have when traveling the world. Often there is the uncertainty of the unknown – many times variables outside of one's control make it impossible to visit somewhere, and in such cases the knowledge of returning there someday is equally as satisfying. I spent two days on a ship circling Bouvet Island in the Southern Ocean. The weather was too bad to make a landing, but its sublime and austere beauty was overwhelming enough to make it a completely worthwhile journey.

One experience which has always been a favorite, and always continues to excite me is taking the Caledonian Sleeper train from London to Scotland. There is nothing quite like waking up in the early morning, crossing the incredibly bleak moors, with mountains in the background, and deer running alongside the slow moving train. Continuing the journey along the winding roads and to the outer isles just makes the journey even better.

What are the main things you seek to experience when you travel (culture, cities, nature, animals, adventure activities, etc.)?

I like to travel for a wide number of reasons. If you go to every country, you will encounter many different experiences, so it pays to have some interest in different things. Mostly, though, I like to witness spectacular nature and landscapes, especially the polar regions and Africa. I could spend weeks on end relaxing in a nice safari lodge, spending days looking at the different animals in the endless vast landscapes.

One of the best ways to see many places in the world is not on the ground but from the air. It is impossible to get a sense of scale and grandeur for many of the natural landscapes in the world, as well as for vast animal movements like the wildebeest migration in the Serengeti. Helicopters are an excellent way to achieve this and provide the best versatility, more so than a light aircraft which needs a lot more space to land and take off. The best journey I made by helicopter, in order to best experience the natural landscape, was up to Lake Turkana in northern Kenya. It is an indescribable journey and an almost similar sensation to eating an extra portion of food you have no space for – it can be a bit of a visual overload as you see so much in such a relatively short space of time. I also recently went to the 'forbidden island' of Niihau in the Hawaiian Islands. The helicopter took us over the whole island before landing. I was truly amazed at the incredible variety of landscapes on the island (roughly similar in size to Santa Catalina in

California). Seeing all of that in just 20 minutes was also a visual sensation and a struggle to take it all in.

My interest in cultures of the world is mostly limited to history, art, music, and architecture. Europe is unbeatable in this respect – it has such an incredible cultural history. I will never tire of exploring it.

Looking back from when you started traveling to where you are now, in what ways, if any, has travel changed you?

I have traveled my whole life, albeit in a different way to systematic planned travel. I still feel like the same person, relatively unchanged in many ways. However, travel has certainly made me more educated, more understanding of the problems which not experienced where I live and more appreciative of the frailty of the planet. Whether or not we ruin our own planet, it will survive, but people have the power to be their own biggest threat – we live in a rapidly changing world.

Travel has also made me able to accept discomfort, difficulty, hardship and schedule chaos, although I always seek to reduce these issues as best as possible.

The more of the natural world I get to see, the more humbled I am and the more I wish to see of it.

Do you speak any foreign languages, and if so, which have been the most useful for you besides English?

English is my native and best spoken and understood language of course. I also speak and understand Flemish and German. I can get by with some Spanish and French, but I am not fluent or even especially good at these languages.

With travel, English has been the only language of use to me. Even in places where there is very limited or even no understanding of English, I never had significant difficulties in being understood. I prefer being with a guide or driver that speaks English, though, in places where it is especially challenging, like Russia and China.

I much prefer to travel and not have to worry too much about language difficulties. I also realize it is not practical or easy to learn many languages to a high standard.

What was the longest extended trip you have ever taken, when was it and where all did you go?

I have traveled with my family on longer trips than what I have done by myself, such as a round the world trip from England to Australia by ship, and a few airplanes across the Pacific and then slowly across the USA by train and another ship to Europe. In terms of my independent travels, set to my own schedule, in 2015, I took an extended trip around the Caribbean, Antarctic and Atlantic islands lasting three and a half months.

Just after New Year in London, I sailed from England to France and took a ship to Martinique in the French West Indies. Despite the time of year, the crossing was fairly smooth and uneventful, and I wasn't ill at all. Soon after arriving, I continued to the island of St Martin, visiting both the Dutch and French halves. Curiously in Marigot, the capital of the French sector, I spotted out of the corner of my eye a plaque marking the 'Consulate of the Principality of Seborga'. Without hesitation, I went inside and met the consul himself, who doubled up as a cigar merchant. He was very glad to receive me and had many pictures of him with the Prince of Seborga. Bizarre is the word to describe it. It was an unexpected find.

In Simpson Bay on the Dutch half of Sint Maarten, I chartered a 55ft catamaran to sail in seven days to Curaçao – a constituent country in the Kingdom of the Netherlands.

En-route to Curaçao I had planned to stop at the tiny Dutch island of Saba and then the Venezuelan island of Aves, right in the middle of the Caribbean. We only got as far as Aves, because of a serious mechanical problem with the boat, there was no alternative but to return to St Martin. This was the first problem which broke up my goal to complete the trip overland. To kill time, I took a yacht over to Anguilla and cruised to Dog Island and Prickly Pear Islands, as it was too far and windy to get to Sombrero Island, with no realistic chance of being able to land there.

I had to take an airplane to get to Curaçao. Once on Curaçao, I got really bad food poisoning so spent much of my time in my hotel. But I was able to have a driver take me on a circular tour of the whole island, lasting about 8 hours, which was enough to see the few sights there are – it is quite an arid, ugly island.

The next stage was taking a ship from Curaçao to Cartagena, Columbia, which went smoothly. I then spent quite a while, unexpectedly, in Cartagena, recovering, rather than pressing southwards to Patagonia overland. It was always going to be a race to cover so many miles in a short amount of time, but in hindsight, being forced to fly ended up being the better option in the end. After a recovery, I then flew to Ushuaia, Argentina.

The main focus of the trip, around which everything else was planned, was a South Atlantic cruise to Praia in the Cape Verde islands. The ship stopped off at King George Island, Antarctica; South Orkney Islands; Southern Thule, South Sandwich Islands; Bouvet Island; Gough Island; Tristan da Cunha archipelago; St. Helena, and Ascension Island.

My original plan was taking a ship from Cape Verde to North Africa, but since the original concept of making the trip overland was ruined, I did away with this, opting to return to England as quickly as possible. Instead, I traveled directly to London, with a brief stop in Morocco. Booked by satellite connection from the ship, it was pre-planned, and fortunately, Praia proved to be an ugly and grim city to spend too long in, so I was not sad to be leaving. Unfortunately, the commercially operated South Atlantic cruise was poorly scheduled, so there was not enough time at each place, and there were far too many unforeseen problems along the way. It is a trip to be repeated, properly, another time.

What two countries have exceeded your expectations and which ones left you feeling underwhelmed, and why?

This question holds little meaning to me; no country is the same throughout, good or bad. The example I give for this is Chad. Over two visits, I managed to avoid, by coincidence not by design, the capital city, N'Djamena. Instead, I flew into the northern desert region direct from Europe and spent eight wonderful days in the remote beauty of the Eneddi region. On the second visit, I transited N'Djamena airport direct onto a charter flight to the south to Zakouma National Park. I had wonderful experiences in the natural landscapes here too. I flew out by charter flight back to N'Djamana via Abéché, a small dusty town in the east. The town is unimpressive but is famous in the region for its trade in leather products. At the time, I was interested in the designs on leather products in the Sahel area, having seen them in other places. It is perhaps odd; I never bought a single possession made of leather. N'Djamena though looks to be very ugly and dirty, perhaps with little to see. I am sure that if I only visited the capital, I would have a completely different and false impression of the whole country. However, I will be interested in returning in the future to see the capital, as well as a few other sites that interest me.

Andorra is another country which exceeded my expectations and has continued to do so each subsequent time I have visited. It is small, efficient, clean, orderly, and scenic and has a pleasant feel to it. For me, it is everything a small state should be.

I dislike saying it, but Germany has often left me feeling underwhelmed on many visits there. It is a pleasant country with a lot to see and do, so it is not completely underwhelming, but it has never quite matched up with my expectations in many respects. To me, it lacks a lot of the feeling I enjoy about other European countries.

When you travel, do you prefer to go with others or solo, and why?

My preference is, generally but not exclusively, to travel with one other, or solo. This gives the maximum degree of flexibility to achieve what I am embarking to do without too many disruptions. However, much of the world is unsafe or difficult to travel through completely alone, so I am never truly solo – drivers and guides are usually present for the majority of the journey.

I very much dislike being subject to the often irrational and disinteresting wishes of a group; I will only travel in a group if I know that we all share, more or less, the same objectives – I've done this many times without problems. It's especially enjoyable on sea voyages, where a lively discussion is a nice way to while away the long hours.

What has been your most uncomfortable mode of transportation?

To reach many truly special places, oftentimes remote places, it has been necessary to travel by almost every mode of transportation, from foot to private jet, and almost everything in between. For getting to many places, it is necessary to suffer from a lack of comfort to a degree. Small comfort issues like being stuck on a bus without air conditioning in a hot country become much worse because of the presence of other people. It is much better to be in a private car and avoid the fatigue created from uncomfortable transport. It increases energy and productivity. On short trips which have tight schedules, this becomes a really important issue.

These small issues pale in comparison to the horrendous combination of being on a small boat in on the high seas. Many times now it has been necessary to charter such vessels to get to places otherwise completely inaccessible. The only way forward really is big seas – bigger vessels. It is almost impossible to find any joy in the emptiness of the seas and the loneliness of the islands when the journey is torturous.

What is the strangest thing you've seen/experienced while traveling?

There have been so many strange and truly bizarre things along the way, and it is hard to pick one single strangest thing. One of the more bizarre things I have encountered was arriving at Minsk airport in autumn 2012. The plane landed and taxied to a remote stand. There were several Belarusian cargo planes lined up, a Middle Eastern private jet, several Arab people around a car with a large Syrian flag on it and soldiers everywhere. Several of the armed soldiers came onto the plane and closed all of the window blinds and kept us waiting there for a long while, all of the other airplanes and the private jet left before we could disembark. The whole experience was strange and slightly unsettling.

What are the best and worst meals you have ever eaten while traveling, and where was it?

Food is not something I ever focus on when I am traveling. It is always a problem, and often a nightmare when traveling and looking to eat both well and with 'exotic' dietary requirements. I go out of my way to avoid most local foods in the majority of the world and try to eat what is safest and most familiar to prevent problems. Most of the world are unaccustomed to someone not eating how they do, so it is always hard. I like to eat well when I am at home and know what I am dealing with. In huge world cities, it isn't a problem, but I do not tend to spend much time in these places.

Out of the thousands of places you've stayed around the world, what have been your best and worst accommodations?

For me, the main issue is getting to the places I wish to see. I have a high tolerance for lack of comfort and convenience to do this, so I can put up with a lot when it comes to bad accommodation. This is not the idea, or a conscious choice, just a realistic acceptance of what is necessary.

Perhaps the all time worst was a very uncomfortable night on the high seas, crossing the South China Seas to Subic Bay in the Philippines. I was on a relatively small sail catamaran without proper facilities like plumbing or cooling. I had horrendous stomach pains and was sleeping on a thin plastic mattress down below in a small galley next to a cook who was chopping up fish while vomiting from seasickness himself. The heat was so unbearable that the paint was melting off the walls and onto my sweat drenched clothes and face. My pain was worsening so much that the captain made several emergency radio calls to nearby ships that could make a better speed. Not a single ship responded, including one sailing just a few miles away and in sight. I was very glad to get to land the following morning and check into a non-descript hotel, but it felt like the best in the world.

My family has been visiting the Hawaiian Islands since the 1920s, and I always find myself going back to the Royal Hawaiian Hotel on Waikiki Beach in Honolulu. They look after me tremendously, and it's a completely unique building, now hopelessly out of place, but a wonderful place to be with beautiful views. Waikiki has grown up around the building.

Another hotel worth mentioning is the Grandhotel Giessbach overlooking Lake Brienz in Switzerland. The views are simply unbeatable, and the lake takes many different colors depending on the time of year.

The best for me is home – wherever that is at the time, for the comfort of peace of mind.

What is your favorite "off the beaten path" destination, and why?

Picking favorites is always difficult, although I would go with the polar regions in general. More specifically, I suppose it has to be Bouvet Island; I will always find myself thinking of it, and planning a return. Bouvet is simply wonderful to admire from the windswept deck of a ship. It is sublime and mystical.

What were your most challenging countries to visit, and why?

So far no country has been especially challenging. Simply having the goal of visiting every country (in a loosely defined way) is not a hard one to achieve. You can fly to more or less every country; there are hotels, there are cars, there are always people willing to guide and assist you to some degree or another. Some places will require visas, but these can be dealt with, it is a question of logistics and knowing what to do or having someone help you who knows what to do. Many Europeans have a lot of difficulty in getting a visa for Angola for example. I recently visited visa-free, so it is all relative and depending on circumstance. Visiting countries is also a question of time, how long you want to spend in each country, this is completely down to personal preference. I have spent far more time than what is perhaps needed in some countries that hardly get a look-in from anyone, and just passed quickly through some major 'must-see' tourist destination countries. In both cases, I haven't felt it wasn't the best thing for me to do.

It is 'places' that are challenging to visit, not specific countries. As an example, it is easy to visit the Democratic Republic of Congo, but it is a real challenge to visit Salonga National Park. The government also limits access to some places, making it a challenge, but again, this is a matter of logistics, and there is always one solution or another if you are keen.

The only really challenging places to visit now really are perhaps some impenetrable jungle or desert regions which would require a lot of trekking or other arduous means of journey. As these hold little to no interest to me, I do not worry about it. The deep sea is a place I am interested in visiting, and this is certainly a challenge due to the few means that exist of reaching it.

Of which travel accomplishments are you most proud?

There are no specific accomplishments I am most proud of, once something is achieved, I am quick to realize there are much more things to see and do. I am generally pleased with what I have achieved so far and where I have been in a relatively short space of time. There is always so much more left to see, though, and once you visit somewhere once, you realize there is a reason to make subsequent trips back. I recently finished visiting every county, region, crown dependency, and island group in the British Isles. But there are still so many places left to visit; it is an archipelago with such variety.

Do you remember encountering particular people that left a lasting impression with you?

Many people along the way have left lasting impressions. To get to the places I have been able to reach so far has involved lots of people along the way who have helped and gone out of their way to make things easier for me, this is always a very warming experience. It has been a great shame to hear of hardship and tragedy for the some of the people along the way, but I am glad for the fond memories.

If you could travel back in time, to which era and place would you go, and why?

There are so many eras and places I would go back to in time. Old family photos of historical ocean liners, airplanes, and the then very exotic destinations make me wish I could have traveled the world in the interwar period. It would have been more difficult in many ways, but the sense of achievement must surely have been higher than it is today, we have never had it so good. My love of Japan's history compels me to wish I could go back and see it on the verge of opening up in the 1850s and then be around to witness the transition from the traditional Tokugawa shogunate to the internationally embracing Meiji government.

Can you describe any particular situation where you felt completely out of your comfort zone?

I am very happy with what I have and what I know. Deviating from this is stepping out into the unknown to a certain degree. However, I am able to remain within a fairly wide zone of comfort, so am fairly unphased by visiting many places which are perhaps not considered to be too safe or easy. I much prefer to be in places where I feel completely safe though - a common trend of danger zones is the presence of people and either economic or political struggles. The wilderness brings its own dangers, but there is definitely a greater feeling of security nonetheless.

What are your three favorite cities in the world, and why?

London, for being the most familiar as well as being a really grand city in the world where everything is available to you; Paris, for being so beautiful, romantic, and enjoyable to get lost in, and Venice, for its complete uniqueness and mystical allure.

What is the ideal amount of time you prefer to travel on each trip before you are ready to go home and take a break?

This depends entirely on the nature of the trip and the destination and also how much time I am willing to spend somewhere. I used to travel to a city, with plans to spend two or three days there, but then enjoyed it a lot and ended up staying an extra week or more. Now my travel plans are more clearly defined, so I do not do this. Some cities warrant a day or two, others a week or more.

Some places you have to spend a long time getting to and from, so if you want to go there, you have to accept this, ideal or not.

Taking extended voyages by sea is ideal, as you can import many aspects of home life with you along the way and still travel continuously.

In your opinion, where are the most beautiful places on Earth?

Beauty is very much in the eye of the beholder. There is also beauty to be seen everywhere. For me, beauty captures both the site and the atmosphere. For this reason, I find London to be very beautiful. Also due to familiarity, and to me, objectivity, Wester Ross and the Outer Hebrides, especially Uist, in Scotland, are the most beautiful places in the world. The polar worlds are also untouched, pristine, silent and sublime to view, so I find those areas very beautiful also.

Places where one least expects beauty, for me, also has a certain beauty to it. Many untamed, rugged, harsh regions like Central Africa have a very certain rough beauty to them, which is also unique, and perhaps difficult to convey as a concept.

An absence of things typically associated with beauty is something I appreciate very much. Empty, uninhabited islands, even ones without dramatic landmarks, will always be viewed as places of beauty to me. I find pure beauty in the barren landscapes of places like Rannoch Moor and the Caithness bogs in Scotland.

It is a dream to fly over the Putorana Plateau in Siberia. I'm sure it will be sublimely beautiful to me.

If you had an unlimited budget and space and time were no object, what would your perfect travel day look like (for example: start your morning in Bora Bora; afternoon on a safari in Kenya; night in Australia, etc.)?

My ideal day in travel, without any time and space issues, would start by waking up to the sunrise over a vast plain in Africa, seeing the animals going about their business. The afternoon would be spent on a ship in the Antarctic, making some landings on the continent and watching the penguins build their nests. I'd then spend the evening watching the sunset over either the West Scottish mountains, seeing them change from green to red to brown to black, or anywhere along the Wild Atlantic Way in Co. Donegal, Ireland, and then return home for the night.

Which three countries would you recommend for adventurous travelers to visit, and why?

China for cultural and linguistic adventure. If one was not familiar at all with the language, struggling to find many people to understand you and was happy to embrace this sort of adventure, China has it all. It is also a beautiful country with tremendous vistas of all varieties to admire.

Canada for outdoor adventure. It's a vast country with so much wilderness and is very much geared up for independent outdoor adventure, be it hiking, canoeing, sailing, flying – anything. It is the only sort of activity I will return to Canada for, as its cities hold little appeal to me.

Central Africa – take your pick of a country and go outside the capital cities – for general difficulty, chaos, and adventure. It is a region I find tremendously scenic and rewarding to visit, but it is a raw adventure and difficulties are abound.

If you had just one travel story to share with someone, what would it be?

One of the easiest and most pleasant travel experiences I have had was arriving by ship to Ascension Island, a remote British outpost in the South Atlantic Ocean. There is no specific story as such, but it was a very pleasant day from start to finish. It looks so arid and strange when anchored offshore, and making out the little buildings made me realize what a desolate place it seems to live. Getting onto the island proved my suspicions about it, but I managed to find a local worker (there are no taxis or tourism services) to drive me around the island to see the spots I was interested to see. It is such a strange island, unlike anywhere else I have been to – completely lunar in appearance, unbearably hot and rather secretive although it was possible to drive right into the airbase without any problems. Later that evening, I went back to the island from the ship and walked over to the beaches. Seeing green turtle hatchlings crawl down to the sea was a beautiful end to a strange, pleasant, interesting and fun day.

Do you ever feel you have missed out on certain aspects of life while away from home as you travel so much?

I have missed several things from home due to being away, but I have never felt I have 'missed out' so to speak. Spending a birthday alone with bad food poisoning on Curaçao was a particular low point. I missed out on taking a yacht to reach Klein Curaçao the following day – but these things happen, it was beyond any control. I always ensure to be around for the things that matter most to me, whether that is at home or away. Occasionally circumstance makes this difficult, but it remains the ideal.

What advice would you give to others who would like to travel to every country?

So many things sprung to mind for this answer. It is good advice to have a knowledgeable travel agent, it is also good advice to say to plan to have the time available for such an endeavor, and it is also good advice to say to do a lot of research and save wasted time down the line. I have tried to live and travel by this advice myself, but without much success. Never have I found a reliable, all-encompassing travel agent who understands exactly what I am doing. I have managed some time badly and not gone somewhere I really should have gone to at the time, and I have wasted time during travel by not planning things ahead.

However, to be held back by these concerns would be very limiting. The best advice really is just to go and do it. If the will is there, everything else should be possible.

For someone who has been almost everywhere, what still gets you excited about packing your bags again?

Packing my bags is never exciting to me, it is the very dull and mundane side of logistics which I dread. Something is always left behind resulting in minor chaos along the way. I often over pack the unnecessary and forget about the essentials, so I always come home with many replicas of things I have. It is perhaps my biggest weakness in travel.

Although, when I am packing my bags, I know a trip is coming up soon (I pack the night before or day of departure – also perhaps adding to the chaos), and this is what I find exciting. I dislike flying, so this is not so exciting, but most other modes gets me excited. When the journey begins, I realize how I'll only be covering such a tiny amount of ground ultimately. Even if I go 'everywhere', I will still only have been to so few places. The world is always able to humble you like this.

Looking ahead, what travel plans and goals are you still pursuing, and what is on your "Bucket List"?

My travels all stem from my generalist's interest in the entire world. Nothing is uninteresting to someone with a general interest in how the world works and exists. As such, every country holds things of interest. In every country, there are things to witness and explore to enhance my theoretical knowledge, as well as new thing to discover. Because of this, I can say that visiting every country will be a result of my goal to explore these things. It is achievable and is all down to logistics. To simply visit every country for the sake of doing so, and that alone holds no interest to me at all. Time is the one asset I can neither buy nor otherwise obtain more of than what I am due to have. I want my travels to have meaning and purpose for me as an individual. This has to be for the purpose of having a deep understanding of all the data points which connect the world together.

There isn't a defined bucket list, and I am not really enamored of these. I would like to continue my explorations of the islands of Sub-Antarctica. These will always be special for me, and I will repeat the ones I've already been to, they're too special to archive away in my mind; they're places to be experienced to the fullest. Alongside this, on the continent of Antarctica, there are also many historical points I am very interested in visiting.

Africa has many regions I am still yet to visit, and out of the way national parks which are rather hard to reach. Russia is a tremendously vast country, and a goal is to visit much more of this country, especially the north and east.

The world is a small place, but there will always be things to experience. The more places I visit and the more things I see and do, the more I realize how little of the world I have seen and how little it will be possible to ever see and do. No matter who you are, what your background is or where you are from, we are nothing in comparison to our home, Planet Earth.

Paul Hurwood, England

Where did you grow up, and what was your early life like?

Born in the city of Hereford, England. I still live there now for six months of the year; this is when I travel around Europe, the Arctic, Africa, the Middle East and Far East (Asia). Then in St. Catharines, Ontario, Canada for the remaining six months. This is when I travel around the Americas, Caribbean, Antarctica, the Pacific and Australasia. Early life outside of school, was traveling with my father; camping, swimming and canoing in rivers and the seas.

What was the first international trip you took, and what do you remember most about it?

In 1969. I was 10 years old at primary school. My parents, (both had served in the British Royal Navy) allowed me to be educated for a few weeks aboard the SS *Uganda* (S.S. stands for School Ship). I traveled from England to Portugal, then onto Spain and Gibraltar, taking in the Iberian Peninsula. I sailed around the Mediterranean, and stopped in Ceuta, Morocco. I remember the different smells and sights of the tour, in particular the spices in North Africa. Also I remember clearly being at the top of the rock in Gibraltar, I peeled an orange for a rock ape, who was as tall as I was at that time. It swiped the orange from my hand, grabbed hold of my hand, and sank its teeth into my upper arm.

When did you go from traveling casually to making this a full-time goal, and what motivated you to travel to every country?

1985. Reading *The Geographical Journal* inspired me. Hearing and reading accounts of Sir Ernest Henry Shackleton and Lt. Col. T. E. Lawrence, and more recently documentaries about polar and global explorer, Sir Ranulph Fiennes. I have had the pleasure on three occasions to listen to Sir Ranulph's lectures, on his life and polar travels.

Also back in the 1980's Michael Palin started to make superb documentaries on his travels. I had the great pleasure of meeting Michael a few years ago at Cardiff University, where we exchanged our future travel plans.

Then in 1993, after being elected a Fellow of the Royal Geographical Society, I had the greatest pleasure to listen to Sir Edmund Hillary, celebrating the 40th Anniversary and his own account, to be the first person to climb to the summit of Mount Everest. This was in the presence of Her Majesty Queen Elizabeth II, Prince Philip Duke of Edinburgh and Anne Princess Royal.

What have you done in your life to gain the freedom and finances to pursue as much travel as you have?

I started my working life in 1975, with three years at sea with Royal Fleet Auxiliary. An old Mariner told me to put money into property. I have to date bought, developed and sold 19 properties, since 1979. Apart from developing properties, I worked for 30 years for British Government and local government, mostly on part-time contracts, allowing me to travel extensively. I retired at 50.

Has there ever been a time where you considered abandoning your travel goals?

On the 8th of January 1989. I traveled overland through Ghana, Togo, Benin into Nigeria on the coastal road. Myself and three others in a 'share' car were held up by bandits. After that happened, I just wanted to be home and never travel again. However, having left Lagos and arriving in Douala, Cameroon, I had time to reflect on the situation and decided to carry on the rest of the tour through Cameroon, Gabon, Zambia, Zimbabwe, Botswana, South Africa, Swaziland, Lesotho and Namibia.

What do you consider to be your two favorite travel experiences, and why?

January 1988, Australia. Climbing to the top of Ayers Rock (Uluru). Incredible views. It is now no longer allowed.

25th of December 1995. Antarctica, 24 hours of light. We were in a Zodiac off the ship and the engines were cut, and a whale came up, and it's head came out of the water. Its eye was black and the size of a small plate, it seemed it was looking into my eyes. I will never forget it.

What are the main things you seek to experience when you travel (culture, cities, nature, animals, adventure activities, etc.)?

All of the above. I love to see animals in their natural habitat. The wonderful ancient and modern monuments and architecture, we have in our world. The countries and peoples of the world, it's amazing.

I am a qualified diver, and still like to dive and see our underwater world, and it's inhabitants. I also parachute, although in recent years I now go tandem, jumping from an airplane from 15,000 feet still causes the adrenaline to flow.

Looking back from when you started traveling to where you are now, in what ways, if any, has travel changed you?

I have spent many years of traveling on my own. In the early days, it was an excellent way to get to know yourself. If you can't live on your own and like yourself, how do you expect a partner to like you? Nowadays when traveling, I just take the journey and try to enjoy every hour of the day.

Do you speak any foreign languages, and if so, which have been the most useful for you besides English?

I have taken both Japanese and Arabic language courses, neither have been effective. When in Japan most people have spoken to me in English, the same in the Arabic speaking countries I have traveled to.

What was the longest extended trip you have ever taken, when was it and where all did you go?

January 1976 to June 1977. Onboard the ship, Royal Fleet Auxiliary. It included Wales, England, France, Gibraltar, Puerto Rico, British Virgin Islands, U.S.A. (on exercise with U.S. Navy). Back to England, Norway, Scotland, Gibraltar (again), Egypt, Malaysia, Singapore, Hong Kong, Thailand Philippines, Indonesia, Sri Lanka, then home to England.

What two countries have exceeded your expectations and which ones left you feeling underwhelmed, and why?

India and China exceeded my expectations. I have spent months in both countries, enjoying the incredible diversity of geography, architecture and nature. From jungles to deserts, from palaces to pagodas in both countries.

Underwhelmed by Nigeria (already mentioned) and South Africa. I did not enjoy traveling around the country while under apartheid.

When you travel, do you prefer to go with others or solo, and why?

Solo. I can stay or move on any time I want to. On the numerous occasions that I have traveled with other companions, accommodation has caused arguments. Traveling by myself to and through countries, I do not mind if I stay at a hostel or hotel.

What has been your most uncomfortable mode of transportation?

Third-class train from Calcutta to Madras, India in 1985. It was a three day and two night journey sitting on a wooden bench in the train, and I slept sitting up as there were so many of us cramped together. Lived on hard boiled eggs and tea for the whole journey.

What is the strangest thing you've seen/experienced while traveling?

In April of 1988, I was traveling by airplane from Panama City to Caracas, Venezuela. I estimated we were flying over the coast of Colombia. I was privileged to look down on a thunder and lightning storm; it was amazing to look down and not up, this spectacular storm had blue lightning, and took place for at least 20 minutes. It was more impressive at that moment than witnessing the aurora borealis (northern lights).

What are the best and worst meals you have ever eaten while traveling, and where was it?

2002. Portobello mushroom, sauteed with onions and balsamic vinegar. Paris, France.

1989. Ate burnt corn on the cob, for two days in Limbe, Cameroon, from a street vendor – I could not find any proper eateries.

Out of the thousands of places you've stayed around the world, what have been your best and worst accommodations?

Best have been the Waldorf Astoria, New York. Also, the Fairmont Royal York, Toronto, Canada. The Ritz in London and numerous Hilton's, Marriott's, Wyndham's and Starwood's (Sheraton) around the world. Not forgetting some beautiful hotels of Las Vegas. Also Sun City, South Africa.

The worst was a hostel in La Paz, Bolivia in 1989. $1 a night, with no running water, no electric and dozens of bugs in the bed and room! I was awake all night.

What is your favorite "off the beaten path" destination, and why?

Rapa Nui, Easter Island, South Pacific. The Moai heads are constantly in my mind. The carving of them I can understand, however, the positions they are situated in on the island, is quite overwhelming along with the numbers of them, some 887 weighing many tons each. While visiting, I was fortunate to witness an excavation, where we found that approximately only one-third of the carved stone is showing above ground. The rest of the torso to the navel is buried below ground.

What were your most challenging countries to visit, and why?

2003, Algeria. It was a challenge just to have the visa issued to visit the Western Sahara refugees. A friend Wayne Price and I ran the Sahara Marathon, south of Tindouf, to raise awareness of the Sahrawi People. At the United Nations Headquarters, Western Sahara is the only country on the map in 'red', which indicates it is under dispute and has been so for more than 40 years.

Of which travel accomplishments are you most proud?

1. Having been elected a life fellow of the Royal Geographical Society.
2. Reaching the 250 countries and island nations award with the Travelers' Century Club. I am now closing in on 300.
3. Being in the top 20 most widely traveled people in the world, with the Most Traveled People website.
4. I have donated numerous objects to the Pitt Rivers Museum at Oxford University; many of those objects are on display at the museum.
5. To have circumnavigated the world, east to west and west to east. And having been many times to both polar regions.
6. Working in orphanages in Jinja, Uganda, and Lima, Peru.
7. Having used and filled up ten passports over the years, and have them all for my perusal.

Do you remember encountering particular people that left a lasting impression with you?

January/April 1987. I traveled extensively around India, Nepal and Sri Lanka. While based in Hikkaduwa, Sri Lanka for nearly six weeks, I met an old man who was only known as "Uncle" by the village people of Hikkaduwa. He took me to a Buddhist temple and taught me many things about Sri Lanka. Also, after a week, he asked me for my birthdate and year. About a week later he brought me pages of writing about my life, up to the age of around 40 years old. It all came true. He told me that through a birthdate, you can tell a person's future through the stars and astrology. He was very old when I met him. I have traveled back to Sri Lanka and Hikkaduwa several times since 1987, and he is no longer there. However, I will never forget him.

A person who has become a close friend in Hereford, England over the past 20 years must be mentioned. Major Robert E. Barnes, who has retired. A man and friend of immense knowledge. When we meet and talk, either for coffee, a pint, or a good Scottish malt, his understanding of any situation is incredible. In the early years of knowing Robert, some statements he made about the world sounded unbelievable, so I would check them out on the computer, and sure enough, it was factual information. He doesn't use a computer; it is all stored in his mind. He is a man who talks to you, not at you or down to you. Through his education and his life, I have to say as a friend he is eccentric, in the most beautiful way, and I am sure his family knows this as well. He has taught me too many things to mention. One, in particular, is to keep a diary, and also that the shortest pencil is better than the longest memory, amongst many other things. I continue to learn from him whenever we meet.

Also my friend and former school master some 50 years ago, David E N B Jones, a Latin and Greek graduate of Cambridge University; again a man of immense knowledge and understanding. In October, 1985, along with Kelman Zempleny II from Los Angeles, we traveled together for weeks around and across the former Soviet Union. Playing bridge on the Trans-Siberian Express at 8'o'clock in the morning, with coffee and caviar for breakfast. Kelman taught me to reward yourself for things that you have done well, because very few others will!

Then I have just a handful of people from Hereford that have left impressions, and we have all traveled at different times together. A world tour with paraplegic adventurer, Pip Lamb; six continents with Mal Weeks; North America and Europe with Gareth Hall; the Middle East with Iain Webber-James; North America and Europe with Gareth

Watson; North America and Africa with Wayne Price; tours together in Africa with Wayne Hanson. Also staying several times with Richard Hunt from Hereford, who works as a teacher at the British Overseas school in Manila, Philippines. Not to forget, my good Canadian friend, Professor Paul Hamilton of Brock University, St. Catharines. When we meet for a drink, I tell Paul about the people and architecture in a particular country, and he tells me the government and political behavior of that country.

If you could travel back in time, to which era and place would you go, and why?

I would liked to have traveled in the Victorian Era, anywhere in the world, when Britain still had a strong Empire.

Can you describe any particular situation where you felt completely out of your comfort zone?

1989, Nigeria. Being held up by bandits, who came out of the jungle to the left of us, on a coastal road from Benin heading to Lagos. Then forced to strip with rifles pushed at you, is a frightening experience. One of the guys in the shared car had a small casket around his neck, a bandit snatched it from him, opened it and started to pour the white powder into his mouth. The guy who owned it was screaming and crying, after they had searched us and taken our belongings. He told me it was his ancestor's ashes in the casket he wore around his neck. My backpack was in the boot of the shared car; they didn't open the trunk. I was carrying more than $2,000 wrapped up in my clothes in the backpack. I remember praying. After taking what they wanted, they went back into the bush jungle.

What are your three favorite cities in the world, and why?

1. Rio de Janiero. Just a fantastic city with party after party, and superb beaches.

2. San Francisco. Because it's San Francisco.

3. New Delhi. It's more manic than London, Paris and New York put together.

What is the ideal amount of time you prefer to travel on each trip before you are ready to go home and take a break?

Between 4-12 weeks. After three months, I start to miss my wife, family and friends.

In your opinion, where are the most beautiful places on Earth?

1. Seychelles. There's a reason why Prince William and Catherine, had their honeymoon there! I believe it is the safest island nation on earth. A most spectacular place.

2. Saint Helena. Beautiful semi-tropical island.

3. The polar regions, both the Arctic and the Antarctic. Probably the cleanest air I have breathed. Superb wildlife.

If you had an unlimited budget and space and time were no object, what would your perfect travel day look like (for example: start your morning in Bora Bora; afternoon on a safari in Kenya; night in Australia, etc.)?

Morning walking along the Great Wall of China; afternoon wandering around the temples of Angkor Wat; late afternoon watching polar bears in Svalbard, and the evening watching the millions of stars visible in the night sky above the Masai Mara. I have done all of these things on different occasions.

Which three countries would you recommend for adventurous travelers to visit, and why?

1. U.S.A. From the beautiful beaches of the West and East Coast, and all the water sports that go with it. The deserts,

and the mountain regions, and all the sports activities that can be enjoyed. Or simply traveling through the different states.

2. Australia. For the same reason.

3. Peru. Walking the Inca Valley from Cusco to Machu Picchu.

If you had just one travel story to share with someone, what would it be?

February 1996, Port Lockroy, Antarctica. Going ashore to the survey station, most of the passengers on the Russian icebreaker were American. When the two staff running Port Lockroy survey station realized I was from England, they asked me if I would take their mail home to England as it could take months before a survey ship would come from the Falkland Islands. The survey ship would then take the mail back to the Falklands, and from there it is flown home. I agreed, and it took me five weeks to get home and post their letters at an English post office. So, for just a short while I was an Antarctic postman. Which brings back memories from April 2012, South Georgia, sub-Antarctica. Stranded in Grytviken for 11 days, with engine failure. I cleaned Sir Ernest Henry Shackleton's grave on two occasions. I will not forget James Wake, the Base Commander, for all your help, with allowing me to use the computers at the station, and not forgetting, John, the doctor. We then transferred ship to an Argentinian icebreaker, then eight days sailing to Montevideo, Uruguay. A wonderful expedition.

And finally, a poem I wrote on travels back in the late 1980's.

The Messenger

Send him east then across to the west,
The poles both north and south,
For there's no greater way of spreading the news,
Than there is by word of mouth.

For the truth to be told by men so bold,
Who'd travel the world so wide,
Would have nothing to fear,
From his fellow man's ear,
Speak it; you've nothing to hide.

So what is this truth you speak of,
Is it in money, gold or charms.
Simpler than that my dear good friend,
Welcome Nations with open arms.

For the sooner, the lesson is heard by all,
The quicker the learning will be,
That the cultures, colours, and creeds of this world,
Can live in peace on this earth you see.

Do you ever feel you have missed out on certain aspects of life while away from home as you travel so much?

My wife Catharine and I met in Antarctica in 1995, aboard a Russian icebreaker. When we married in 2000, when we were both in our 40's. Never had children, my one and only regret.

What advice would you give to others who would like to travel to every country?

You must have a financial strategy that does not run out, and a plan to travel to countries, or it will never come to fruition. Traveling around the world to all of the countries and island nations, even on a budget, will cost an incredible amount of money.

For someone who has been almost everywhere, what still gets you excited about packing your bags again?

At the time of this interview, I am heading out to El Salvador, Colombia and San Andres again in two weeks time. I still get the "jitters" before leaving for a trip, tour or expedition. However, that for me is the drug, and it is very addictive.

Looking ahead, what travel plans and goals are you still pursuing, and what is on your "Bucket List"?

To complete all 193 countries – I have five more tours to do. I am planning to do this over the next 6 or 7 years, before completing all.

Luis Filipe Gaspar, Portugal

(In Ecuador)

Where did you grow up, and what was your early life like?

I was born in Lisbon in 1958. I made my first travels with my parents when I was still a child. We would drive to Spain and France. That is how I acquired a taste for roaming. At that time, after returning home, I would look at the world map and question myself since I felt that I still had "so much world" to discover. I began to understand that my curiosity might take me far. Reading, searching, observing, recording, taking pictures became part of my everyday life. And that is how I am today.

What was the first international trip you took, and what do you remember most about it?

It was my first InterRail on which I traveled to ten countries in Europe. I sold books and ice cream at the Lisbon Popular

Fair, saved some money, and my father lent me some small change, and I set off on my adventure. Twenty-four hours later I arrived in Paris. Carrying my backpack, I went door to door searching for the youth hostel I had booked beforehand. Some were closed, and others were full. In the end, I spent the night at Gare d'Austerlitz and promised myself that never again would I bother to book a hotel – something that I still fulfill, religiously, to this day.

When did you go from traveling casually to making this a full-time goal, and what motivated you to travel to every country?

I became an untiring traveler while I was still young. At sixteen, I traveled around Europe for a month with a friend. When I got home, I made some calculations. In a somewhat unique equation, I calculated the number of years that I expected to live, the amount of holidays I would have throughout my life, and the places in the world that I would like to visit. When I saw the result, I realized that I was "already lagging significantly behind." From then onward, my mission became to "mend the damage". Since then, and with this reckoning in mind, I have sought to balance this ratio. I traveled extensively in Europe, and when I felt that I knew the Old Continent like the back of my hand, I decided to take on the world. I know a significant part of the world, which allows me to have a comprehensive knowledge of other cultures. Whenever I visit a country, getting to know UNESCO World Heritage Sites is one of my priorities. This is a commitment that I have undertaken. After traveling for so many years, I still feel that traveling is worth living for.

What have you done in your life to gain the freedom and finances to pursue as much travel as you have?

Based on the decisions that I have made over the years, I am aware that my life and my routines are different from the majority of people. From a personal and financial point of view, I have obviously made choices and continue to do so. I would not be able to face life in any other way. A mixture of adventure and romance vs. oddness and seduction. In practice, it has meant a careful management of my investments, more specifically my holiday plans and my expenditures. Over the last years, the issue of my holidays has become easier since I am self-employed. As for the family, that has to some extent also been overcome since I do not have a traditional family nucleus and, as a consequence, I am not subject to the constraints that this would imply.

Has there ever been a time where you considered abandoning your travel goals?

My architectural background and because I have worked in various places around the world has allowed me to harmonize discipline and rigor, two of the features that define me, with being a passionate man open to the world. I have never regretted it, but I am fully aware that the path I have embarked upon is complicated, because to take this route I had to relinquish other life projects, perhaps easier or perhaps more trying.

What do you consider to be your two favorite travel experiences, and why?

Since forewarned is forearmed, I always have a well-delineated program of what I want to see and to do, but I always leave one or two days for unforeseen events, whether they are hitches or new opportunities, that could enrich my journey. One time, when returning from a trip to Bolivia, the plane was delayed six hours. I availed of the spare time, called a cab and asked the driver to take me to a Jesuit Mission in the middle of the forest. When I arrived at the hamlet, it was pitch-dark. In the midst of all the blackness, the light from the candles that lit up a magnificent painted wooden church where Easter Mass was being held stood out. I shall never forget that place, the people and the hymns that appeared quite by chance on a trip that supposedly had already ended.

What are the main things you seek to experience when you travel (culture, cities, nature, animals, adventure activities, etc.)?

Like any other traveler I could organize my trips around food, beaches, hotels, sports, work, exhibits, and congresses, among other things. There's an almost infinite array of topics. The fact that I have ambitioned, from a very young age, to know the world, presupposes considerable strictness and determination, which I believed that I possessed. Right from the start I assumed as a life project and guiding principle that it would be the UNESCO World Heritage Site since it would allow me to combine my vocation for the arts with my passion for traveling.

Looking back from when you started traveling to where you are now, in what ways, if any, has travel changed you?

I admit that because I have overcome several obstacles and reached several goals and, above all, considering what I have achieved so far, I can consider it a gain. I found myself between the will to start off on an adventure at the beginning of each trip and my training as an architect, in particular in architectural renewing and renovation, which allows me to have a different view of everything around me. It is in these two closely related worlds that I find the "almost" perfect balance. Despite my long track record as an irredeemable traveler, and regardless of how plain the destination may be, I still feel that each new trip has enriched me in some way. I find that traveling boosts our universe and gives perspective to the universe of our being. Only in this way can we understand the true dimension of our littleness and our small world. After each trip one feels smaller, humbler and, above all, more human, not only from the cultural point of view but above all as a person.

Do you speak any foreign languages, and if so, which have been the most useful for you besides English?

I am fluent in English, Castilian, French, and in Portuguese, my mother tongue. Of course, English, considered a universal language, has helped me in many situations. However, more than speaking any language, it is important to be able to communicate and to relate. I recall a situation during my trip to Iran. I was asked whether I wanted a driver who could speak English and I answered that it did not really matter. In the end, I got a driver who only spoke Arabic. That man was extremely affable, one of the features of the Iranian people, and he accompanied me all the time during my seven-day stay. I never had any problems nor did this ever keep me from doing what I had planned for this trip.

What was the longest extended trip you have ever taken, when was it and where all did you go?

The longest trips that I have ever made lasted five weeks. Among them I can highlight my trip to India and Nepal, two countries with very unique features and that I always like to mention when speaking about my life project. The cultural, religious and social diversity and even the different approach to life is one of the things that fascinate me most in India. You can see contrasts around every corner, and for someone who tirelessly seeks diversity, India is a real treasure and an authentic rainbow. Jaisalmer is "The Golden City" (because of its dune colored houses), Jodhpur is "The Blue City", Jaipur is "The Pink City" and Udaipur is "The White City", also nicknamed "The Venice of the East". To the color mixture is added the mixture of the many spices and, of course, the mix of lifestyles, of religious beliefs and habits. A trip along the sacred Ganges or a visit to Varanasi, a city where thousands of pilgrims gather, will certainly linger in the memory of each visitor as they linger in mine. As to Nepal, where the Everest is located, it is truly the "top of the world". The Kathmandu Valley, with its countless temples, is truly magical and proves the country's religious and legendary diversity. Lumbini, the birthplace of the Lord Buddha, is also a must-see, as well as the Royal Chitwan National Park or the Sagarmatha (the park inhabited by the Sherpas, who devote themselves to helping mountaineers climb the Himalayas). The Phewa Lake, the Devi Waterfalls, the World Peace Pagoda or Kangchenjunga are other places that I could not miss on this long, enriching and demanding trip.

What two countries have exceeded your expectations and which ones left you feeling underwhelmed, and why?

Of all the countries I have visited, I cannot choose the number one because the places and the cultures are not comparable. One cannot compare New Delhi and New York. There are places that have given me more while others have given me less! India always gives me a lot, while China always gives me less than I expect.

When you travel, do you prefer to go with others or solo, and why?

To travel, always! Be it solo or with others. I am flexible regarding the choice of company, but that does not mean that I give up my plans and my way of traveling, quite the contrary, as far as that is concerned I am rather "uncompromising."

What has been your most uncomfortable mode of transportation?

I could mention a few weird means of transportation used in India or some countries on the African continent. But I shall never forget a train trip on my first trip to China.

Hundreds of people crammed in the rail cars, some sitting, others standing, mixed with food scraps, an unbearable greasy smell wrapping everything. That was rather uncomfortable, something that I still remember to this day.

What is the strangest thing you've seen/experienced while traveling?

Because I prepare my travels in great detail, I cannot say that I have ever been really surprised. Of course on all travels and depending on the place where you are, there will always be one or another situation that surprises or marks you more, but I have never actually been surprised. Also, because I never set out with definite ideas about the places that I have set out to discover, I set off on my voyage of discovery without preconceived ideas. Therefore, the "strangest" things that happen to me become, in the end, an important trait of this will to know more – to know every corner of the world in a different way.

What are the best and worst meals you have ever eaten while traveling, and where was it?

Although I enjoy good food, I find that it is not the same as a good meal. This can be only a piece of chicken with white rice accompanied by a very cold beer. It depends on the place and the circumstances, and that is what I value most. However, I recall an excellent foie gras on Madagascar and an appalling fried fish in Mali.

Out of the thousands of places you've stayed around the world, what have been your best and worst accommodations?

In India, a country of extreme beauty and contrasts. In Rajasthan, I stayed at a hotel that was a true Maharajah's palace, covered with gold and precious stones, silver cutlery and plates and everything else that my retina and my memory did not have the privilege to record. As to the worst, there were a few, but a small "hotel" on the banks of the Manaus river, in an area called "Triple Frontier" – Brazil, Tabatinga, Peru, Santa Rosa and Leticia, Colombia. I fell asleep with the bed up against the bedroom door. When I woke up in the morning, I saw that there was a pool of blood next to the hotel entrance!

What is your favorite "off the beaten path" destination, and why?

I can think of four places where I would like to settle. New Zealand and Australia because of the relaxed lifestyle, the opportunities, the people and the freedom it represents traveling in those places just with a backpack. Hawaii, because it is an island paradise where you have access to everything you need to live comfortably and because that story about love and a cottage only works for half a dozen months. And Canada, because it is sort of Australia in the Northern Hemisphere.

What were your most challenging countries to visit, and why?

Some of the countries in Central Africa, both on account of their political regime and on their standard of living. Despite most of its people being kind, the governments exert a great control, which often prevents us from getting about and restrains our movements, such as taking pictures and getting close to a place or a monument. On the other hand, due to the emerging danger and the level of poverty, traveling inland is quite challenging, not only because of the means of transport but also because of the accessibilities that are practically non-existing.

Of which travel accomplishments are you most proud?

Each madman has his obsessions, and I have a whole collection of them. I am particularly fascinated by trains, trains that no longer run and that in some cases have been abandoned. In order to see them and to record them, I am capable of traveling hundreds of kilometers. And it is while traveling that I get my hair cut, twice a year, in places you would never imagine. I always have more than one trip thought out. I only use old *Lonely Planet* travel guides. I may not remember names or faces, but I have a gift for remembering - with impressive detail - a place where I once ate, tens of years ago, in some far-away place. As I have an adventurous spirit, I pepper my journeys with more or less radical experiences. I have climbed Mont Blanc with the greatest Portuguese mountain climber João Garcia, I have skydived, skied, and I have also dived with sharks. Another of my passions is photography. It enables me to capture places, moments and things that I want to perpetuate in my memory and share with those who consider themselves as accomplices of my adventures.

If you could travel back in time, to which era and place would you go, and why?

If I had the power to travel back in time, I would surely go back to the 15th and 16th century, to accompany the Portuguese seafarers who adventured out to sea in search of new worlds. I can completely identify with the desire to go beyond what is known, to go beyond what we see on the horizon. So, therefore, going on board a caravel and helping discover the sea route to India, a place that still fascinates me to this day every time I go there, would be a tempting adventure. Who knows, this tendency to want to sail in "uncharted waters" – as one of the most famous Portuguese writers of all times, Luís Vaz de Camões, once said – is not in the blood of the Portuguese. But it is in mine, that I know for sure!

Can you describe any particular situation where you felt completely out of your comfort zone?

It is true that I have been in some difficult situations. I have landed in some countries where I was the only passenger to get off the plane in that place (all the other passengers were only in transit). One example is the African countries, where political and social stability is still far from being achieved. In Guinea or Liberia, for instance, I did indeed feel out of my comfort zone. It is not easy to travel in the country; it is not easy to find a place to eat, or even to walk down an avenue without more or less threatening stares. The same happened on a recent trip I made to Somalia. Traveling around the country, in particular in Somaliland, an area that is claiming its independence is not exactly comfortable. I experienced another less-than-pleasant situation when I was assaulted by the police in Ukraine. Albeit it is not a confidence inspiring situation, this did not keep me from moving on.

What are your three favorite cities in the world, and why?

From my point of view, and seeing that they conciliate and "carry" a number of values that are so dear to me, historical, artistic, cultural, environmental and urban, it would be Lisbon and Berlin. And Sydney, for its beauty and enviable lifestyle.

What is the ideal amount of time you prefer to travel on each trip before you are ready to go home and take a break?

Instead of saying how much time I spend in one place before I feel the need to go home, I think it is easier to say the minimum amount of time I feel that I need to be in a given place to get to know it: never less than three weeks. All of this is, of course, very subjective and full of constraints, namely the places that I find that I must visit if I am in a country without having a marked destination if one place makes me stay longer than I had initially foreseen. Returning home is always good, but for someone who travels desperately and who escapes whenever he can, as it is my case, the breaks are not exactly a necessity.

In your opinion, where are the most beautiful places on Earth?

UNESCO World Heritage Sites never disappoint me, whether they are natural or cultural heritage sites. As to the wonders of nature, I would place the Perito Moreno Glacier on a pedestal, as one of the last life glaciers on Earth and which occupies part of the Argentinian Patagonia. And as far as cultural heritage is concerned, I have a weak spot for temples (perhaps an occupational "fault"). I was very impressed by the temples of Angkor, in Cambodia, built with a remarkable architectural and urban accuracy. With the Giza pyramids and the temples of Luxor and Aswan in Egypt, and regardless of how much I think about it, I still cannot grasp how they managed, in those days, to work and transport the granite blocks. Or with the fascinating city of Lalibela, in Ethiopia, the main pilgrimage center of the Christian Orthodox Church and famous for its mysterious subterranean churches sculpted in monolithic rocks and that historians today still question how and why these churches were built. To me, a trip always enriches you. For instance, I was once not really fascinated by deserts, but today I am passionate about them, about their colors, lights, and shadows.

If you had an unlimited budget and space and time were no object, what would your perfect travel day look like (for example: start your morning in Bora Bora; afternoon on a safari in Kenya; night in Australia, etc.)?

This question is indeed a challenge, and I could give many different answers. However, this one day plan seems quite attractive. I would wake up, with the sun shining, in Angkor Wat, in Cambodia. I find the magic that involves that space that has close to one thousand temples, quite fascinating. For breakfast, I would travel from Asia to Central America and would sit on the Jardim de la Union, in Guanajuato, Mexico. Without pressure constraints, I would spend the morning diving at 50-meters in that same area, in the Caribbean Sea, on one of the most beautiful beaches for diving, the Grand Anse Bay, in Grenada. For lunch, I would choose the restaurant La Varangue, in Antananarivo, Madagascar (one of my favorite restaurants in the whole world, if I may say so). If I had spent the morning in the heat, in the afternoon I would climb Mont Blanc and afterward I would go parachuting. I would end the afternoon with a good gin at the Victoria Falls Hotel, in Zimbabwe. Then I would fly back to the Americas, this time to Buenos Aires, for dinner at the Cabaña Las Lilas restaurant. I would have my coffee on the Strawberry Hill in Jamaica. After the coffee break, I would go to Iceland to see the Northern Lights (Aurora Borealis), and finally, I would lay down in a sleeping bag in the Sahara Desert, in Egypt.

Which three countries would you recommend for adventurous travelers to visit, and why?

It is difficult to choose only three, but I would suggest Bolivia, India, and Australia.

Bolivia, on account of the great diversity of its landscapes, which pose a true challenge: Nevado Sajama, more than 6,500 meters above the sea, Salar de Uyuni, the largest salt flat in the world, the huge lakes and the Lake Titicaca or the Altiplano.

India, for its cultural diversity, and its mixture of colors, landscapes and traditions. The country has mountains, the Himalayas; it has beaches, deserts and in all those landscapes there are so contrasting ways of life that it is a pure adventure to let oneself be carried away by the spirit of discovery and get to know such a multitude within the same country.

Australia, one of my countries of choice, is entirely different. The landscape variety in Australia is also a challenge. Diving in the Great Barrier Reef is mandatory for whoever loves water sports, because of the unique explosion of colors and life that you find there. The rocky formations in the desert in the country's interior are also unique. A trip on the Indian Pacific Railway is the most magnificent way to get to know the Australian Desert. The country has glaciers, lush forests, in addition to very interesting cities, like Sydney, Melbourne or Perth.

If you had just one travel story to share with someone, what would it be?

I have many stories, but if I were to choose one I would tell about my arrival in Iran, precisely to prove how traveling with defined ideas is not the right attitude. I must admit that when I arrived in Tehran at two o'clock in the morning, I felt uneasy concerning what was in waiting for me. However, from the moment I arrived until I left, everything went just fine. The people are very friendly, and you can see that they are pleased to show tourists the past and richness of the country, which mainly involves beautiful palaces surrounded by vast gardens. It does not make sense to be fearful because, after all, I traveled quite calmly through Iran, not having experienced any problems regarding safety and always with the immense friendliness of the Iranians.

Do you ever feel you have missed out on certain aspects of life while away from home as you travel so much?

I feel that I am a citizen of the world, and I really cannot face life in any other way. On account of the fact that I have overcome several hurdles and reached several goals, for all that I have achieved so far, I consider it a gain and never a loss.

What advice would you give to others who would like to travel to every country?

My traveling philosophy is very simple: "squeeze the places". That is why I created several rules that have simplified my life. One is never to spend the first day at the place of arrival; I gain more if I leave it for the return. Another is not to travel with luggage in the hold, so as not to lose it and not to be subject to anyone putting (or removing) anything from your luggage. As to hotels, I try to find them when I can. If there is a bed, fine, if not there is always the car, a railway station or a park bench where you can spend the night. As a forewarned person, I travel with a well-outlined plan of what I want to see and do, but I always leave one or two days for unforeseen events, whether they are hitches or new opportunities that could enrich my journey. Another golden rule is not to start off with presumptions regarding the places and the people. That is a serious mistake that I have been able to confirm on several occasions.

For someone who has been almost everywhere, what still gets you excited about packing your bags again?

One day being able to leave without knowing when I shall return, i.e. without a set date and time.

Looking ahead, what travel plans and goals are you still pursuing, and what is on your "Bucket List"?

As far as traveling is concerned, I am tireless, wherefore there are always new places that I want to visit and where I want to adventure. Furthermore, as I have always mentioned, I always leave one or two things to see in each destination so that I have an excuse to go back there. Visiting all the countries is not enough for me, so to speak. It is obvious that the countries that I have not yet visited are at the top of my list, and they are the ones to which I currently direct my attention to. Gazing at my world map, the few African countries that I still do not know jump out, and especially countries in Central Asia and the Pacific. In Oceania, I already know Australia and New Zealand, but there are many more that I still do not know, some of them true paradises on Earth for those who appreciate a landscape with sun and sea. The Fijian islands, Palau or the Marshall Islands are in my plans, as well as Samoa or Vanuatu, with their unique cultures and which will certainly mark or even surprise me, despite all the experience that I have accumulated so far.

Artemy Lebedev, Russia

(After having reached the Geographic South Pole, 2012)

Where did you grow up, and what was your early life like?

I was born in Moscow at the Grauerman Maternity Hospital on February 13, 1975 (birth height: 50 cm; birth weight: 3500 g).

I was a regular Soviet school student in a working class outskirt of Moscow. The only thing that connected me with the world was the political map of the world which hung on my wall. I was looking at countries, learned some funny city names like Bujumbura or Bandar Seri Begawan (both sound sort of weird in Russian), and never had the slightest hint that someday I will visit any of those. Foreign travel was not an option in my country.

What was the first international trip you took, and what do you remember most about it?

My first trip abroad was Greece in 1987. It became possible only because of the Perestroika. The best a Soviet citizen could dream of before that could be Bulgaria or Mongolia, but even for that, you had to qualify.

The choice of Greece was because my grandmother is Greek, but she was brought to the USSR at the age of 12 in 1935, and she had a chance to see her homeland after me.

I remember two things: a trip on a cruise ship *Pegasus* around the Aegean Sea (a gift from some Greek relatives) and when I was changing price labels on boxes in a supermarket to pay less for the goods (it was a time they could be repasted, and cashier actually believed in the numbers on the stickers).

When did you go from traveling casually to making this a full-time goal, and what motivated you to travel to every country?

Russia's borders have been wide open since 1991, but only had Greece, Ukraine, Poland, Germany, Mexico and U.S. on my list of visited countries before the year 2000. I never thought of becoming a traveler.

But one day it all changed, and I used travel as a remedy for my laziness.

After visiting Cuba and Great Britain in one year, I had a plan: I have to visit one new place every month. It could be a country, it could be a city, but it has to be a new location. Otherwise, I would be sitting eternally in my chair in front of the monitor. I wanted to have a reason to have a break that I cannot ignore. So since then I have had no gaps in my monthly travel plan.

What have you done in your life to gain the freedom and finances to pursue as much travel as you have?

It all progressed very naturally. I never had a plan in advance. I didn't have a plan to visit all the countries before half of them were done.

In 1992, I opened my first design company, and in 1995, I founded the first Internet design studio in Russia, which happened to become the largest design company in the country. Today there are more than 350 people employed, and we've just celebrated our 20th anniversary.

My website is Art. Lebedev Studio (www.artlebedev.com) if you want to see what I do besides traveling.

Has there ever been a time where you considered abandoning your travel goals?

Somewhere along the road I've realized that I travel too much. And I've come up with a new plan: travel no more than one week a month after visiting all the countries. More or less this is what I'm sticking to now because I have so many things to do at work.

What do you consider to be your two favorite travel experiences, and why?

My memoirs could fill up the rest of this book. But I will randomly pick these two stories.

1) When in Guinea, I got almost killed by the street gang. It was the day they announced presidential election results. And it's a day you don't want to be in an African country. Not on the street at least.

I managed to arrive in Conakry at night. The city was completely empty. And suddenly there were rocks on the road. So many rocks that our car couldn't get past them. We stopped and then there were rocks flying at us. And then 10 or 15 people appeared. And then they took everything from us. They robbed me, my guide and my driver. Somehow our driver overcame the initial shock and managed to make a U-turn, so in the end, we all survived. But I clearly remember my thought: this is it.

2) When in Antarctica, we were waiting for good weather to fly to the South Pole. The camp on the glacier is the most boring place on Earth. There was a limit of one glass of wine per person, and the food was bad, too. Some of the folks, who spent $50,000 US were not excited about this level of service.

Luckily for us, the weather was perfect. And we jumped the relic DC-3 that flies to the South Pole itself. Flight time is about four hours. So I had some time to chat with the pilot. When he found out that I take helicopter lessons, he immediately offered me the right seat and gave me controls. I tried several aircraft's in my life, and DC-3 was a particular pleasure to operate. You just have to be gentle with it.

When we finally arrived at the Amundsen-Scott Station, the weather was so good that we didn't need any of the fur hats, gloves and parkas. A guy from the U.S. station came out to greet us – and he was wearing Crocs!

When I got to the stick indicating the Geographic South Pole, I took it off the snow and moved it ten centimeters north (actually, any direction from the initial position is north, it is fascinating). So I am responsible for the new position of the South Pole now.

What are the main things you seek to experience when you travel (culture, cities, nature, animals, adventure activities, etc.)?

I hate nature. There are so many absolutely fantastic photos of every beautiful place, taken at every possible time of the day, that I feel no need to come and witness if the sunset at this beautiful place indeed appears at this spot at this time of the year.

I love cities. They are underexplored. They always change. No one captures those changes. That's where I come in.

I love side-streets, phone booths, street lights, trash cans, benches, doors, and windows. I make a profile of every city I visit (1332 at the time of this interview, March 2016) and in ten years it will be different.

Some things have completely disappeared from our knowledge that could have been recorded by people living then. Like, how did a garbage dump look at the time of Leonardo? Or how a trash can looked in Saint Petersburg in 1900? Or how a street sign looked in Moscow in 1915? You only may guess today because no one was willing to take a close-up photo or make a drawing of that.

Looking back from when you started traveling to where you are now, in what ways, if any, has travel changed you?

The biggest result for me is a complete lack of xenophobe. People are people everywhere. And I am comfortable everywhere people are – on the 100th floor of an NYC skyscraper and inside a Mauritanian tent with goats and flies. Before traveling, I was afraid of most of the places. Just like people are scared of Afghanistan, Palestine or Somalia now. When you come there, you see that it's really nice.

Do you speak any foreign languages, and if so, which have been the most useful for you besides English?

I speak Russian and English. When in school I was taking lessons in French with zero success. And some Greek, but the lack of practice eliminated any progress I had. Actually, English today is the most universal language in the world. You may safely travel with it.

What was the longest extended trip you have ever taken, when was it and where all did you go?

That was my first Ethnographic Expedition. I bought a Range Rover, covered it with sponsor stickers, and drove all the way through Russia until Nakhodka. The car was so bad, and I spent most of the journey fixing it. The biggest problem was that the engine's supports were not strong enough, and – this is no joke and no exaggeration – my engine fell out four times.

It was 1998, and guys at Land Rover didn't care about the Internet. At the same time, I had a pretty large audience reading my blog and for many years, Range Rover become a symbol of inferior car quality and lack of customer service.

In the end, I had to leave my car at the official dealers in Ulaanbaatar for a month, and for half a year in Krasnoyarsk.

The whole trip took more than a year.

What two countries have exceeded your expectations and which ones left you feeling underwhelmed, and why?

Portugal and Malawi are real hidden gems.

The Galapagos Islands and Easter Island were a real disappointment.

The Galapagos is where you can see some turtles and wish there were better hotels and restaurants. Most of the tourist attractions are really boring, predictable, and it all looks like a local zoo.

The giant panda sanctuary in Sichuan is a hundred times better.

Easter Island is an example of an overrated destination. There's nothing on the island itself, just couple of villages. There's general knowledge that scientists are fascinated by the moai. Some people think they came up from space, and some people believe they were carved a thousand years ago. Everyone thinks they are extremely heavy. But in reality, they are light and were cut out right on the island just 300 years ago, when St. Petersburg was founded in Russia.

The rock gods on Mount Nemrut in Turkey are the real thing if you want to see really impressive and ancient statues in a remote location.

Generally, I would say that South America is very much underestimated and most of Africa is very much overrated.

When you travel, do you prefer to go with others or solo, and why?

I prefer to be alone, because I don't need breakfast, and everyone else cannot go without it.

What has been your most uncomfortable mode of transportation?

There were many. When in school we were traveling to mountains in the back of a truck with so little space that three girls had to sit on my legs. After that, I could not walk for 20 minutes.

Recently I was traveling in China on an overnight sleeping bus. That is very memorable and really uncomfortable. Even a train with no A/C in India in the summer is better.

What is the strangest thing you've seen/experienced while traveling?

I'm lucky to see strange things every day. One example: there is a tradition in Peru to be in yellow underwear when New Year comes.

What are the best and worst meals you have ever eaten while traveling, and where was it?

I keep an excellent memory of the Wagyu beef in Japan. I don't remember the name of the restaurant, but it seems like it's perfect everywhere.

At the same time, I can't understand how people in Scandinavia can eat licorices. Eeew.

Out of the thousands of places you've stayed around the world, what have been your best and worst accommodations?

I remember literally hundreds of good and bad accommodations.

The bad one: a room with the toilet bowl right in the room and no windows, in a Liberian village.

The good one: a ride on a private Boeing to Italy, then helicopter transfer to a villa in Sicily, then a Zodiac ride to the 100-meter long private yacht with black caviar and some good wine and good company. Not sure if I could tolerate that for more than couple of days.

What is your favorite "off the beaten path" destination, and why?

I love to walk the streets of old Moscow at 5 am on a Sunday in the summer. It is the beauty and tranquility without a single person around.

What were your most challenging countries to visit, and why?

I tried to get visas to Turkmenistan for ten years and to Saudi Arabia for seven years. That was hard.

Tokelau was particularly hard to get to, because I was denied access to it on one atoll, so we sailed to another and I tried to get ashore before the immigration office woke up. And I made it. My illegal entry became legal when I talked to guys there and got the Tokelau stamp in my passport.

Lesotho was tricky because the British embassy in Moscow said, "It's OK, you may go." So I went. And there was no one at the border. So I spent some time in the country. And on the way back, immigration sees no entry stamp in my passport, and they go, "Whaat!?" So I was denied my outward flight and spent the whole day knocking doors trying to get proof that I was already inside the country.

Just to mention a few...

Of which travel accomplishments are you most proud?

I am proud to be the first Russian to visit all the countries and territories. There's one guy who did 193 UN countries one month before me (and he started ten years before me). But he doesn't count any of the non-UN countries, like Taiwan or New Caledonia. I do count them.

Do you remember encountering particular people that left a lasting impression with you?

Yes. From almost every country. My best memories are about people from the Russian North.

The North is a place that does not forgive ignorance, and everyone is willing to help everyone because one day they may need to help themselves. Completely the opposite thing is happening in the South, where one may ignore people's problems for days, and they will not die because of that.

Several times my car was about to stuck forever in permafrost due to unforeseeable technical problems. And every time there was a knowledgeable, competent, helping man to fix everything and ask nothing in return.

This is a good time to say thanks to Alexey from Novorybnaya, who gave me shelter for the whole day, and Jenya the Greek from Hatanga port who serviced my Toyota in the middle of nowhere.

If you could travel back in time, to which era and place would you go, and why?

I would like to press several buttons, please. Prehistoric times just to get an impression; Roman time is incredible, and I want to go there; 19th century fascinates me as well.

Can you describe any particular situation where you felt completely out of your comfort zone?

While traveling, I came up with a very handy rule: never let anyone take you out of the comfort zone.

When Chinese border patrol officers started to browse all my private photos, I was OK. When a Swiss customs officer almost undressed me searching for something, I was OK. When I was interrogated in Djibouti for eight hours for taking a picture of a goat next to an American embassy, I was OK.

So no one, so far, has been able to take me out of my comfort zone.

What are your three favorite cities in the world, and why?

Besides Moscow, it would be New York, Istanbul, Tokyo. These cities know everything about people, and they give everything to people. And to the occasional traveler, too.

What is the ideal amount of time you prefer to travel on each trip before you are ready to go home and take a break?

One day, one city is my favorite rule. I'd rather came back sometime again to see more if I like it.

In your opinion, where are the most beautiful places on Earth?

Cities where you can see old architecture, water, and mountains at the same time.

If you had an unlimited budget and space and time were no object, what would your perfect travel day look like (for example: start your morning in Bora Bora; afternoon on a safari in Kenya; night in Australia, etc.)?

Morning in Japan, daytime in Moscow, lunch in Europe, dinner in New York City, and an overnight in Chile. Just one of the hundreds of scenarios I can come up with.

Which three countries would you recommend for adventurous travelers to visit, and why?

Somalia, Antarctica, Palestine. Why? It's hard to get to, and it's against common sense to go there.

If you had just one travel story to share with someone, what would it be?

It could be any of my hundreds of stories. Every time someone travels and says afterward, "We've traveled without any adventures", I feel like they've wasted their time.

Do you ever feel you have missed out on certain aspects of life while away from home as you travel so much?

No way!

What advice would you give to others who would like to travel to every country?

Avoid war zones. Everything else is fine.

For someone who has been almost everywhere, what still gets you excited about packing your bags again?

The knowledge that there are so many more interesting places to see. Really, I have a feeling that I've just scratched the surface and got an impression, but there's so much more to learn and to discover.

Looking ahead, what travel plans and goals are you still pursuing, and what is on your "Bucket List"?

My plans:

2016: Penza, Saransk, Maykop, Evenkia, Russian islands in the Arctic Ocean. Puntland and Iraqi Kurdistan. Spain.

2017: Australia, Canada, Argentina.

2018: Brazil, Africa.

At the moment, I'm using The Best Travelled (www.thebesttravelled.com) as my reference of what to see. But after that, I'll have no guidelines to travel.

Jagannathan Srinivasaraghavan (Dr. Van), India & USA

(Kabul, Afghanistan, February 2011)

Where did you grow up and what was your early life like?

I was born in a village near Thanjavur, Tamil Nadu, India. My father was a physician with the Indian Railways, and my mother was a homemaker. In my very young age, traveling essentially meant visiting relatives since my father got transferred from one city to another. Adjusting to the new environment and friends was inculcated in me at a very young age. When I was 12 years old, our family traveled to Northern India, visiting New Delhi, Agra, Mathura, Hardwar, and Rishikesh. That is the big trip that I remember with my parents, a brother, and a sister. Even within India, there are so many languages and cultures, and it was fascinating to me, even at that age. I lived in college hostels (dorms) from age 16 until 23. In my late teens, I explored on my one-speed bicycle, even taking trips up to 300 miles in 3 days. I was in medical school from age 17 to 22, and I often fantasized leaving medical school and becoming a pilot, and at other times dreaming of a practice in Beverly Hills, California. From my early 20's, I explored new places in India every chance I got. In fact, due to my father's employment in the railways, I was entitled to use free passes as well as discounted tickets. My father would even joke later that "I worked 32 years for the Indian Railways, and my son used all my passes." When I finished medical school, I decided to travel the world and figure out how I could achieve that. The three options that I narrowed down to were: (1) to move to the United States and make enough money to achieve my dreams. (2) To go to Australia and do the same. (3) Join the merchant navy as a physician. The first overseas trip that I took was in 1974 to Singapore and Malaysia to take the ECFMG examination. This was a requirement for foreign medical graduates to get into residency in the United States, and was also honored by a couple of states in Australia. Though I passed the examination in 1974, I immigrated to the United States, only in January of 1977.

What was the first international trip you took and what do you remember most about it?

My first international trip was to Singapore and Malaysia in July - August 1974. Reaching Singapore late in the evening, the place looks marvelous, and the city was so clean that it was a new experience. However, in the hotel restaurant, when I asked for a vegetarian meal, all I got was salad, and I felt like crying. In Kuala Lumpur, I stayed with a wonderful family who took me to the Hindu Temple before taking me to the examination site. After the examination, I took a night train to Panang, I took a shower in a mosque, and went around the town, later taking another night train, and the next day visited a hill station: Fraser Hill. There were Indian families in that area, and they arranged for a boy with a Yamaha motorcycle to show me around. On our way back spending three nights in Singapore, I was able to borrow money from a shopkeeper to be paid to his relative in India at a premium rate, so I could buy a 2 in 1 radio and cassette tape recorder and a Yashica camera. There were numerous friends of friends whom I met for the first time, helped me that I cannot forget.

When did you go from traveling casually to making this a full-time goal, and what motivated you to travel to every country?

Every time I visited a new place or a country, I was so excited that I kept traveling. Initially, I was not even counting every country but was mainly concentrating on the sights I wanted to visit. I took nearly six months off after completing my residency in psychiatry, three months off after two years in my first job and took a year off after six years, and each time circumnavigating the earth, visiting new countries. Marriage and children did not slow me down a great deal – my wife is a member of the Travelers' Century Club (TCC), and my two sons traveled to more than 90 TCC country locations by the time they were in their late teens. I never imagined I would do as much as I have. Initially, I was aware of the TCC in the 1990's. However, I did not become a member until I had traveled to more than 200 locations. In fact, by 2006, I had just visited 140 U.N. countries. When the goal seemed more reachable, I accelerated the process, especially after 2008 when I retired as Professor of Psychiatry.

What have you done in your life to gain the freedom and finances to pursue as much travel as you have?

Though I could have had a very comfortable life in India, in 1977, India had very little foreign exchange reserves. In fact, I was given $6.50, when I left India, as I had an immigrant visa to the United States. A year after residency, when I got my unrestricted Illinois license. I was moonlighting so much that I was working nearly 120 hours a week so that I could afford to travel the world. In fact, during three years of my psychiatric residency, I had taken two trips around the world, each lasting one month. As an academic psychiatrist, I made decent money, and I did not have other expensive vices. I was able to travel to some countries to lecture, and thus get a visa (Saudi Arabia and Cuba), as tourist visas are not available to visit. In fact, I have lectured in 30 countries on six continents. I have retired from my federal government job, and as a professor at the University. I continued to work, making it feasible for taking exotic trips. I have attained a status that I work when I want to and take time off anytime without asking permission from anyone. Luckily, there is demand for what I do, and I can cover my expensive trips.

Has there been a time when you considered abandoning your travel goals?

Since I did not plan to be competing, and considered life itself as a journey and enjoyed my travels, I never considered abandoning travels. Even now, I could think of so many places that I have not visited, and time is so short that one cannot visit every place. Abandoning travel goals is not an option that I ever contemplated.

What do you consider to be your two favorite travel experiences, and why?

Two great years of travel for me were 1980 and 1985. In 1980, I circumnavigated the globe twice in addition to six weeks of train travels through Europe, including some Eastern European countries. In 1980, I bought a PanAm Passport with 30 tickets, which entitled me to travel anywhere PanAm flew for 30 days, in business class. I went from the United States to Argentina, Uruguay, Brazil, Australia, New Zealand, Japan, Hong Kong, Singapore, India, UK and Kenya. When I realized I visited six continents in 30 days, it was exciting. I flew over 81,000 miles and spent eight nights on the plane. I visited my family for three days in India during that trip. That was a memorable experience. While returning from Argentina I met a few Americans returning from Palmer Station in Antarctica, and that made my resolve to go to the seventh continent. The most memorable experience of my travel was in January of 1985, sighting Smith Island of Antarctica for the first time. My ten-day cruise from Ushuaia, Argentina, visiting Antarctic Peninsula, and returning to Punta Arenas, Chile, was one of the most memorable trips. On April 23, 1985, I planted the Indian flag at the North Pole, and I believe that I am the first Indian citizen to achieve that goal (only in 1986 did I become a U.S. citizen). Returning from the North Pole, I spent a night in an igloo drinking brandy with ice shavings from the wall. What an experience, probably never to be repeated! Later the same year I went to Churchill. Manitoba to photograph polar bears!

What are the main things you seek to experience when you travel (culture, cities, nature, animals, adventure activities, etc.?)

I am a people person, and I always try and connect with people. Having said that, it is not always easy where the language barriers may be an obstacle. Honestly, each place has its strengths. I visit some places due to its history and monuments. Others for nature and wildlife, and yet others for a sense of adventure. I have visited hospitals in many developing countries to learn how they cope with illness in general and mental health in particular.

Looking back from when you started traveling to where you are now, in what ways, if any, has travel changed you?

Travel was always a fun activity, even when I ran into difficulties. I could always think back and laugh at incidents. For many years as I was practicing full-time my profession. I could only take off possibly 20% of my time for travel, including professional conferences. After retirement from two jobs, now I seem to be spending 40-50% of my time traveling. Last year in 2015 I made 13 international trips, big and small. I have learned, no matter what country you go to, all the people have the same kind of expectations and dreams, they all want to have a safe, comfortable life, and they want their children to do better than themselves. Sometimes the people with minimal resources tend to share what little they have more than the people from rich countries. In general, people are all good at heart, though every country has its share of bad apples, too.

Do you speak any foreign languages, and if so, which have been the most useful for you besides English?

I speak my mother tongue, Tamil. This does not add a significant advantage except in some places such as Malaysia, Singapore, and Sri Lanka. I can understand Hindi, the national language of India, though I cannot converse fluently. This is helpful in many parts of the world where Indians and Pakistanis live. My Spanish is rudimentary but what little I know helps me a lot. I wish I knew more of French and Russian. I know a few basic phrases in many languages, and make it a point to learn while I am traveling that breaks the ice with a stranger and opens up communication, and I am amazed how much you can do with non-verbal communication. Recently with the internet everywhere and translations of text, I have been able to communicate easily with almost anyone.

What was the longest extended trip you have ever taken, when was it and where all did you go?

I took a year off from September of 1986 to September of 1987. The first four months, I traveled to Alaska, Hawaii, Guam, Japan, South Korea, Taiwan, Philippines, Indonesia, (including Borneo, Sulawesi, Spice Islands and Irian Jaya provinces), Singapore, India, Nepal (including a 20-day trek to Mount Everest Base Camp), Bangladesh, Switzerland, and Germany. I spent the month of January, 1987 in the U.S. getting additional visas before venturing out in February, to the U.K., Morocco, Canary Islands, Senegal, Mali, Ivory Coast, Togo, Benin, Cameroon, Kenya, Tanzania (including a 5-day trek climbing Mount Kilimanjaro), Zimbabwe, Zambia, Malawi, Botswana, Ethiopia, India, and Spain. I came back to the U.S. on May 31st. I got married in May and took a honeymoon trip, spending seven weeks visiting Switzerland, Liechtenstein, Austria, Hungary, Bulgaria, Turkey, Greece, and Egypt, completing the year away from my jobs by the end of August 1987.

Which two countries have exceeded your expectations, and which ones left you feeling underwhelmed, and why?

During my first trip to Europe, in 1978, I was so impressed with Switzerland that the services were top notch, and the people seemed to genuinely care about tourists. I was so impressed that I have visited Switzerland many times over the years, and in fact, I have a friend there whom I met in 1980 and still maintain a friendship with. The other country that impressed me on my first circumnavigation of the globe in 1979 was Japan. It is so organized, and in spite of the crowds, they move around without ever getting into one another's personal space. Everywhere people were quiet, and there was hardly any chatter in trains. They were extremely polite and helpful.

Among the places that exceeded my expectations, I have to include Pitcairn Island. There are only 46 people living on the island, and it is at least 36 hours travel from the nearest island, Gambier, in French Polynesia. I could not believe how well the houses were and all the material comforts they could get on that island. It is a part of the UK and thus most of the food is imported to the island. Telecommunication is connected to New Zealand and thus a call to Pitcairn Island costs the same as calling New Zealand. They buy TV time from different programs, and I could not believe that I could be sitting on Pitcairn Island and watching an Indian program, or *CNN*.

The places that underwhelmed me would include some countries in Africa. For example, I was in Guinea and went to the bank to change money, and a bank employee took me outside to the roadside vendor to change my money. And at the border with Sierra Leone, a police guy was so arrogant, and he tried to stop me entering Sierra Leone, saying I did not have a visa when I had one, and delayed me for a couple of hours, trying to extract a bribe. I could not believe that policeman was driving a Mercedes Benz.

When you travel, do you prefer to go with others or solo, and why?

Even though I like traveling with others, I tend to travel most often alone. By going alone, I tend to meet more locals and learn a lot more about their culture. For example, I have traveled to China in a group full of American visitors, and we hardly mixed with the locals. On many of my trips, I have traveled by myself and have found it to be much more thrilling and enchanting. However, there are places that you are forced to go in a group, and I do not mind that.

What has been your most uncomfortable mode of transportation?

In February of 1987, traveling from Bandiagara to Kani-Kombole, in Mali, on a two-wheeler as a pillion rider. It was a non-existent road full of stones and bumps that half the time we had to push the two-wheeler and on top of it, we had a flat tire that had to be repaired. On the same trip, returning from Djenne to Bamako, Mali, I was on a so-called bus with chickens tied to the side of the windows. If you are careless, and you put your elbow out through the window, the chickens would come to peck at you. I have also traveled in overcrowded buses where 50 people are sitting, another 50 people standing, and some more on top of the bus, and some hanging from the stairs, on a few journeys, lasting a few hours, in Asia. It is amazing surviving such journeys, and I can truly laugh about them.

What is the strangest thing you've seen/experienced while traveling?

In 1986, I had a multi-destinations pass on Garuda Indonesian Airways. When I was in Jayapura, Irian Jaya province, I was able to get special permission to travel to the highlands where Dani people lived. When I reached Wamena, I stayed in a basic hotel as the rooms in a better hotel were all booked for government officials visiting the area. Right after landing I spotted Dani men walking only with a penis gourd and women walking with grass skirts and a few shell necklaces only. Yet I was able to go to a bank and cash my traveler's check. In 1973, apparently a missionary family was killed on Christmas Eve and even talk of cannibalism involved. Yet I ventured on a hike to visit a village where the chief had kept the mummified body of his ancestral chief. I met with the chief and his four wives and also took a picture with the mummified body. Among the four wives, only the youngest was wearing a T-shirt while the rest were bare on the top. I asked through my interpreter why that was so. To my surprise, the oldest of the wives commented that it was because of us that they are losing their culture and customs that the youngest wife was refusing to follow their customs. There are so many churches of several denominations, and there was tension especially where the church teachings conflicted with the Dani way of life, such as polygamy. (I have shared this story with many friends, and a psychiatrist friend has added spice to the story indicating that I provided psychotherapy to the youngest wife to follow the customs of her tribe and got the t-shirt as a souvenir!).

I would add one more story from January 2015. I was in an Indian restaurant in Da Nang, Vietnam eating lunch when I saw an Indian couple come in. I met them and inquired whether they were working in Vietnam, I presumed in Information Technology. They told me that they were visitors from Chennai, India. My relatives all live in Chennai, and so I introduced to them with my last name, and the gentleman replied that was his name too. Though not uncommon, it is not that common except in one community, and it was indeed a surprise. Next, I asked the lady where she hailed from, and she stated the name of her native village, and now I was taken aback. She was asking me whether I was from the general area, however when I told her that I hailed from the same village, and our ancestral homes are on the same street. It was indeed a pleasant coincidence, and we have become good friends, and they joined my wife and me on a trip to Mustang region of Nepal in November 2015.

Out of the thousands of places you have stayed around the world, what have been your best and worst accommodations?

One of the best places that I have stayed was Hotel Ounasvaara in Rovaniemi in Finland. Every room came with an attached bathroom, and a sauna. In front of the hotel was the start of cross country skiing, and in the back of the hotel was downhill skiing, and you could go for a snowmobile ride on the Kemijoki River nearby and also get a reindeer sled driver's license. One of the most expensive places I stayed was a nice, beautiful bungalow in Desroches Island, in the Seychelles.

What is your favorite "off the beaten path" destination, and why?

Hiking in the Himalayan Mountains in India and Nepal. I loved traveling in Gulmarg and Pahalgam on the Indian side of Kashmir in 1975. The mountains are fascinating around Darjeeling, Gangtok and further into Bhutan.

What were your most challenging countries to visit, and why?

One of the hardest countries to visit was Saudi Arabia as they did not allow any tourist visa. With my professional contacts, I was invited to give a talk in Jeddah, and thus, I was sent an invitation for a so-called business visa for a month. That enabled me to travel to places such as Mada'in Saleh, a UNESCO World Heritage Site. I was almost the only individual traveler there. Other foreigners whom I met either were working in the country or visiting a relative in the country. I was also able to visit Mogadishu, Somalia for one night, and I was able to travel to the beach and some places in the city with two armed bodyguards for a large sum of money. In Libya, a travel agent arranged a visa for me to give a talk at the university, and I traveled freely with a Libyan driver and a Libyan English-speaking guide to many places. There were checkpoints manned by young adults carrying machine guns. If anyone wanted to take my camera away from me, there was no place to report the crime. I was assumed to be local, and we were waved through. I visited UNESCO World Heritage Sites at Sabartha, Leptis Magna, and Cyrene in February 2012 for one week and I hardly saw any other foreign tourists. Libya was my last country to visit.

What are the best and worst meals you have ever eaten while traveling, and where was it?

I am a vegetarian, and my favorite cuisines are Indian and Italian. I have found so many excellent restaurants all over the world, even in unexpected places. For example, when I was in Tashkent, Uzbekistan, I visited a restaurant, Raj Kapoor, named after a famous Indian movie star, and had Masala Dosa. Of course, in Desroches Island of the Seychelles, the Indian chef prepared fabulous dishes for me. Maveli Tiffin Room (MTR) in Bangalore, India is such a fan favorite for locals and foreigners alike.

The worst food I had was again in Bandiagara, Mali. I waited for an hour in a small restaurant for an omelet, before I found out the food was never going to come and had to settle to get something on the road side. There was no electricity, and I was not sure what kind of shape the salad I got was in that the vendor served me, but I was so hungry and had no options.

Of which travel accomplishments are you most proud?

I have circumnavigated the earth seven times. I am certainly one of very small number of people who have set foot both at the North Pole and the South Pole. And of course, I am proud to be the first Asian Indian who planted the Indian flag at the North Pole, on April 23, 1985.

If you could travel back in time, to which era and place would you go, and why?

Personally, I believe we are living at the best time in human history. If I have to think of a period, I would like to have lived during Emperor Ashoka's reign. Some of the monuments from his period are still standing attesting to the engineering skills from over 2000 years ago. Ashoka chakra, or the spiked wheel that decorates the Indian flag, is from his period.

Can you describe any particular situation when you felt completely out of your comfort zone?

In 2009, in the beach area of Libreville, Gabon. I was mugged by three youngsters, and they snatched my bag containing my passport, money, and also robbed my camera. They had pushed me down and relieved me of my possessions, and if I had resisted, they could have stabbed me. I was completely dazed and had to cross a creek that was flowing into the ocean to get to the other side where there were many people, and get to the police station helped by a local and three school students. I spoke no French, and the police were unhelpful. Once I went to the U.S. Embassy, the consulate was superb and helped me out in every way she could. With the aid of the consulate, we were able to press the police to take some action, and four days later the police arrested the three criminals. When they picked up the criminals, I was brought to the police station where, seeing the treatment they received, was very painful, and I was tearful when my 20-year-old interpreter, showing no mercy for the youngsters, commented, "You can't feel sorry for them. They're criminals." It took eight days before I got a new passport, and subsequently, I had to get a police report saying that I had lost the passport and change my travel plans, as I did not have the visa to go to the Democratic Republic of Congo as I had originally planned, and I had to fight the corrupt officials in the airport to let me leave the country. Basically, the officials wanted me to pay 100 Euros for a visa since the new passport didn't have Gabon visa, in spite of knowing my passport was stolen in their country. I refused, and it was 'Who blinks first' kind of a game. Just before the flight was about to take off, they stamped my passport and allowed me to go.

What are your favorite cities in the world, and why?

I love Rio De Janeiro for its beautiful beaches and wonderful Corcovado and Sugarloaf Mountains. Saint Petersburg for the Hermitage Museum and Petrodvorets (Peterhof Palace). Singapore for its cleanliness and ever-changing skyline and the people.

What is the ideal amount of time you prefer to travel on each trip before you are ready to go home and take a break?

In the past, I used to travel for 2-3 months at a time. In 2015, my longest trip was about 35 days, including 29 on a ship from Ushuaia, Argentina to sub-Antarctic islands including the circumnavigation of Bouvet Island, and touching Tristan da Cunha, St. Helena, and Ascension Island. Then I flew to the Falkland Islands and Chile, before returning home. I prefer 2-4 week trips now.

In your opinion, where are the most beautiful places on earth?

I love mountains and ocean. There are so many places that would cover both. The Himalayan regions in India, Nepal, and China, the Alps in Switzerland, Austria, France, and Italy, the fjords of Norway, and South Island of New Zealand. Further, I would add Faroe Islands, Lord Howe Island, Cocos (Keeling) Islands, Fiji and Rangiroa Island of French Polynesia.

If you had an unlimited budget in space and time, but not object, what would your perfect travel day look like (for example: start your morning in Bora Bora; afternoon on a safari in Kenya; night in Australia, etc.)?

I do not wish to dream of a perfect day that I can be in multiple destinations. My perfect travel day would be on a space shuttle traveling at 17,300 miles per hour, circumnavigating the earth every 90 minutes and seeing possibly eight sunrises and sunsets in a 12-hour period. I had made a reservation on the Phoenix-E program to reach the low orbit and travel for 8-12 hours and return to earth the same day in 1985. It was planned to be one week program including the weightlessness training for a few days before the flight itself and a day for a debriefing on return. The first such flight was planned to commence on 12 October 1992 for the 500th anniversary of Christopher Columbus's discovery of the Americas. My priority number was 35, and I would have certainly been on the first or second flight carrying 20, as I had figured out that some people ahead of me may choose to opt out from the first flight to avoid being the guinea pig. Alas, when the space shuttle Challenger tragically crashed on January 28, 1986, we were heartbroken when the US Government put a stop to all private space shuttle ventures.

Which three countries would you recommend for adventurous travelers to visit, and why?

I would recommend Papua New Guinea as there are so many distinct cultures and customs. Mali, as the place is so remote and interesting. The third would be Libya, with wonderful Roman ruins and the Sahara Desert.

If you just had one travel story to share with someone, what would it be?

Of all the travel stories, picking one is not an easy task. Arriving in the USA in January 1977 was suspense ridden until it truly happened. After passing ECFMG examinations, I did not secure a residency position applying from India. Those who dared to travel to the USA without a job had a significant advantage, as they could be personally interviewed. Since I did not get a position to start in July 1976, I was pretty much sure that my next opportunity was to consider July 1977, and in the meantime, I could complete

Internal Medicine residency that I was training for in India by March 1977. In October 1976, President Ford signed a bill that Congress raised immigration policies against International Medical graduates. Those in my situation had to be physically in the USA by 9 January 1977 in order to get a visa and thus pursue residency or else will have to go through more rigorous qualifications involving additional examinations, including a clinical examination only available in Philadelphia. I had no close relatives in the USA who could provide me an affidavit of support to affirm and support me until I am self-supporting. Luckily one of my teachers who had been in the USA only two years sent me an affidavit, but he had five children so I could not live in his place. I had a classmate who was in New York and started his residency only in July 1976, and he offered me to stay with him initially. I received the immigrant visa to the USA on 3 January 1977 and left Chennai, India on the 6th of January. Just before the flight, I was moving between the hospital where my sister was delivering twins to catching my flight in the evening, and that was true also for my father. I had to change flights in Mumbai (then called Bombay). In spite of my father's advice not to leave the airport, I managed to visit with a friend working for a telephone company and made a phone call to Chennai and found out that my sister had delivered two boys about the same time as I was flying out. On the 7th of January, the British Airways flight arrived at Gatwick instead of Heathrow airport due to a strike by its employees. Obviously, we missed the connecting flight to New York. We were given a train ticket to Victoria Terminal and given the address of BA office to sort out our stay and onward flight. India restricted foreign currency to those leaving India with an immigrant visa, so I had $6.50 only. It was not pleasant when you are traveling with suitcases in those days with no wheels and further I was carrying all kinds of gifts for known and unknown people as I was hoping to get a residency position. British Airways suggested that I could fly with them on the 10th of January as he was sure that the strike would be over. I knew that the cost of my ticket was not based on an excursion fare up to London but was a regular fare from London to New York, and I insisted that they arrange on any airline the next day and also provide a room, meals, and transportation. They obliged knowing that I was aware of my rights, and the next day I boarded Iran Air to arrive in New York on 8th of January 1977. My friend was not at the airport, and I had to tell the taxi driver that he has to find my friend's address in Queens in order to get paid. Within a month after arriving in the US, I bought a ticket on the Greyhound that entitled me to unlimited travel for nine days for $99. I had residency interviews at the Chicago Medical School and University of Nebraska, Omaha. Except for two nights that I spent with friends in Chicago, I spent seven nights traveling on the bus using coin showers and lockers. I hardly spent an additional $50 on that trip. When I got back to New York, both programs called to confirm a position for me. I tentatively accepted both positions giving myself time to review the contract at a later date. By mid-February, feeling that I had achieved what I wished, I borrowed money and returned to India in early March. I traveled one last time using my father's railway passes before getting back in June 1977 to Chicago to start my residency. I had a single dorm room without attached bath on the hospital grounds. Most people would have cringed but it was wonderful that I could walk to the hospital, and the librarians would lock me in the library so I could study for the next exams until late hours and walk back to my room. Within six months I bought a new car, and my first-year vacation was with Eurail pass all over Europe in June 1978.

Do you ever feel you have missed out on certain aspects of life while away from home as you travel so much?

You always have to give up something if you wish to gain something else. Relationships suffer when you're gone for a long time. There are festive occasions that I have missed in spite of careful planning. Investments have suffered at times since I have not been too obsessive in following the market on the road. I was due for promotion in my job when I decided to take a year off to travel. Though I have missed out on certain aspects of life, looking from an angle of benefit vs. risk, I would always choose to travel, and I have no regrets whatsoever.

What advice would you give to others who would like to travel to every country?

I would advise to start early and keep doing it. As life itself is a journey, I have often seen people work so hard thinking they would do multiple things when they retire. However, when they have the money they may not have the motivation or their health may not cooperate. Further, when you are young, there are a lot of uncomfortable situations that could be handled much easier than when you get older.

For someone who has been almost everywhere, what still gets you excited about packing your bags again?

I am always excited about visiting new places, and meeting people from these places. I do not get tired of that, and it hardly takes me any time to pack my bags as I am efficient.

Looking ahead, what travel plans and goals are you still pursuing and what is on your bucket list?

I'm currently working on adding another 20 to 25 Russian oblasts, krais, and republics. As I have visited about 57 of the 85. I Also hope to add four more provinces of China, leaving only a few of the islands of China unvisited. On the Travelers' Century Club list of 325, I have British Indian Ocean Territory (BIOT), Midway Island, Socotra, Tokelau, and Wake Island to complete the list. I hope to visit them within the next few years when an opportunity presents itself. In 2015, our chartered boat was denied permission to land on an island of Tokelau as we did not get prior permission. A chartered flight to Wake Island was canceled in December 2015. Socotra in Yemen was added to the list this year, but the civil war in Yemen renders it impossible to visit at this time. In addition to that, I'll be visiting some uninhabited islands with a group of fellow travelers to add to the mosttraveledpeople.com (MTP) list, where as of March 2016, I am ranked among the top 10 travelers.

Made in the USA
Lexington, KY
27 August 2016